Shaffer

LANGUAGE THOUGHT AND PERSONALITY
in Infancy and Childhood

By the same author
INFANT SPEECH
LANGUAGE IN SCHOOL
LANGUAGE IN SOCIETY
THE IMPORTANCE OF ILLITERACY
HOW CHILDREN LEARN TO SPEAK

M. M. LEWIS

LANGUAGE THOUGHT AND PERSONALITY
in Infancy and Childhood

BASIC BOOKS, INC., PUBLISHERS
New York

© 1963 by M. M. Lewis
Library of Congress Catalog Card Number: 64-15444

Contents

Introduction   7

PART ONE
INFANCY

1. The Beginnings   13
2. The Growth of Meaning   27
3. Language and Thinking   47
4. Language and Personal and Social Development   58
5. Language and Exploration   80

PART TWO
EARLY CHILDHOOD

6. General Characteristics   101
7. The Growth of Reasoning   118
8. Ethical Development   134

PART THREE
LATER CHILDHOOD

9. General and Linguistic Characteristics   165
10. Language and Concrete Thinking   176
11. Social and Ethical Development   203

Notes   229
References   248
Index   253

Introduction

THE intention of this book is to give a systematic account of the growth of language in relation to general development in infancy and childhood. During the last thirty years there have been innumerable studies of different aspects of language and of its place in human behaviour, more particularly by workers in U.S., in U.S.S.R., in Switzerland and France and in Britain. Much of this has increased our understanding of specific characteristics of children's language; but there appear to be few, if any, attempts to give an ordered account, in the light of this recent work, of the progressive development of language in relation to general growth from birth throughout childhood. Even so excellent and comprehensive a summary as that of McCarthy presents a series of encyclopedic articles without attempting to combine these into a unified statement of progressive change and development. It would seem that there is a place for a survey that will try to take into account detailed observations of children and experimental work with them, and bring these together in an ordered and coherent picture of growth.

We may say growth; for the more we learn of the day-to-day changes in the speech, language, thought, feeling and social behaviour of children the clearer does it become that we are witnessing a process in which the innate potentialities of a child are realised within the conditions of his social environment. It is a continued and gradual process in which day by day a child becomes a person. As he grows, there is no moment of which we can truly say, Here something new has suddenly appeared. He grows, and his speech is transformed into language; his language influences his thought and feeling; his thought and feeling influence his speech and his language.

In attempting to follow these complex processes in the lives of children we have had much to guide us during the past thirty years. Our knowledge and understanding have been greatly enriched by fundamental studies of language itself and of the relations between language and all other aspects of human behaviour; to name only the most obvious, the work of F. C. Bartlett, Cassirer, Freud, K. Goldstein, Head, G. H. Mead, Osgood and Skinner. We are indebted to many other workers for studies of the specific characteristics of children's language as such. Statistical studies; the value of these cannot be gainsaid. The refinement of the techniques now used, and of the criteria to which the treatment and presentation of data are subjected, give statistical statements increasing validity as a contribution to our knowledge. Studies, again, of children's speech; we owe much to the evidence made possible by the apparatus now available for the recording of vocal utterance, offering invaluable information of phonetic, syntactic and lexical characteristics. And, coming more closely to our special concern here, are enquiries into various aspects of the integration of children's language with their general development. There are the seminal studies of such pioneers as Piaget, Vigotsky and Luria, illuminated by a host of detailed experimental investigations into particular functions of children's language.

One additional and largely new source of knowledge needs special mention. We are now able to draw upon evidence hardly available, if at all, thirty years ago; studies of children whose linguistic development has been retarded—children with impaired hearing or those brought up in an environment unfavourable to their linguistic growth. The increasing attention given to these children, with the aim of devising remedial or even prophylactic measures, has thrown much light upon the linguistic development of children not so afflicted. The benefits are mutual. The treatment of the less fortunate children has gained from a greater knowledge of the development of the more fortunate.

In striking contrast to this wealth of widely-ranging work is the continued poverty of close and detailed records of language at successive moments in ordinary children's everyday lives. What a child says, when and to whom; how others respond to him, he to others. Here unfortunately we are little better off than we were thirty years ago.

I have used whatever I have been able to find. For the earliest months I have had to fall back upon some of my own records, so that the first part of the book is a reconsideration of my previous study, *Infant Speech*, in the light of the work that has been done since then. For the period following infancy I have in the main drawn upon the observations of Louise Ames, Susan Isaacs and I. and P. Opie.

A word must be said about the arrangement of the book. Anyone who attempts a survey of children's development is faced with a problem of presentation; whether to follow, one by one, particular strands through from beginning to end or, alternatively, to give a series of composite pictures stage by stage. With the former choice he is confronted with the difficulty of bringing together the isolated strands. With the latter choice he runs the risk of presenting a succession of discrete steps and, perhaps, appearing to conceive of development as a process of maturation more or less independent of learning. As my main concern here is to attempt to relate language to other behaviour, my survey has tended to arrange itself in the three broad stages of infancy, earlier childhood and later childhood; in each of which, although diverse aspects of development are considered, they are frequently combined into a comprehensive picture of children at that period in their lives. It is hoped that this treatment will not leave an impression of a series of unconnected stages, but will succeed in showing the language and general development of a child as a process of organic growth within a social environment.

PART ONE

Infancy

NOTE

The figures in brackets, which occur throughout the text, refer to the Notes beginning on page 229.

I

The Beginnings

A CHILD is born a speaker and born into a world of speakers. To recognise this is of the utmost importance for our understanding of the growth of language and its place in human development.

The linguistic growth of a child in his social environment moves forward as the continued convergence and interaction of two groups of factors—those that spring from within the child himself and those that impinge upon him from the community around him. The growth of many other creatures has of course this dual character. Where a child's development differs is that he is so much more richly endowed with the potentialities of speech and that he grows up in a social environment permeated by symbolisation, the most potent form of which is language.

THE ROOTS OF SPEECH

To say that a child is born a speaker means this: that he has innate capacities, the roots of his linguistic growth—that from birth he vocalises and responds to sounds.

He vocalises; there is even some evidence of pre-natal vocalisation (1). Certainly when he draws his first breath, every child cries. The expulsion of breath is an element in his violent reaction to his new environment; there are movements of his vocal organs, the result of which is heard by us as a cry. Other urgent bodily conditions soon manifest themselves in a similar fashion—hunger, pain or other discomfort. Contented, the child in his earliest weeks is usually silent or he sleeps; later, he begins to make noises characteristic of his contentment. As soon as his mother responds to these discomfort-cries or comfort-noises we have the rudimentary conditions of a language—one person makes sounds to which another responds.

The child is also innately disposed to respond to sounds. It is possible that this too may occur before birth (2). Certainly, most newborn children respond to loud sudden noises, even on the first day, by changes in the rate of respiration or pulse, in some cases by more overt bodily movements.

Have children, however, an innate tendency to vocalise as a specific response to the human voice? One interesting fact suggests this: a child, often as early as his second week, may start crying when he hears other children cry. But a cautious interpretation of this would be that it is simply an instance of the child's general tendency to respond to loud shrill noises. A further common observation, however, takes us a little further. In his early weeks a crying child will normally be soothed by the voice of his mother or whoever looks after him. In this a child is like those other young animals who from an early moment in their lives respond to the calls of their parents. Biologists today are disposed to believe that the young creature is born with a tendency to react to a range of not very specific sound-patterns and that the responses become more specific to those patterns which are heard coming from the parent. It would seem justifiable to explain a child's responses to the human voice in the same way (3).

We have, then, already in a child's earliest weeks the two convergent groups of factors that will continue throughout his linguistic growth: the child utters sounds and responds to the human voice, his mother responds to his sounds and speaks to him. If any of these four necessary conditions is impaired, the child's linguistic growth may suffer. Obviously, defective hearing is likely to be a potent and cumulative cause of linguistic retardation. No less powerful, and more immediate, are the effects of a child's failure to receive the care that normally a mother is able to give. When, for instance, because of a mother's illness her child spends his early weeks in a hospital or other institution, the frequency and the variety of his early sounds may be notably below the average (4).

THE BEGINNINGS

For normal healthy growth both groups of factors must be present. The child's own discomfort-cries and comfort-sounds constitute his own contribution to his growing language. The complementary contribution comes, of course, from without—from his mother and the other people around him. To understand his growth we need therefore to consider each of these two contributions, beginning with his own cries and noises.

THE DIFFERENTIATION OF UTTERANCE

Discomfort-cries and comfort-noises are quite characteristic and distinctive. Every mother soon recognises whether the child, though out of sight, is 'crying' or 'just making noises'. Each characteristic complex pattern of sounds, intonation and pitch comes to have its meaning for her.

What is not so obvious, though no less true, is that for the child himself his early utterance has its rudimentary 'meaning'. As we have said, the sounds he makes are the vocal elements in his reactions to changes in his bodily conditions. When he cries or makes comfort-sounds, his auditory and kinæsthetic experience—his 'awareness' of his utterance—comes to him embedded in his experience of his bodily condition at that moment. So, since form and function are inseparable in his rudimentary linguistic behaviour and since his later language grows out of this rudimentary behaviour, the nature of his early utterance—in form and function—is a potent influence in the growth of his language.

THE SEQUENCE OF THE EARLIEST SOUNDS

In order to understand the course of a child's development we have to observe the actual sounds as they emerge, the order in which they occur and the circumstances in which they are uttered. Allowing for individual differences, we find that the sequence is broadly the same in all children everywhere. We can distinguish three stages in the emergence of the discomfort-cries and three in the emergence of the comfort-sounds. The earliest vowel-like sounds are augmented by two successive groups of consonantal sounds.

The discomfort-cries: at the outset these are vowel-like in quality —mostly 'front, narrow' vowels, ranging from e to æ, shrill and frequently nasalised. Soon, in the stream of discomfort-cries, consonantal sounds begin to emerge, sounds approximating to w, l, ŋ, h. Then, as a third stage, sounds rather like labial and dental consonants appear: approximately m and n.

In the development of comfort-sounds there are three broadly corresponding stages. First, the rudimentary vowel-like comfort-sounds are much less distinct and clearly defined than the earlier discomfort-cries. The comfort-sounds are 'back, open' vowels, rather of the order of a, o, u; relaxed in quality, rarely if ever nasalised. Then, when the first consonant-like comfort-sounds begin to appear, these too are mostly produced in the back of the mouth—sounds like g, x, ɡ, k, r. The third stage is the emergence of labials and dentals, usually not nasalised as p, b, t, d, occasionally nasalised as m and n. The actual dates of the occurrence of these successive sounds vary of course from child to child, but from many observations in different parts of the world we can safely say that the order of the stages is broadly everywhere the same. They are summarised in Table I.

This is not merely a phonetic classification. The successive stages become deeply significant of the child's growth in language as soon as we consider the sounds in relation to the circumstances in which they are uttered (5).

THE DISCOMFORT-CRIES

Why are the earliest discomfort-cries vowel-like, narrow, shrill and nasalised? The main clue is given by Darwin in *The Expression of the Emotions in Man and Animals*. Pointing out that a child's cry in discomfort is the vocal manifestation of his total reaction to the disturbing stimuli, Darwin shows that in such a state the contractions of the facial muscles would result in a 'rectangular' narrowing of the mouth cavities, producing narrow and tense rather than open and relaxed vowels. Following this, we can add that the intensity of the child's reactions would tend to raise the pitch to shrillness and also that, in the effort to increase the volume of sound, the child would involuntarily bring the nasal resonance-chambers into play and so produce nasalised sounds (6). Thus the phonetic characteristics of the first stage of discomfort-cries are seen to be the vocal aspects of the physiological features of the child's reaction to his condition.

With these clues in mind, how do we explain the second stage of discomfort-cries: consonants of four types—w, l, ŋ, h? These sounds are produced by closure or partial closure at points ranging from front to back of the mouth. If in the course of uttering a vowel sound, the lips are brought close together, the result is a kind of w; bringing the front of the tongue close to the gum-ridge will produce l; bringing the back of the tongue close to the hard palate produces ŋ; and h is the sound that appears when there is partial closure of the glottis, while the other vocal organs are in position for uttering a vowel.

TABLE I

The Stages of Early Spontaneous Utterance

Stage	Discomfort-cries	Comfort-sounds
I. Vowel-like.	(i) Onset: immediately after birth. (ii) Narrow vowels: e, ɛ, æ, a. (iii) Often nasalised.	(i) Onset: when the discomfort-cries have already begun to appear. (ii) Open vowels: not clearly defined, a, o, u. (iii) Rarely nasalised.
II. Earlier consonantal.	Sounds made by partial closure: w, l, ŋ, h.	Mostly back consonants: g, ɡ, x, k, r.
III. Later consonantal.	Front consonants, usually nasal: labial, m dental, n.	Front consonants, usually oral, sometimes nasal: labial, p, b, m. dental, t, d, n.

The explanation of the emergence of these four sounds, w, l, ŋ, h, is clear. The child does not utter one long uninterrupted cry. His crying is punctuated by momentary closure or partial closure of some part of his vocal apparatus; and according to whether this is at his lips, gum-ridge, hard palate or glottis we hear w, l, ŋ, h.

Finally, as Stage III, we have the emergence of the very important front-consonants, the nasal labial and dental, m and n. Their connection with sucking has often been suggested, but once again it is the clue given us by Darwin that enables us to recognise the nature of this connection. Like the earlier sounds these too are the vocal manifestation of physiological functioning. The act of sucking consists of bringing the lips together and simultaneously or immediately afterwards bringing the front of the tongue hard against the upper gum-ridge. If this is done whilst one is vocalising nasally, the resulting sounds will be m and n. Now many observations go to show that a child, from about a month onwards, begins to make anticipatory sucking-movements when he is hungry, often when the preliminaries to feeding are in train. His mother, for instance, is bringing the bottle towards him, or—at a later stage—is tying a bib under his chin. These are among the most striking examples of the processes of learning in early infancy (7).

Now if a child, while uttering his nasalised vowel-like hunger-cries, begins to make anticipatory sucking-movements, the consonantal sounds m or n will be heard. So the characteristic hunger cries of children—spontaneous and 'expressive' of their normal physical and psychological development—are *mama* . . . and *nana*, sound-patterns that, as we can see at once, come to play essential parts in linguistic development.

THE COMFORT-SOUNDS

In similar fashion, the phonetic characteristics of the successive stages of comfort-sounds reflect the child's reactions to his bodily conditions when he is contented. The child's innate tendency to vocalise gradually spreads from the urgency of discomfort to all other bodily states. From what we have said about the discomfort-cries we can see, by contrast, how the first comfort-sounds are likely to be vowel-like *back* sounds, such as a, o, u. The child will be lying contented, relaxed, most usually after he has been fed. In such a condition, with the mouth slackly open, and with the back of the tongue lolling against the soft palate, back vowel-like sounds will be produced.

So in the second stage, when consonant-like sounds begin to appear, it is evident that they are likely to be back consonants such as g, x, g, k, r. Several factors may combine to produce this result.

Sounds of this kind are formed when there is partial or complete closure at the back of the mouth, particularly by the movement of the back of the tongue towards the soft palate. As in Stage II of the discomfort-cries, if the child when vocalising pauses for breath, the momentary partial or complete closures will be heard as consonant-like sounds. In a state of contentment these will be back consonants because, as we have seen, in this condition the child is lying relaxed with the back of the tongue lolling against the soft palate. Further, after feeding—the commonest state of contentment at this stage—there may be an excess of saliva in the mouth which, when the child vocalises, will produce a 'gurgling' noise. In addition there may be some regurgitation or belching after a feed, again tending to produce back consonants. By a combination of these factors we get the characteristic 'goo-goo' noises of the contented infant.

With Stage III of the comfort-sounds we come once more to labial and dental consonants. These, as we have seen, are the vocal manifestations of sucking-movements. But why should these movements occur in a state of contentment? To answer this we must remember that a child will make sucking-movements not only in anticipation of food, but also after he has fed. There will be a tendency for the sucking-movements to be repeated—something of the nature of perseveration (8). So, in a state of relaxation, when a child vocalises, there will be a recurrence of labial sounds; consonantal sounds ranging from p to b—according to the amount of 'voicing'—and a similar range of gum-ridge sounds, t to d. If there happens to be any nasalisation at the time, sounds such as the labial m or the gum-ridge n will appear (9). So in this third stage of the comfort-sounds the characteristic sound-patterns will be *papa, mama, tata, dada*, with occasional *mama* and *nana*.

Thus we see that three general observations combine to explain the forms of 'expressive' utterance in discomfort and in contentment. A child's vocalisations are shaped by his physiological reactions to his condition; his utterance is punctuated by complete or partial closure at different points in his vocal organs; before or after feeding he makes anticipatory or perseverative sucking-movements.

In order now to understand how these patterns of utterance take their place in his growth, we have to look at two important features of vocal behaviour: babbling and imitation.

BABBLING

One of the chief characteristics of a child's vocal behaviour is that during the early months—usually not before the sixth week—he will begin to babble; that is, when contented he will utter repetitive strings of sounds. It is important to recognise the difference between this babbling and 'expressive' comfort-sounds, the manifestations of his contentment. When a child is babbling he gives us the impression that he is making sounds 'for their own sake', that he derives satisfaction from the utterance itself, that he is 'playing with sounds', playing with his vocal organs in the same way as he plays with movements of his fingers and his toes (10).

What is the place of babbling in linguistic development? To understand this we must first ask how it is that babbling arises.

This question of the source of babbling is part of the wider problem of the source of play in general. Few psychologists would be content to dismiss the problem by saying that play is simply an innate tendency or instinct. McDougall, for example, insistent as he is on instincts as the basis of human behaviour, nevertheless makes a special point of asserting that play cannot be regarded as an instinct. His discussion of play in general is a good guide to our understanding of babbling in particular. He suggests that in play creatures are 'exercising their various motor mechanisms and finding pleasure in so doing' (11). An obvious criticism of this is that it is a description rather than an explanation; but in fact there is little more to be said. Children—and indeed adults—enjoy their own activity. One thing may perhaps be added. We may hazard the suggestion that—at any rate, after a time—one element in the child's pleasure is likely to be the 'sense of achievement', the experience of finding that one can do what one intends to do. We know that this is a source of potent satisfaction as a child grows older, to say nothing of adult life. It would seem reasonable to recognise its rudiments even in the earliest months.

We would say, then, that when a child babbles he makes sounds that he has uttered in discomfort or contentment, now finding satisfaction in producing at will those sounds which at first have occurred involuntarily. It would seem that this satisfaction is at two 'levels'. First there is the pleasure in each sound itself—the complex stimulus of motor and auditory sensations. The child learns to repeat a particular sound, or group of sounds, in order to experience this satisfying stimulus. As a result of this repetition, satisfaction at the second level enters. The child begins to find pleasure in the regular pattern constituted by repetition—a very complex pattern in which no doubt, rhythm, stress, variation of pitch and regular variation of sound-groups are all elements.

What then is the place of babbling in a child's development? In babbling we have the rudiments of two important aspects of this development.

First, it is evident that the child's enjoyment of making sounds and hearing himself make them is one of the roots of his subsequent enjoyment of literature, written and spoken. From these early moments and throughout childhood he is likely to show, again and again, his pleasure in the phonetic and syntactic patterns of language. This is that element in æsthetic creation and enjoyment which consists in the pleasure provided by the material medium of a work of art—what has been called 'æsthetic emotion'. As Alexander has said, 'Words or other expressive products become the material of art when they are used not for the sake of the things which they mean but in themselves and for their own sake.' (12).

The second important characteristic of babbling is that it is a means by which a child, through repeated practice, acquires skill in making sounds. As other forms of play give a child the rudimentary skills upon which his later complex skills are based, so babbling gives him the beginnings of the highly complex skills that go to the production of the sounds of speech.

In a variety of ways both the enjoyment of the patterns of speech in themselves and the enhanced skill in producing these patterns, will contribute to a child's language. In particular, they open the way to the intervention of others. For while a child is playing, those around him—through a diversity of influences—will usually act in a selective way upon his actions, shaping them and directing them towards the skills that he will need as he grows up. We encourage him to experiment and play with toys, tools and instruments, all of which—under the influence of our approval or disapproval—guide his growing competence towards the mastery of those skills that will best serve his future needs. A child's play—even when, in its beginnings, it is highly egocentric—is in some measure socially determined; as he develops, play becomes more and more a social activity. It is social influence which is a powerful factor in making play a preparation for 'real life'.

All this is true of babbling in relation to linguistic growth. In babbling the child explores the possibilities of his vocal apparatus and so produces an enormous diversity of sounds, out of which a comparative few will ultimately form the speech-sounds of his mother tongue (13). In this gradual process of selection the potent factor is of course the unremitting influence of his social environment—he practises in his babbling the sounds that he has heard. In this way a child born in England learns to imitate the English spoken around him (14). To the nature and the development of the beginnings of imitation we must now turn.

IMITATION

Imitation is so characteristic of the behaviour of every child that it might well be thought to be an inborn power. But here again even McDougall is doubtful and subsequent evidence has confirmed his doubts. Imitation has to be learnt.

In linguistic development this means that in the course of acquiring the mother tongue by imitation, a child has to learn how to imitate speech. Observers of children are by no means agreed on the manner in which this learning of imitation proceeds. Here we would suggest that there are three stages: what we would call rudimentary imitation during the earliest months is followed by a period in which imitation is in partial or complete abeyance, after which there is a vigorous rebirth of imitation (15).

The observers who do not accept this account do not dispute the facts. They maintain, however, that the behaviour observed in our first stage is not imitation at all and that imitation therefore really begins in our stage three.

What are the facts—what do we find when we observe the progressive changes in children's vocal responses to the human voice? At first, as we have mentioned at the beginning of this chapter, the only response of this kind is crying when other children cry. Later—perhaps in his fourth week, although the actual date of onset varies from child to child—we see the beginnings of responses to adult speech. These earliest responses are not vocal. When a child is crying, the sound of his mother's voice may soothe him into silence. Later, the responses to speech become more positive. Hearing his mother's voice he may 'smile' or make other facial or other bodily movements. Then—perhaps in his third or fourth month—the rudiments of *vocal* response to speech appear. When a child of this age is lying contentedly silent and someone speaks to him, he may be stimulated to make noises; if he happens to be making comfort-sounds or babbling, there is a marked increase of this sound-making. This is a matter of common observation; more systematic records have been made by various observers, for instance, Valentine (16).

Now it is quite true that the responsive sounds that a child makes at this stage may be very different from the sounds that he hears. He is stimulated to make his own sounds; can this be called imitation? Clearly there is something new in his behaviour: where previously on hearing speech he remained silent he now responds vocally. To this extent it is imitation—that the child now speaks on hearing someone speak; but it is only rudimentary imitation in that there is little or no similarity.

We have to recognise that whenever we speak of imitation—in whatever field of behaviour—we cannot make absolute correspondence our final criterion. Indeed if absolute similarity is our criterion we are forced into the absurdity of saying that a child of five who says *fing* for *thing* is not imitating, that imitation only begins when he can say *thing*. It is surely reasonable to say that the child's *f* is his imitation of *th*.

In a child's earliest months his vocal responses to our words do not, of course, closely resemble them. But there is usually a regularity in his responses to particular sounds; and it is this regularity which is the source of his ultimate ability to imitate. To take a typical instance: a child in his fourth month said *weh* when he heard somebody say *goo*—one of his own familiar sound-patterns. After a time this became quite regular; it is reasonable to say that at this stage *weh* was his response to *goo*—although *goo* often appeared in his own babbling.

This kind of imitation occurs in the normal course of everyday life in an ordinary home. It is one of the chief means by which a child learns to imitate speech. We imitate his sounds and express satisfaction when he responds, particularly when his sounds resemble ours (17).

The nearer the approximation of his sound-group to ours, the more marked will be our show of approval—by a smile, maybe, or tone of voice. This approval gives a special character to any sound-group that approximates to the one we say to him. The child has an increased incentive to repeat it; it becomes one of the sound-groups most likely to recur in his babbling. As he practises making it, it becomes more habitual to him than other sound-groups, and so there is a selective effect, resulting in his utterance of sound-groups which come nearer and nearer to those he hears—the phonetic patterns of his mother tongue.

The importance of this early everyday intercourse between a child and his mother or other members of his family can hardly be overestimated. We have seen that already in the earliest weeks the frequency and variety of sounds may be restricted through inadequate fostering by adult care. There is an impressive accumulation of evidence that children brought up in an orphanage or other institution are—compared with those brought up in a family—often retarded in the continued development of their speech, from the beginning and throughout childhood. The routine and comparatively unvaried life of an institution is less likely to evoke utterance from a child than the variety of everyday life in an ordinary home; and in an institution there are rarely enough 'mothers' to play speech-games with a child. Where this is recognised and special care taken to encourage speech, the potentially harmful effects of life in an institution may be obviated. And even when some harm has been done in infancy, it would seem from recent work that subsequent remedy is possible (18).

To continue our account of normal progress; we have said that after a time the early rudimentary imitation diminishes or lapses altogether. Why is this? The answer is provided by looking forward to the third stage, when imitation begins again with much greater frequency, vigour and accuracy than in the rudimentary stage. We find that this rebirth coincides with the time when the child would be described as 'beginning to understand what we say to him'. The child begins to respond in specific ways to particular patterns of heard speech, in relation to the circumstances in which they occur. He learns that when he makes certain responses to these sounds he obtains the satisfaction of approval by those around him. He learns also that he can bring about action in others by making these sounds himself. The sounds of the mother tongue become even more important in his daily life; there are still more powerful incentives to produce these sounds himself. He has reached the stage of imitation with meaning.

How does this explain the previous period of lapsed imitation? Imitation is likely to lapse as the child becomes more attentive to the *circumstances* in which he hears speech—and his attention, for the time being, is diverted from these sounds themselves which, in stage one, were in the forefront of his attention. His response is now dominated by the particular and important experience that each sound-pattern regularly brings in its train.

The three stages of imitation, we see, are intimately bound up with the whole development of a child's responses to the meaning of what he hears and his own meaningful use of speech. Stage one is the period when the sounds of human speech are beginning to attract his attention and this sharpening of awareness stimulates him to respond vocally. Then he begins to be aware of the circumstances in which others speak to him, and the sounds he hears become a stimulus for him to attend to these circumstances. The sounds now call forth from him many other kinds of response than the purely vocal. We see this as the lapse of imitation. Then as he begins to attend to heard sounds in relation to circumstances, imitation is reborn. He utters imitated sounds with meaning.

With this, the child is moving into a remarkable stage in his life—the emergence of his response to the meaning of what he hears and with it the growth of meaning in his own utterance. To this development he brings some characteristics which he shares with other living creatures, and some which sharply marks him off from them. In four respects, we have seen, he is like some other animals. He is born to utter certain sounds and born to respond to sounds—probably in a special way to those of his own species; he plays with his sounds; he learns to imitate the sounds of others. In three respects he is marked off from any other animal. He has probably a capacity for making a greater variety of vocal sounds. He certainly has a brain potentially better fitted to recognise and manipulate relationships. Above all, he is born into a world of speakers, whose behaviour is permeated by symbolisation through their speech.

It is with these primary capacities and in this community that he comes to understand the speech of others and to say things that others understand. To these changes we must now turn.

2

The Growth of Meaning

THE child's responses to the speech that he hears and his own use of this speech with meaning develop side by side—in general his progress in responding to words preceding his use of them. Here we begin by outlining the course of the development of the child's responses to the meaning of what he hears, we continue with the growth of meaning in his own utterance and then consider how the two factors—response and utterance—combine to contribute to his linguistic and general development.

THE DEVELOPMENT OF RESPONSE

In the last chapter we traced the early course of a child's responses to human speech, from the moment when he is set crying on hearing other children cry, up to the time when another person's voice may stimulate him to utter his own comfort-sounds.

Let us now go back and observe the beginnings of a child's response to the meaning of what he hears. We find the rudiments of this in the emergence of different characteristic responses to the intonational qualities of what is said to him. We saw that, perhaps as early as his fourth month, he may utter sounds expressive of contentment when someone speaks pleasantly to him. About this same time, or perhaps a little later, he will begin to show distress and cry when he is spoken to sharply—whether 'in reality' or 'in play'.

The next important stage in this progress is the appearance of specific actions in response to specific words. For every mother this is a great landmark in her child's life, for now she can begin to use words to control his behaviour. Typical instances are these observations of a boy in his tenth month: when he was about to put a piece of paper into his mouth and someone said *No!* he desisted; when someone said *Say Goodbye!*, he waved his hand (1). We say to ourselves, He has begun to understand us!

What has happened here? Of course it is an instance of 'learning' —and in saying this we at once recognise that it is not simply the establishment of a response to a 'neutral stimulus', but a highly complex process. The child's response is strongly motivated and highly charged with affect, which is contributed in varying degrees by each of the three elements to which the child responds: the word itself, the person who speaks it and the situation in which it is spoken.

The word itself as a pattern of sounds has qualities which directly evoke an affective response from the child. The tone in which it is spoken is more or less harsh or musical and, as we have seen, from a very early time children normally discriminate between unpleasant and pleasant sounds (2). These intonational qualities are greatly strengthened and sharpened when the child is responding to human speech. The spoken word will tend to arouse those responses which are specially evoked by persons—crying by the sound of others crying, smiling by the sight of a familiar face, babbling by heard words. So when a child of ten months hears *No!* or *Say Goodbye!* each of these sound-patterns must arouse in him, through its intonational characters—particularly pitch, stress and volume—'expressive' responses (3).

As for the person who is speaking to him—there is no need to emphasise how affectively significant she is likely to be for him, particularly if it is his mother who is speaking. But above all, it will be what she is doing at this moment in this situation that will evoke affective responses from the child. As she says *Goodbye* she waves her hand—a movement charged with affect for him because it has come to mean the moment of parting. He has learnt also that if he waves in reply, this evokes from his mother an expression of pleasure, so that he is encouraged to wave—or, as some psychologists would say, his response by waving is 'reinforced'.

Again, when a child is intent upon some act which interests him and is suddenly brought up sharp by his mother's *No!*, strong feeling must be aroused. He learns that to desist evokes an expression of pleasure, or, at the least, the cessation of her displeasure.

It is not surprising therefore that Pavlov, recognising the unique role of speech in human behaviour, was impelled to say with special emphasis that a word as a conditioning stimulus is never as 'neutral' for a person as a buzzer is for a dog; because of a person's 'previous life experience', a word comes to be connected with a wide range of stimuli (4). In addition, it is evident that those around the child do not merely present him with words which are stimuli to which he himself learns to respond; by a diversity of means, intended and unintended, they *actively* lead him to approved modes of responsive behaviour.

Not only this: we must remember that the word that the child hears is a stimulus of a very special kind because he himself is a speaker. Now, in the later part of his first year, he has repeatedly known the experience of utterance: has not only heard himself speak but on each occasion has experienced a complex kinæsthetic pattern as he speaks. His perception of the word is likely to bring with it incipient utterance, which itself may do something to promote the response he is learning to make.

From the beginning, and throughout the time that he is learning to respond discriminatively to the speech of others, there is a progressive development of meaning in what he himself says. To understand, therefore, how a child comes to wave his hand on hearing *Goodbye!* or desist from an act on hearing *No!* we must therefore trace the growth of meaning in his own speech.

'MEANING' IN A CHILD'S SPEECH

A child's first utterance of words with meaning seems even more spectacular than the beginning of his responses to words. He has spoken his first word! He has begun to speak!

It is sometimes said that there is a particular moment in a child's life when his first word suddenly appears; and alternative explanations of this supposedly sudden event have been put forward. On the one hand, it is held that there is a spontaneous tendency for a child to utter certain patterns of sounds in particular situations; for instance, that he is innately disposed to say *mama* as part of his responsive behaviour to his mother. On the other hand, it is held that he learns to say this word with this meaning by imitating its use by those around him. Each of these views has some truth in it. In the beginnings of a child's utterance with meaning, there is a combination of innate tendencies, of imitation and of the experience of a variety of situations in which he and others use words.

What are we describing when we say that a child has spoken his first word? We mean that he has uttered a group of sounds recognisably like one of our words and apparently with some specific reference to a person or situation. If this seems to be a new step, it is only because we have failed to notice his rudimentary approaches to the present achievement. The apparently sudden advance has, in fact, a long history in the child's life.

To examine this, let us look more closely at the typical emergence of *mama*, which is certainly one of the commonest and most important of 'first words'.

It is evident that this word, both in form and in meaning, has roots that go back deep into the child's earlier life. As we saw in Chapter 1, *mama* is the sound-pattern that appears when a child makes anticipatory sucking-movements in the course of uttering discomfort-cries and, later, perseverative sucking-movements during comfort-sounds. It is therefore spontaneous in its form—in that its pattern, phonetic and intonational, arises from the physiological functioning of the child. It is also spontaneous in its meaning to this extent—that it is primarily a vocal manifestation of sucking in a state of discomfort or contentment. From these primary roots a process of extension takes place; the child comes to say *mama* in states of discomfort other than hunger, and in contentment other than satiety. Then, out of this wide range of situations, a narrowing of usage takes place. But much must happen before a child's *mama* can be said to be a name for his mother.

To understand the course of this development, our view must once again widen to take in the child's partners: we must notice the responses aroused in others by his utterance of such a sound-pattern as *mama*. These responses are broadly of two kinds, which may be called the manipulative and declarative effects of what he says.

MANIPULATIVE AND DECLARATIVE EFFECTS

A child's utterance is manipulative in effect when it causes someone to perform a task—ultimately, with growing experience on both sides, a task which satisfies him. His speech is declarative in effect when it arouses in another person an expression of feeling—ultimately, with growing experience on both sides, an expression which satisfies him. The distinction is important for our understanding of development; although many of a child's utterances—and indeed, language throughout life—may have both manipulative and declarative effects.

The word *mama*, for instance, begins to have a manipulative effect when the child urgently utters this at a moment of need, and his mother—or some other person—comes to his aid. The effect of his cry is to cause some other person to manipulate something for him. A typical early instance is this:

> 0;9,29. The child is sitting alone in his play pen. His ball rolls out of his reach. He stretches towards it, but unsuccessfully. After several efforts he begins to say *mamama* while still reaching for the ball. If then his mother comes and gives him the ball, the word *mama* has had a manipulative effect.

Distinct from this is the child's utterance of *mama* when in a state of contentment, the effect then being to evoke an expression of pleasure from another person. It is a rudimentary declaration of satisfaction, resulting in something of an affective communion with the other person. For instance, from the record of the same child:

> 0;9,6. He says *mammam* in a very contented tone, while lying in his mother's arms and looking up at her. If then his mother smiles and perhaps speaks to him, his *mammam* has had a declarative effect.

It need hardly be said that in these two early uses of words we have no more than the beginnings of manipulative and declarative speech; that these two effects emerge as distinct functions only as the result of the co-operation of others with the child—that indeed his words acquire these functions only through this co-operation. It is in this way that, as time goes on, and with constant interchange, sound-patterns which are at first expressive become functionally effective.

At what point in the life of a child he begins to speak manipulatively or declaratively, with *intention*, we cannot say. He speaks and there is a response; how soon does he recognise this sequence and begin to speak with the intention of securing the response? We can do no more than consider the process by which intention is likely to develop. It is evident that one of the chief factors in this process must be the stabilisation of the usages of words, the development of regularities of meaning, in the child's communication with other people. To the beginnings of this we now turn.

THE STABILISATION OF MEANINGS

How does the word *mama*, for instance, come to mean the child's mother? Of course, when she hears him cry *mama* she approaches him, gives him his food, relieves his discomfort. He stops crying. She may be pardoned for assuming that he is giving her a name if he cries *mama* when she is absent and ceases when she appears. But close observation of children's early uses of *mama* shows that this assumption is far from justified; as a rule, over a period of some months the word has a wide range of 'meanings'. It is only through a long course of varied experiences, through repeatedly saying the word and evoking a response, hearing the word and responding to it, that the child comes to have the word as a name for his mother.

For instance, the record of the boy whom we have cited includes, from his tenth to his nineteenth month, the utterance of *mama* in a wide variety of circumstances of need and satisfaction, often without anything that could reasonably be called a reference to his mother. For instance, on one occasion at the beginning of his fourteenth month when a visitor new to him was in the room he picked up his playthings one by one and brought them to her saying *mama* each time (5).

It is obvious that a range of meanings as wide as this becomes narrowed down to mean the child's mother because of the manner in which she responds to his *mama*. She brings herself into the forefront of his experience. By relieving his discomfort when he cries *mama*, or enhancing his pleasure by smiling with him when he murmurs *mama* in contentment, she gives his word the rudiments of a manipulative or a declarative function.

She does something more than this: when she comes to him she says *Mama is here!* or something of the kind. She imitates his *mama*, imitating not only his word but also its 'meaning', for she brings the word into the situation which is already for him functionally bound up with this word. And he in his turn will imitate her—and this is the extent of the justification for the view that he learns to say *mama* by imitation.

The complexity of the process that emerges even from our brief analysis is remarkable—and even so there are probably factors that we have missed. Certainly one thing is clear—the child's first steps in the mother tongue move forward by constant inter-relation between him and those around him. Here, at any rate, a term sometimes too loosely used has an accurate application: <u>a child's linguistic development is a social process.</u>

BASIC BABY-LANGUAGE

Mama is not always a child's first word. It may be the commonest, because of its intrinsic relation to a child's bodily states, the situations in which he hears and speaks the word and therefore its traditional meaning in so many languages, which in turn reinforces its use by so many mothers. In other first words some if not all of these processes are also at work. In the further development of the main discomfort and comfort sound-patterns which—as we have seen in the last chapter—have their roots in the child's bodily states, we find, as in *mama*, an extension of usage to allied states, coupled with the social intervention which leads to an ultimate narrowing of the field of meaning.

As a result there are what may be called six archetypal nursery-words throughout the world; six sound-patterns broadly of these kinds: *mama, nana, papa, baba, tata, dada*, with local variations and with fairly well-defined ranges of meaning or areas of reference. *Mama, nana*—the more intense nasalised forms—come to be used in circumstances of urgency and for those persons who minister to the child's primary biological needs: food, sleep, mother, nurse, aunt, grandmother. *Papa, baba, tata, dada*—the more relaxed non-nasal forms—come to be used in states of contentment and for the persons, things and acts that evoke or contribute to these states; father, the child himself in play, playthings and games. It is easy to see how *papa*, a word spoken by the child in contentment, can come to mean a person who plays with him; how *baba* can come to mean the child himself, or *tata* a game such as hand-waving. This is a fascinating side of linguistics, the exploration of which would take us too far afield (6). Here we can do no more than recognise that, on the basis of the primary expressions of discomfort and comfort, the child's reference is directed—and the meanings of these six archetypal sound-patterns developed—by the socialisation of the child's utterance and his responses to the speech of others.

It is clear also that imitation and babbling will play their part in reinforcing the use of these sound-patterns. The patterns that are of most significance in the child's experience are those which will most readily be imitated by him and subsequently appear in his babbling. In this way, a process of selection takes place by which in every society, the child's primary wide repertory of sounds (see page 22) becomes limited to the phonemes of the mother tongue. His ability to utter other sounds become atrophied by disuse. An English child who at first can say *ch* as well as any German or Scottish child, later may be 'unable' to do so, and must be laboriously re-taught.

SECONDARY BABY-LANGUAGE

This archetypal basic baby-language is usually augmented by a repertory of words which, while they do not directly develop from the primary discomfort and comfort patterns, are yet related to these and at the same time to the patterns of the adult language. A sort of transitional language appears which acts as a bridge between the child's basic expressive utterance and the conventional linguistic forms of the mother tongue that he is acquiring. Words in this secondary baby-language enable the child to pass from his own primary utterance to the mother tongue by having affinities with his expressive forms and at the same time picturing—in sound or in pattern—the things or situations they come to mean.

Let us take as an instance the more or less onomatopoetic word *bow-bow* or *wow-wow*, which is among the earliest recognisable words of many children (7). It need hardly be said that this word is not as a rule a child's own imitation of a dog, but usually—perhaps always—his imitation of somebody else's *bow-wow*. Yet it is more readily acceptable to the child than a purely conventional word, for it has affinities both with his primary baby-language and also with the object it comes to mean. In form it is a front-consonantal reduplicated word (phonetically in the same class as *baba*)—and therefore the child more readily produces an imitation recognisable by himself and others. Secondly, the meaning of the word for the child—his tendency to utter the word when he perceives the dog—is greatly fostered by the word's picturing of the dog's bark. In brief, what happens is that an adult introduces into the child's experience a word which does not expressively arise from him; but which nevertheless has an affinity with his own expressive words and at the same time has an obvious representational link with the thing it is intended to indicate.

As well as onomatopoetic words, adults sometimes introduce words otherwise 'iconographic', where the word pictures not only the sound but other features of the thing meant—for instance, *tick-tock*, which represents to some extent the alternations of stress and pitch that seem to occur in the ticking of a clock. Now it is very interesting to notice children's transformations of this word. Among the records of the earliest words of four children (two German, one English, one American) we find these versions: *didda*, *dida*, *titit*, *titta* (8). It is clear that in all these cases the form of the word is assimilated by the child to the forms of his own reduplicated front-consonant words. Something of the pictorial character of the word is no doubt lost; what is gained is greater ease in reproducing it. And if—as is so often the case—the adult in turn imitates the child's version, so that *didda*, for instance, becomes the nursery-word for clock, his imitation of both form and meaning is greatly helped.

EARLY WORDS AND GENERAL DEVELOPMENT

We now have to ask what is the relation between the emergence of these early words and a child's general cognitive development and his affective and conative development. Here, because of the intimate relations between affective and conative growth, especially in infancy and childhood, we shall speak of 'orectic' development, using a term which in recent years has gained increasing currency (9).

What we can say of the divers aspects of development at this stage can, of course, only be by way of inference from what we can see of a child. We have to remain unaided by anything the child can tell us of himself; we have to infer what is going on 'in his mind' from what we can observe of him, other children and ourselves.

In uttering or in responding to a word a child, we may reasonably suppose, is helped by the word to attend more readily to the situation in which it occurs and so, as time goes on, to particular features of the situation—the word aids the child's perception. For this we have evidence both from experiment and from systematic observation.

One experiment may be cited. Two Russian workers in the tradition of Pavlov—Shipinova and Surina—'established conditioned reflexes' in children between thirteen and thirty-one months old. Repeatedly shown a red box and a green box, they came to recognise that it was the former that always contained a sweet. The 'establishment of the reflex' was often very difficult; 'it was easily extinguished and had to be worked out afresh next day.' But with a sample group of the children the (Russian) word *red* was spoken by the experimenter at every correct choice. The differences in results were striking. The sample, experimental, group needed up to fifteen trials to establish the connection, the control group two-and-a-half to three times as many. After the lapse of a week the experimental group recovered the connection much more readily than the control group, for whom the connection tended to be very unstable. Further, while the experimental group were capable of perceptual transference, 'losing no time in looking for a sweet under a red cup, a red box or a piece of red material', no transfer of reflexes was observed in children of the control group (10).

It would seem reasonable to suppose that the word *red* acted in a rudimentary way not only as a sign for the cup but also as a means of relating the cup and the sweet. This does not mean that the child understood the word as we understand it, but only that the word, carrying with it the stimulating power of the human voice, greatly aided the child's perception.

But in speaking of the power of the human voice we are implying also that the word evokes an orectic response from the child. This must be accepted. At this stage of development, affect and conation act together as a powerful selective influence upon the child's perception. When in the early days of modern child study, this became very evident, the case was no doubt over-stated. Meumann,

THE GROWTH OF MEANING

for example, said in 1902, 'The child's earliest words are exclusively emotional or volitional in meaning' (11).

What we can more certainly say is that at first affect and conation attract and direct the child's attention and that out of these cognitive and orectic beginnings the child's cognition grows, by a dual process —cognitive development and linguistic development influencing each other. On the one hand, the child's growing cognition, even where it is not mediated by language, influences his linguistic growth; on the other hand, the growth of language promotes his cognitive growth. We can illustrate this from a series of observations from the record of the child cited on page 31. During the first half of his second year, there were illuminating changes in the functions of *mama* for him (12).

1;0,6. The child is gnawing at a crust. His mother says *Baby, give mummy crustie*. He holds up the crust. His mother has tried this on several occasions in the past three weeks, but with no effect.

1;1,6. Father and mother with child, who is gnawing a crust. When Mother says *Give daddy crustie*, the child offers it to her. When she says *Give mummy crustie* he offers it to his father.

1;2,1. By this time the child is using *mama* in a variety of circumstances, as mentioned on page 32.

1;4,2. If Mother says *Come to mummy*, the child responds according to circumstances. If he is tired or needs help, he comes at once. Sometimes, however, he will scuttle away in play, hide his face and then look up roguishly.

1;6,13. When Mother says *Where's auntie?* the child imitates *ah-tee*, pointing in the right direction. To *Where's Dempy?* he replies *deh-deh*, again pointing in the right direction. But to *Where's mummy?* he points in the right direction, but remains silent.

1;6,15. From his baby-carriage he catches sight of a poster on a hoarding—a picture of a smiling woman. Immediately he says *mama, mama*.

Even these few salient instances from the full record of this child suggest that the process of the growth of meaning is a highly complex inter-action of cognitive and orectic factors. We notice that from the beginning the child normally does not hear the word as an isolated unit; it comes to him in a verbal context (*Baby, give mummy crustie*) and also in a context of action—his mother, for instance, bends forward, smiles, holds out her hand. And his responsive behaviour is likewise complex—it includes, in addition to his overt physical act, some cognition and some affect. He hands the crust; he is aware of his mother, the crust and the act of giving; he experiences pleasure in his own achievement and in the encouragement expressed by his mother at this achievement.

If we were to infer from this incident at 1;0,6 that the child has firmly associated *mama* with his mother, the next observation, just one month later, should disabuse us. It is clear that all that has been established is a loose linkage between the broad pattern of the mother's behaviour and the broad pattern of her child's response. So long as his mother's gestures and expression and the over-all pattern of her remark are relatively constant, the child responds with the act of giving; but there is not yet a stable association of the word *mummy* with his mother (or of *daddy* with his father). The linkage becomes closer in the following months, not only through the child's repeated experience of the word spoken by others but also, as we see, for instance, at 1;2,1, through his own uses of the word, constantly encouraged as he is by those around him.

The observation at 1;4,2, reminds us that the link, stronger though it may be, is by no means a simple cognitive relationship. The child's response to *Come to mummy* is influenced by his affective state before he hears the words and by his affective response on hearing them. The record on this occasion suggests not so much a specific, stabilised, response to each of the words *come* and *mummy*, as this—that the phrase as a whole still evokes from the child a broad pattern of action, in this case the incipient response of going to his mother. Whether this potential response then issues into the act of going or whether it is replaced by some other behaviour, will depend upon the affective factors.

Two months later, at 1;6,13, the continuing strongly affective character of the child's response to *mummy* is shown in a very striking fashion. To *auntie* and *Dempy* he responds with the expected act—he points and imitates the word. Not so when he hears *mummy*. He points silently. This word has of course an immeasurably fuller significance for him than the other words. Of an adult or an older child we might say that he is too shy or inhibited to utter, in play, a word that has so rich an emotional meaning for him. Of a child of this age it would perhaps be more accurate to say that he 'cannot' speak this word unless the appropriate affective conditions are present. He cannot 'play' with the word *mummy* which has so strong an affective character for him. It is now a word whose utterance is evolved by a pressing need—something much more powerful than the routine of a game. It is still, then, far from being a name for his mother.

The episode two days later seems, at first sight, to weaken this interpretation, but closer consideration shows that this need not be so. When he catches sight of the poster, the child's cry of *mama* is probably much more than a sound-pattern he has learned to utter on perceiving his mother. On this occasion, in fact, it was a cry of delight—an expression of feeling, an affective response to the smile depicted there, his pleasure on seeing the face of his mother and also, perhaps, his pleasure in the experience of recognition itself.

PERCEPTION AND LINGUISTIC DEVELOPMENT

What has a record such as this to tell us about the growth of perception in children? It suggests that a not uncommon view of the genesis of perception is false: the notion that the power of perceiving becomes more refined and discriminative merely as the result of experience in perceiving. It is clear, rather, that the development of perception is influenced by, and influences, other aspects of a child's development—in other words, when we are describing the development of perception we are drawing attention to one aspect of his total growth. Observations such as those we have just discussed lead us to these inferences. A child learns to perceive the world around him in the course of his physical activity, in his manipulation of his world. This growth of perception is related to the orexis aroused in him by his experience of this world; at the same time his growing perception is influenced by, and influences, his linguistic development.

In view of our specific concern here, let us consider the last of these a little more fully. Perception will develop in the absence of language or indeed of any other symbols. If we may imagine a child deprived, or almost entirely deprived, of language—as for instance, a blind and deaf child, or a child living a highly solitary life—we should suppose that there would nevertheless be some growth of his power of perception, partly through the maturation of his sensory and motor organisation, partly through a process of learning during the repeated experiences of perceiving the world around him. One may well suppose also that, since perception often involves some recall, this deprived child would develop a symbolism of his own, some sort of imagery—not necessarily visual—which would contribute to his recognition of objects and to his awareness of similarities and differences (13).

In normal children language enters this process of symbolic mediation to reinforce it, to shape it and ultimately to become its chief means. How soon this entrance of language begins it is not easy to say; Piaget suggests that the 'sensori-motor period' may last until the end of a child's second year, when he will still be acting 'directly'—that is, without using inner language. A typical instance is a child of this age who draws his bed coverlet towards him to get something lying on it. This happens, says Piaget, without the mediation of inner language (14).

The evidence given in the earlier part of this chapter makes it difficult to accept this statement at its face value; it is difficult to believe that even during his first year a child's behaviour towards his mother, for instance, is uninfluenced by the fact that he says and hears the word *mama*. Everything goes to suggest that while a child's earliest perception may be non-symbolic, symbolism soon enters; and that with the advent of verbal symbolism, the functions of language become wider and more powerful as perception develops. Language helps to intensify the child's awareness of specific features of his environment, both when others speak to him and when he speaks to them. Further, language, by reinforcing attention, fosters retention; so that the repetition of a word by the child himself or by others helps him to recognise things—as, for instance, the child who said *mama* on seeing the poster.

One of the chief clues to our understanding of this is given by Bartlett, in his well-known study of remembering. To explain how past experiences influence present behaviour he advances the hypothesis of the 'schema'—the effect of past experiences persists as a pattern of readiness with which we meet the present situation. This pattern or schema is not merely a static impression made by the past experiences—a schema is an active, dynamic process. In the interval between the past and the present there is a cumulative development—a schema is 'an active organisation of past reactions and past experiences.'

Now while schemata may operate without our being aware of them, we often need to bring them consciously into relation with the present situation. A person then, says Bartlett, 'turns round upon his schemata'; he becomes conscious of these schematic organisations within himself by symbolising them; either by non-verbal means—such as 'images' or other bodily patterns—or by language (15).

We are not supposing that a process as definite as this necessarily occurs as early as a child's first year. But we may well believe that the beginnings of it are emerging in a child's perception of his mother when he says *mama*, having previously seen her, been fed by her and played with her on innumerable occasions.

THE CONCEPTUAL ASPECT OF EARLY PERCEPTION

Now as soon as we observe a child recognising something we may also wonder whether his perception of this is not to some extent conceptual. A widely-accepted view of the nature of conceptual thinking does imply this. A concept, says Price in his analysis of thinking, is a 'recognitional capacity' (16). If this is what we mean by a concept, then a child who recognises his mother or his teddy bear is already perceiving these in a somewhat conceptual fashion.

That this is possible is also implied in generally accepted views of the relation between perception and conception; Blanshard, for instance, in his study *The Nature of Thought*, says 'We may say confidently that there is no stage in experience, not even pure sensation, if such a stage exists, in which universals are not present.'

The part that language plays in this was long ago made clear by Stout when he pointed out that the 'universal' is present in perceptual as well as conceptual thinking. 'Implicit in the percept, it is explicit in the concept.... The universal must, so to speak, be dragged from the dim background of consciousness and thrust into the foreground, there to be scrutinised and manipulated by the mind. It is language which makes this possible.' In another place Stout points out that even a proper name is conceptual in function in that it symbolises for us 'the unity and connecting identity of a person's manifold and varying states, relations, qualities and activities' (17).

This suggests that when a child of eighteen months says *mama* on seeing his mother, the word is symbolising for him his identification of her in diverse circumstances. There is surely some truth in this. At least, there are the small beginnings, the rudiments of conceptual thinking, of recognition in the course of perception. But we must be careful not to picture this recognition as a purely cognitive process. As yet we have no more than the potentiality of cognitive growth in what is still a predominantly orectic event. Seeing his mother he expresses his pleasure in a variety of ways; if he says *mama* it is as much an expression of his feelings as a mark of his recognition of her.

Certainly, the more often he responds to his mother in the same way, the more probably will he become aware of similarity in what he perceives. And the growth of this awareness will depend to some extent on the responses that other people make to him. By their attitudes, their gestures and their words they may either reinforce or weaken the growth of his rudimentary recognition.

In brief, so far from *mama* having become for this child at eighteen months a name for his mother, we are still witnessing the beginnings of the process through which the word ultimately comes to be a name. It will be for us to describe this further process—the manner in which the development of language and the development of cognition result in 'names'.

To understand this, we must look beyond conceptual thinking, to a development of supreme importance in a child's life—the emergence of ethical behaviour. We are using the term 'ethical' in the widest sense; we are thinking of a child's ethical development as the growth of his behaviour in relation to the approval and disapproval of conduct—his own and others'. And we have to ask what is the place of language in this development.

LANGUAGE AND ETHICAL BEHAVIOUR

From a very early time a pattern of approved behaviour is being fashioned in the child. We say fashioned, because while much of his

THE GROWTH OF MEANING

purely cognitive development takes place through his own direct experience of his environment, with some incidental direction from others, his ethical development mostly occurs through their deliberate intervention. He learns how to behave under the pressure of their approval or disapproval.

This ethical development is of course both cognitive and orectic. Since, as we have seen, the beginnings of cognition may be non-symbolic as well as symbolic, ethical development may also have rudimentary beginnings which are non-symbolic. In the early stages the child modifies his behaviour in response to the physical—non-linguistic—behaviour of others, including gestural and facial expressions of approval and disapproval. With his linguistic progress this development is likely to be greatly accelerated. For disapproval the gain from language is greater even than for approval. A child behaving in an acceptable way needs no more than a smile or a gesture to encourage him to continue. A child doing, or about to do, something harmful or potentially harmful must be stopped at once. For this, nothing is so powerful an instrument as language. The parent's admonitory *No!* rapidly becomes the means of prohibition at a distance.

In the normal course of development, this is seen in the fact that *No!* enters earlier into the child's linguistic experience than *Yes!* To take a typical instance: the child K was first observed to respond to *No!* at 0;9,15, while his first response to *Yes!* was at 1;9,3. His first own use of *No!* was at 1;7,6; his first *Yes!* at 1;8,27.

The fuller record of this child illustrates in a striking way the manner in which the response to and utterance of these two words combine to influence behaviour.

0;9,5. He has seized a piece of newspaper which he is about to put into his mouth. I say *No!* in a loud voice. Immediately he stops the movement of his hand and looks towards me. He keeps his eyes steadily on me for a minute or so, then turns back to continue the movement of the paper towards the mouth. I say *No!* again. Again he turns towards me and stops the movement of his hand. This time he looks at me for quite two minutes. I look steadily back at him. He begins to cry and continues for some minutes.

Two things happen here: the child desists from his intended action and shows, by crying, that the situation is unpleasant for him. At this stage the child's response must be to the intonation, pitch and suddenness of the word rather than to its phonetic form. The child is startled by the sound and his act is interrupted. As time goes on, he learns by repetition of this sequence of events that the act of putting paper to his mouth will be followed by the unpleasant experience of hearing *No!* For instance:

> 1;1,27. He begins to play with a forbidden object. His mother says *No! No!* He stops at once.

A week later he is beginning to anticipate and so avoid the unpleasant *No!*

> 1;2,3. Whenever recently he has attempted to open the lid of a coal-box, his mother or father has said *No!* Today he attempts to open the lid; his father says *No!* The child looks up at him, whimpers a little and crawls away from the box. Ten minutes later he is again at the box and catches hold of the lid as though about to lift it. Then he looks up at his father, drops the lid and crawls away.

This, in adult terms, could be described as the child 'remembering' that attempting to lift the lid is followed by *No!* It is, of course, possible that the child does not, at this stage, actually remember past occasions of this kind when he has heard the word *No!*—that his past experiences influence his present intended behaviour without any recall of these past experiences.

But there comes a time when the child himself begins to say *No!* in a situation where his behaviour is prohibited. For K the first recorded instance of this occurred about five months after the last observation.

> 1;7,6. He takes up a book. His mother says *Don't tear it, will you?* He replies *No!* Later she tries this again twice, with the same response each time.

Here the recall of *No!* has certainly emerged into utterance. Again assuming as little as possible, we can say that, hearing the prohibitory admonition by his mother, the child completes the now accus-

THE GROWTH OF MEANING

tomed pattern of experience by saying *No!* The child's mother takes this, of course, as an expression of his assent and so, in fact, the beginnings of this verbal assent are fostered, as we see three days later:

> 1;7,9. He reaches out for a medicine bottle. His mother says *No bottle, baby.* He replies, *No!* and desists from trying to touch the bottle. Later in the day this happens again.

A further development becomes evident less than a week later:

> 1;7,15. He is offered, for the first time, some clotted cream in a spoon and takes it. His mother offers him more but he turns away his head and says, *No!*

Here, it would seem, he marks his own refusal by saying the word that has become the linguistic element of the act of desisting. In this way *No!* begins to be an expression of refusal.

About a month after this we find the first record of his use of *Yes!*

> 1;8,27. His mother asks: *Do you love daddy?* He replies, *Yes!*

These early uses of *No!* and *Yes!* are, we may well suppose, still largely expressive; they are part of the child's total response to the situation—they have not yet become responses, in themselves, to the situation. As time goes on, these words begin to emerge, with increasing clarity, from the situations in which they occur. They are on the way to becoming verbal substitutes for disapproved or approved acts.

We see this first in the manner in which his responses to these words begin to change. He begins to deal with them verbally. Instead of embarking on an act and waiting for the word *Yes!* or *No!*, the child verbally anticipates what he might be about to do and then acts in accordance with the reply he obtains.

> 1;9,2. There are two low cupboards side by side, one of which is forbidden to him. He points to this cupboard saying *eh, eh* (a customary way with him of indicating a wish or request). When his mother replies *No!* he points to the permitted cupboard, again saying *eh, eh.* His mother replies *Yes!* All this is repeated about a dozen times. Later there is a similar episode in connection with a forbidden bottle and a permitted box.

The very interesting advance here is that the child is beginning to precede an intended act by speech and gesture and, finding that these receive the response *Yes* or *No*, he repeats all this as a sort of game, one result of which is that his *eh eh*, which has been an expression of need, now begins to take on an interrogatory function. We have here the rudiments of what ultimately becomes the child's act of seeking permission, asking whether what he would like to do is acceptable to others.

The further freeing of these words from immediate situations is seen when the child begins to use them himself in relation to anticipated behaviour, action that is still in the future—though still, of course, closely bound up with the present situation. An instance of an early use of both assent and refusal is seen in the following observation of K:

> 1;9,23. His mother, who is wheeling him in his pram, asks, *Want to walk?* He replies, *vaukie, vaukie*, is put down and walks a little. Later, back in his pram, he says, *Vaukie*; and when his mother says *No!* he tries to get down out of the pram himself (18).

This is clearly a step towards the substitution of words for physical acts—the words are beginning to be freed from the context of the situation in which they have previously been embedded. To ask permission the child, instead of uttering expressive sounds such as *eh eh*, uses a word of the mother tongue which much more effectively indicates what he intends. Instead of responding to *No!* automatically—with a specific response that he has been 'trained' to make—he is now beginning to 'comprehend' it; he now responds to the word in the context of the situation and his own impulses.

Now as these words *Yes* and *No* become increasingly freed from specific situations and responses, it becomes more possible for the child to speak them to himself and even merely imagine them—as some psychologists would say, he may begin to 'internalise' them and so use them as guides to his own behaviour. This is evidently a development of the greatest importance in a child's life. To consider how it takes place we must first notice now his thinking develops and the part that language plays in this.

3

Language and Thinking

WE have now to observe more closely how the child is initiated into the language spoken by those around him and at the same time initiated into their modes of thought. We have to see how the growth of his language and the growth of his thought influence each other; how the words of his baby-language, with their functions in his behaviour, come to be supplemented and ultimately superseded by the words of the mother tongue with their current meanings.

Throughout all this we see a continuing process, the beginnings of which we have already witnessed—the process of mutual adaptation between the child and his society. For his part, the child both transforms his own language in the direction of the mother tongue, and the mother tongue in the direction of his own language. For their part, those who speak to him sometimes adopt his speech and sometimes adapt their speech to his. The child moves towards conformity with the usages of his society, but his conformity is, of course, never complete—whilst he changes he tends to cling to his habits of speech and thought. Whilst he accepts, he resists. So throughout life his speech and thought retain their individual idiosyncrasies.

CHANGES IN THE FORMS OF SPEECH

Let us look first at the typical changes in the forms of a child's speech as he moves forward from his baby-language. Nothing is more striking in children's development than their strange transformations of the mother tongue. At first sight they may appear wayward, casual and wildly different from child to child; yet they are, for the most part, in accordance with a fundamental principle of human development—the child's attempts to master the unfamiliar forms of the mother tongue are constantly determined by the familiar forms of his own speech (1). He assimilates what is new to what has become habitual; he adapts what he has been accustomed to say to what he hears. In the act of reaching forward he is harking back.

The growth of a child's vocabulary is sometimes thought of as the 'acquisition' of words, as though each new word were one more ticket or label added to his collection. This notion comes perhaps from thinking of a language as a social institution, an established system which a child takes over, step by step; or, maybe, from an undue emphasis on the written rather than the spoken language, or perhaps from observing what happens in learning a foreign language. A schoolboy who learns that *homme* means *man* is adding to his collection of words. But a child's progress towards the mastery of the mother tongue is not, in the early stages at least, this kind of addition. It is, rather, a continued process of modification of the patterns of his linguistic behaviour. These patterns are schemata which have developed in the course of the child's experiences.

In the last chapter we noticed how his schemata may influence changes in a child's *uses* of a word, its functions. At the same time he is influenced by schemata of the *forms* of words, which we may call his phonetic schemata—the persistence of earlier habitual forms of speech, now showing themselves in his transformations of the mother tongue. As Bartlett says, 'determination by schemata is the most fundamental of all the ways in which we can be influenced by reactions and experiences which occurred some time in the past' (2).

The detailed recording and analysis of transformations that occur in children's speech exemplify this very clearly. For instance, a child at the beginning of his third year was saying *vide* for *ride* at a time when in other contexts he was making a clear *r*-sound. Why this discrepancy? This child's record shows that *v* had appeared earlier in his history than *r*. Now, in his imitation of *ride*, he assimilates the initial sound to his more familiar schema *v*. The same child said *ninnie* for *Winnie* at a time when he was saying *w* in different

LANGUAGE AND THINKING

contexts. Not only had *n* appeared three months earlier than *w*; the form *ninnie* shows the persistence of the schema of 'reduplication' or doubling which, as we have seen, is characteristic of primary baby-language. Many similar examples can be cited from the records of children in different countries (3).

THE EXPANSION AND CONTRACTION OF MEANINGS

In a child's further semantic development, the persistence of schemata as he encounters new situations is no less evident. Sometimes the effect is to extend the application of a word, sometimes to narrow this. Here again, instead of simple acquisition, there is a constant process of progressive adaptation, in which the meanings of any one speech-form tend to expand and contract under the influence of his intercourse with others. We have seen a notable instance of this in the last chapter, in our survey of one child's progressive use of *mama*.

A more general consideration of such changes of meaning will help us to understand how these are related to a child's general development in his inter-action with those about him.

Extensions of meaning are among the most characteristic features of children's speech. Often bizarre, amusing and 'clever', examples have been recorded by a multitude of observers (4). One of the earliest instances we owe to Darwin, whose boy 'when just beginning to speak' said *quack* with reference to a duck and then applied the word to water; then to birds and insects on the one hand and to liquids on the other. Later, having seen a representation of an eagle on a French coin, he named other coins *quack* (5). We may cite one other example, from the record of their daughter by the Chamberlains: at nineteen months she saw the moon through the window and was told *moon*. The same evening, with half a circular biscuit in her hand, she said *mooi*. Subsequently she applied this word to cakes, round marks on a window, writing on a window, writing on paper, stains on the ceiling, 'round things in books', patterns on the bindings of books, faces, postmarks and the letter O (6).

Examples such as this might suggest that extension of meaning occurs in this way: a child, having imitated a new word with a particular meaning, then applies it to other 'similar' or 'related' things. But the whole story is longer and less simple. The wide use of a particular sound-group is, as we have seen, already characteristic of a child's linguistic behaviour long before he imitates conventional words. When by imitation he comes to replace one of his own sound-groups by a conventional word the process of extension to other situations may continue. For example:

> 1;9,15. On seeing aeroplanes through the window, he said *eh-eh* (a 'word' used by him in a variety of situations). Twelve days later, seeing an aeroplane, he said *pay pay* (plane): next day he said *pay* when he saw a kite (7).

To casual observation it might seem that the process of extension of meaning began only when the child, having learnt *pay* for aeroplane, went on to use it for kite; and that his previous use of *eh-eh* for aeroplane was mere noise-making or playing with sounds. But the fact that the child was already using *eh-eh* for aeroplane before he adopted—and then adapted—the conventional word is very important. We cannot understand the nature of a child's extension of the use of a conventional word unless we recognise that this is a continuation of a process already at work in his use of his own speech-forms.

We must also recognise that a child's progress does not consist only in the extension of the application of a word: he learns also to limit its application. Examples of this are not so often recorded. The reason is obvious. It is striking and perhaps amusing when a child, having learnt the word *pay* for aeroplane, applies it to a kite. But when he goes on to imitate and use the word *kite* correctly and thereafter limits *pay* to aeroplanes, nothing remarkable seems to have occurred. But in a child's development this process of limitation is no less important than the process of extension.

To understand these two processes we need close and detailed observations. Unfortunately the great majority of records of children are less useful than they might have been, since they fail to detail the circumstances in which a child uttered a particular word or responded to it. It is not enough to have a list of the successive 'things named' by the word. We need to know something of the situation, something of the behaviour of the child himself and others, on each occasion.

Here we shall survey a single example in detail, considering both

TABLE II
EXPANSION AND CONTRACTION OF MEANINGS

Age of Child	Cat	Cow	Horse	Large Dog	Small Dog	Toy Dog
1;9,11	→tee					
1;10,18		→tee				
1;11,1						
1;11,2			→tee			
1;11,24			→hosh		→tee	→goggie
1;11,25	pushie		tee		goggie	
1;11,26		→moo-ka		→hosh		
1;11,27				biggie-goggie		
2;0,10						
2;0,20	pushie	moo-ka	hosh	biggie-goggie	goggie	goggie

→ First use of a word.   ──── Word no longer used.

expansion and contraction of a word and allied words during a period of some three months; Table II. At the beginning of the period the child, who for some time past has used *tee* for a cat (Timmy) now extends its use to include a small dog. At 1;10,18 he uses it for a cow and at 1;11,24 for a horse. There is then a contraction of its meaning when he acquires *hosh* for a horse, but this word in its turn is at 2;0,20 extended in meaning to include a large dog. At the end of the period he has four different words—*pushie*, *moo-ka*, *hosh* and *goggie*—for four animals all of which, at some time during the period, have been indicated by the word *tee*. The whole series of observations, typical of the manner in which children acquire the conventional words for animals, is worth studying in some detail.

How are these changes related to the child's behaviour in his intercourse with others? We begin with the fact that he has imitated *Timmy* by saying *tee* when he sees the cat. Now he says *tee* when he sees a dog. What has happened?

It is an instance of what Pavlov has called generalisation. But, as some of his followers have pointed out, this is not logical generalisation, the result of cognitive analysis and synthesis. It is only the beginning of the process of development that ultimately leads to logical generalisation.

Certainly at this stage there are the rudiments of conceptual thinking. There is a recognition of the objective similarity between the dog and the cat—the dog, in some respects, 'looks like' a cat. By saying *tee* on seeing the dog the child shows that he has the 'recognitional capacity' that Price has identified with conceptual thinking.

But this is far from being the whole story. The child's recognition is certainly not confined to the objective similarity between the dog and the cat. There are other elements in the situation which combine now to evoke the word *tee*.

The child brings to this situation schemata of past experiences—of his use of the word *tee* and of his experiences of cats and dogs. These schemata are not simply cognitive— they are likely to be both functional and orectic as well (8). And the child is probably saying the word *to* someone—there is communication.

To say that there is functional similarity is to suppose that the child perceives the dog as something that may have the same function in his experience as the cat has had. He can expect the dog to behave to him, in some measure, like a cat; he can, for instance, play with the dog as he has played with the cat. To say that there is orectic similarity is to suppose that the dog arouses in the child something of the affect and conation that the cat has aroused.

As to communication, it is clear from the actual record of this episode that the child is not merely 'naming' similarity—putting, so to speak, a label on a concept. The child—as far as we can judge from the record—is using *tee* declaratively; he is communicating to others his response to the dog, inviting them to share his experience. He is using a habitual linguistic act—the word *tee*—as a means of declarative communication in a situation which is partly new and partly like past situations. And it is in extending his use of the word in this declarative way, that he is providing himself with a symbol of similarity. So the word *tee* begins to be a means of thinking conceptually about the dog and the cat.

This close analysis gives us a guide to understanding the further development of expansion and contraction by which this child, during a period of three months, arrives at a group of names for animals, approaching conformity with adult usage.

The child, already using *tee* for dog, now at the end of a further month (1;10,18) says *tee* for a cow. A fortnight later a very interesting development occurs. He has taken over *goggie* for his own toy dog (1;11,1). Then he extends this to include a dog (1;11,2); and this extension, we see, at once involves a contraction of the previously wider use of *tee*.

But while contracted here, the use of *tee* is extended in another direction. At 1;11,24 the child says the word on seeing a horse. His father gives him the word *horse*; his exclamation *hosh* next day suggests that he has adopted this. But no; things are not so simple. The following day, seeing a horse, he reverts to *tee*; his father says *horse* which he then imitates.

The events of these last three days illustrate in a very striking way both the child's conservatism and the manner in which he moves forward under social pressure. The child is conservative in that he persists in using his familiar *tee*. Social pressure then comes in and he adopts the new word *hosh*.

The sequel to this is again very illuminating. A fortnight later, the child, seeing a large St Bernard dog, says *hosh*—a not unnatural extension. No doubt someone then said to him something like: 'No! That's not a horse—that's a dog!' How bewildering, perhaps, for the child. This large creature, which looks so much like a *hosh* is, he is told, a *goggie!* A difficult lesson; but he learns it. Ten days later he is saying *biggie goggie* for the St Bernard.

It is by some such dual process of extension and contraction that children learn to classify and name animals as we do. In the course of three months this particular child has, from time to time, extended the use of *tee* to apply to cat, cow, dog and horse; but by subsequent contractions it has been replaced by four new words; *pushie, goggie, moo-ka* and *hosh*.

One of the most striking features of these changes is the manner in which the child's adoption of the new is modified by the persistence of the habitual, whether in the forms of his words or in their meanings. The word *tee* itself is already a combination of the child's utterance of *Timmy* and his habitual front-consonant baby-language —*tee* is, in fact, a typical 'early word'. As for its meaning, we have seen how the child tends to use it conservatively, applying it in turn to each new animal he encounters—a familiar schema in a new situation. Again—when under the pressure of social intercourse, he adopts *pushie, goggie* and *moo-ka*, notice how the form of eaeh of these, again, is an amalgam of the old and the new. The word *goggie*, for instance, has two characteristics of baby-language—the consonant is a back comfort-sound and there is doubling. Finally, the extension of the new word *hosh*, once adopted, to include the St Bernard is parallel with using the new word *pay* for the kite.

Thus the child moves towards the mother tongue through a continued process of convergence between the old and the new, the personal and the social. He utters patterns of sounds and he uses them in ways which are influenced both by his own habits and the habits of those around him. Ultimately those speech-forms and those meanings persist which are given social approval during the child's intercourse with others.

Declarative and manipulative factors. Such records of a child's actual growth remind us that a concept is not simply an imprint on the mind, impressed there by a succession of perpetual experiences. The development of conceptual thinking is the growth of an ability, of the operation of a 'recognitional capacity'. A child, when he applies a habitual word in a new situation—for instance, his encounter with a new animal—is not merely naming the animal, in the sense that the word is evoked from the child by the mere force of association or conditioning. The child, in uttering the word, is performing an act, *doing* something. And we must not fail to notice that he is doing this in concert with others through intercourse with them.

Because we have a word *horse* which for us is the name of the animal—a word by which we refer to any horse—we may, hearing a child say *hosh* suppose that it has the same function for him; that having learnt that this is the name of that animal, he then applies it to other similar animals. But if we consider the situations in which, at this stage, a child speaks this word we see that this interpretation is false. The child is still only on his way to naming: it is through what he is doing now that he will ultimately come to have names for things.

What, then, was this particular child doing when he said *hosh*? The most important part of the answer is that he was using the word communicatively. He was speaking *to* someone, not merely in the presence of someone. No doubt his utterance was in some measure expressive—in Darwin's sense; what he said was the vocal part of his total response to the situation. But clearly he was also addressing himself to a listener, drawing the attention of some other person to the situation.

We can, of course, only infer this from observation of the child's behaviour. All the circumstances, as recorded at the time, suggest that when he said *hosh* on seeing the St Bernard, he was speaking declaratively. He was perhaps expressing his pleasure at the sight of the large animal, pleasure mingled perhaps with awe at the size and vigour of this fine creature; maybe also his pleasure in his own recognition of its similarity to the horse previously encountered. And if he received in reply some expressive response from the person he was speaking to, his word was not only expressive but had achieved declarative communication.

Manipulative communication will also, through extension and contraction, contribute towards naming. We take an instance of this from the record of the same child. He had been using the word *boh* for various boxes, including the box containing his toy bricks. At

1;7,8 he wanted some of his bricks which were lying scattered about beyond his reach. The box was not there. Stretching towards the bricks, he said repeatedly, *boh*, *boh*, *boh*, until the bricks were handed to him. To test whether he was really extending the use of *boh* to include the brick, his father said, *Give daddy boh*, whereupon the boy handed him a brick. Nearly three months elapsed before the child began to use *biki* for brick; this adaptation of the adult word brought with it a limitation of the use of *boh* (9).

Let us ask, When this child extends the manipulative use of *boh* from the box to the bricks, what happens? In the past, he has used the word *boh* as a means of securing an 'object as a whole'—'the-box-containing-bricks'. He is now under the urgent necessity of drawing attention to what has been part of this object, the bricks. He can do no more than try with the word *boh* that has already proved effective in drawing attention to the whole object. He is understood; he is successful; the word *boh* achieves for him manipulative communication as a means of securing the bricks. But at the moment when he is handed the bricks he also receives the word *bricks*; and in ultimately adopting this as *biki*, and simultaneously learning to limit the use of *boh*, he is being helped to discriminate between the box and the bricks—in the manner reminiscent of the famous episode in the life of Helen Keller when she first came to discriminate between the mug and the water within it (10). From instances such as this it is evident that the continued process of manipulative extension and contraction must play a large part in the growth of conceptual thinking.

What emerges from our account of this transition to the mother tongue is that a child moves towards the naming of objects as the result of the impact of conventional words and their meanings on the patterns of linguistic behaviour that have long been habitual with him. He has been seeking to satisfy his needs by means of his own rudimentary declarative and manipulative sound-patterns; in seeking the co-operation of others he is impelled to extend and to contract the application of these patterns. His adoption of a conventional word, in place of one of his own, accelerates this process while it enhances the efficacy of communication. So he learns to use words of the mother tongue as names for particular things or groups of them.

We have, therefore, to qualify the not uncommon statement that a child begins the process of generalisation and classification by first learning a name for a thing and then extending and limiting the application of this name (11). The truth is, rather, this. A child's instrumental uses of his own speech, which have their roots in his earliest expressive utterance, are means by which he experiments in satisfying his needs through extending and contracting the application of his sound-patterns, under the constant responsive guidance of those who share his experiences. In the course of time the adoption of conventional words in place of his own primitive sound-patterns ultimately leads him to recognise that words may be the names of things. This is certainly a most powerful factor in his cognitive development, helping him towards the modes of abstract thinking current in the society in which he lives. But the course of this cognitive development has its beginnings in the earliest moments of his life. It is carried forward by the daily interchange of his behaviour with others; it moves in directions determined by his needs, his emotions and his purposes. The beginnings of his awareness of his own orectic experiences—of his emotions and his intentions—we have noticed in the last chapter. We now have to observe the further development of this awareness.

4
Language and Personal and Social Development

THE DISCRIMINATION OF ORECTIC ATTITUDES

WE have seen that a child's progress in the accepted classification of things—for instance, animals—is as strongly orectic as it is cognitive. With the aid of language, whilst he is moving towards current modes of thinking, he is moving towards current patterns of feelings and attitudes. We have now to observe how he comes to differentiate the diversity of orectic attitudes—his own and others'—as he acquires more precise and specific means of symbolising them. We shall see that this again is not simply a process of attaching verbal labels to already existing attitudes. On the other hand, the word does not give birth to the attitude. As with cognitive development, the child's orectic behaviour begins early and his attitudes are expressed by his own primitive sound-groups. The growing pressure of the need to communicate leads him to adopt conventional words, which in turn modify his attitudes. There is constant mutual inter-action between the growth of language and the growth of orectic behaviour.

It is a process of increasing differentiation and discrimination. The child learns to differentiate more effectively between approval and disapproval, and at the same time to discriminate diverse modes of approval and of disapproval. From the broad orectic opposition of discomfort and contentment, satisfaction and dissatisfaction, there begin to emerge specific æsthetic and ethical attitudes.

(i) *Orectic discrimination of situations*

An important phase of a child's orectic, as of his cognitive, development is his adoption of conventional words in relation to particular situations. When K, who has been saying *a . . . a . . . a* on seeing the cat, now says *tee*, he is specifying this situation not only cognitively but also orectically. The same primitive sound-group *a . . . a . . . a* has up to this moment served to express a feeling of pleasure in many different situations; *tee* expresses pleasure evoked more specifically by the cat.

Two other series of episodes from the record of the same child illustrate this more cogently: his adoption of *fa* for flowers and *shee* for sea (1).

fa

Since his tenth month the child has frequently said *a . . . a . . . a* in a tone of delight in a variety of situations.

1;4,12. His mother brings him near some jonquils growing in a bowl. She says: *Smell the pretty flowers.* He bends over and smells them, saying *a . . . a . . . a.*
1;4,13. The child is crawling about the room. His mother says: *Where are the flowers?* He crawls towards the jonquils and holds out his hand towards them.
1;4,16. In another room there is a bowl of tulips. His mother says: *Baby, where's the flowers?* He points to the tulips.
1;6,14. His mother is holding him by a window, through which he can see a bowl of hyacinths in the room. He puts his hand on the window-pane and says *fa fa.*

It is clear that in replacing his primary expressive *a a* by *fa*—his adaptation of the adult word—the child is making a dual advance. He is able to communicate his delight more effectively, to draw his mother's attention to the flowers and not to any other object in the room. At the same time he is enabling himself to link up his feeling of pleasure with the flowers, to bring this feeling more closely into relation with the flowers. The expression of approval and the attitude of approval itself are both becoming more discriminated.

The second series of observations illustrates a similar development in the expression of disapproval:

shee

Since his eleventh month the child has frequently said *a a* or *eh eh* in a tone of displeasure in a variety of situations.

1;9,23. At the seaside. His mother has taken him for a walk by the sea and has said the word *sea* to him several times. Later, out of sight of the sea, she says: *Where's the sea?* He points in the right direction.

1;9,28. He is in bed. There is a thunderstorm. His mother hears him crying and goes to him. He is standing up in his bed in agitation and fear. He points in the direction of the sea, saying *shee, shee!*

Here, by using the adult word *sea* instead of his primitive *eh eh*, the child is able to make known that it is the noise of the storm—'mistaken' for the sound of a rough sea—which is the object of his fear.

In each of these series there are the same characteristics as we have already seen in the child's cognitive development—the broad use of a primary sound-pattern made more limited in scope and more definite by his adoption and adaption of a conventional word. In this way the child reaches a stage where an orectic attitude—approval or disapproval, delight or fear—is expressed not only by intonation, facial movement, gesture, bodily posture, but by a specific phonetic form. For the adult this is the name of an object; for the child a sound-pattern linked to a situation.

Great as this advance is, it is still only a step towards the symbolisation of an attitude so that it is clearly specified to others in communication and to the child himself. *Fa fa*, for instance, spoken in a tone of pleasure may express delight; uttered in a tone of disapproval it may express refusal. Similarly the word *shee*, here used to express fear, might with a different intonation be used to express pleasure. The child now needs to acquire verbal means, a distinctive phonetic pattern, by which he can reinforce intonation, gesture, posture and movement in drawing attention more precisely to the orectic attitude itself, whether approval or disapproval.

This advance occurs as the child takes over and adapts conventional names of attitudes. By the end of his third year, for instance,

K was using a variety of words for different kinds of approval: *pretty, nice, clean, good, better, best, lovely, right*; or disapproval: *horrid, dirty, naughty, shocking, nasty, untidy, wrong*.

How do these discriminatory words emerge in a child's speech and what functions have they for him? Certainly it is not enough to say that through imitation he has acquired a repertory of adjectives. The child has adopted a word which in the current language is adjectival in function. To know what functions it has for the child and how these have come about it is essential, here as always, to observe closely the successive situations in which he responds to and uses the word.

(ii) *The differentiation of approval*

From the record of K, serial observations of two words—*pretty* and *nice*—illustrate the differentiation of words expressing approval.

We have seen that at least as early as 1;4,12 he responded to *Smell the pretty flowers* by bending over, smelling them and saying *a ... a ... a* in a tone of delight; and that about two months later he was observed, for the first time, replacing this primary expression by his adaptation of the adult name for the flower, *fa ... fa*—his orectic attitude still being expressed by intonation, gesture and allied behaviour. For this attitude his mother has a symbol: *pretty*. But it is not until three months have elapsed that we observe the child's first use of this word.

pretty

1;9,12. He picks up a piece of pink ribbon and says *pittie*. Later he does this with a green pencil and a decorated box.

1;10,13. In a bus with his mother. Looking at a pretty young woman, he says *pittie ahtie* (auntie).

1;11,8. His mother having changed her dress, he looks at it and says *pittie fokkie* (frock).

2;1,0. Switching on a light he says *pittie lykie* (light). Then, holding his toy dog up to it, *goggie, pittie lykie*.

2;1,26. Walking in the park, he looks round, then says *pittie*.

2;2,18. Looking at a picture of birds: *pittie birdies*.

2;3,2. Just before going to bed last night he received a present of a fine wooden train. Early this morning he awakes and asks for his train. Told that it is still too early he says *pittie puff-tain!*

2;3,16. Pointing to a ruby glass reflector on a bicycle: *jats pittie!* (That's pretty!)

2;4,10. Seeing his mother wearing a new necklace: *dats pittie; pittie beads.*

What is happening during these seven months? To say that the child on seeing the pink ribbon imitates the word *pretty* and subsequently extends its use tells us little. Certainly there is imitation of the word and extension of its use to situations in which the child has probably not encountered it—for instance, the ruby glass reflector. There is even extension to refer to something not actually present—the train. But all this is still an inadequate account of the functions of the word for the child.

To understand the course of development we have to go back a little. The child has heard the word *pretty* used by others in a variety of circumstances and in such a way as to invite a pattern of response which includes a physical act and an orectic attitude. When his mother, for instance, says *Smell the pretty flowers*, she speaks both manipulatively and declaratively. Her manner, gestures and intonation all invite the child to imitate her own action in smelling the flowers—and this he does. She also evokes an orectic response, of which his *a ... a ... a* is the declarative expression.

It is evident that, as time goes on, the word *pretty* will lead the child to expect a pleasant experience—maybe a pleasant smell, associated perhaps with pleasant visual impressions. The word will come to evoke a complex orectic schema.

By the time that he himself first uses the word—at 1;9,12 for the ribbon—its function has become considerably more specific. From this time onwards, it is applied to a visual experience and the orectic attitude evoked by this. Again we might explain what has happened by saying that the child has heard the word used in a variety of situations in which the common visual character is prettiness, that he has recognised this common character and with it its name, *pretty*. But again this will not do. What visual pattern is common to ribbon, pencil, box, woman, light, birds, train, reflector, beads?

We can say that all of them give a visual experience of colour and

LANGUAGE AND PERSONAL AND SOCIAL DEVELOPMENT

brightness. But even this is adult thinking, our abstraction. The diverse situations must be different in colour and brightness for the child. If for him they are alike enough to evoke the same word *pretty*, it must be for their *orectic* character. They have orectic similarity for him.

In considering the development of conceptual thinking—illustrated by K's classification of animals—we saw that even where the similarity of situations is mainly cognitive and functional, orectic similarity may play some part. Conversely, in the differentiation of orectic attitudes, we have similarity which, while partly functional and cognitive, is predominantly orectic. We are led to conclude that, at this stage, the child's use of *pretty* is not the result of abstraction—a recognition of a common perceptual pattern to which he attaches a name. It is rather that the similarity of the child's orectic experiences in various situations and the fact that he uses the same word in them all, is taking him on the road towards the abstraction of the concept of prettiness.

These suppositions are borne out by our observation of the same child's uses of *nice*.

nice

1;6,9. His mother, standing by the drawer in which chocolate is kept: *I've got something nice for you!* He replies, *gogga!*

1;6,23. Walking with him in the street, his mother says: *I've got something nice for you!* He replies *gogga!*

1;11,2. Says *nice!* on various occasions, e.g. while his hair is being cut, as the scissors touch his neck, he grins and says *nice!* Again, while smelling lavender water; while drinking sweetened milk.

2;0,7. Patting his mother's face, he says *nice!* She asks, *What's nice?* He replies, *Mummy, nice mummy.*

2;1,8. His mother occasionally puts a spot of eau-de-Cologne on his hands after washing him. Today after being washed, he goes to her cupboard, takes out the eau-de-Cologne, saying *nicie-handies* until she puts a spot on his hands.

2;1,18. Pointing to a bottle of lotion sometimes used for his nose, he says *nicie nosie!*

2;6,14. After a fortnight's absence from home, looking round his room he says, *It's nice to be home!*

The parallel with the development of *pretty* is evident. The child, having encountered the word in certain situations, imitates its use and extends it to new situations, all of which appear to have for him some common orectic character. But how are they perceptually similar to him? Certainly not visually. Perceptually, they are all, to some extent, combinations of tactile, olfactory, gustatory and vaguer organic experiences. Their effectiveness for the child must be in the common orectic attitude which they evoke and which may perhaps be described as a feeling of well-being. Here again, this is not to say that the child, even by the end of the series, has abstracted a common quality of 'niceness' and labelled this *nice*; but rather that in a variety of situations, a certain similarity of orectic experience and his response to and use of the same word all combine to lead him, as time goes on, towards the ultimate abstraction of the common quality.

Throughout all this, what cannot be too strongly emphasised is that the process of discrimination takes place in communication between the child and others. He responds to what they say; he imitates them; but above all he uses speech to draw attention to his declarative and manipulative needs and, increasingly, with a deliberate intention. In the two series we have just considered, *pittie* is for the most part used declaratively, as an expression and symbolisation of the child's pleasure; but it would seem likely that *pittie puff-train* at 2;3,2 was used with something of a manipulative intention, a demand for the train. In at least two of the instances of *nice*, the manipulative as well as the declarative intention is beyond doubt: at 2;1,8 and 2;1,18 where the child is asking for something to be done for him. There is no doubt that what mainly promotes a child's discriminative use of words symbolising attitudes is his need to evoke a desired response from another person.

The emergence of *pretty* and *nice* for one child, may be taken as typical of the process by which different kinds of approval come to be symbolised by different words.

(iii) *The differentiation of disapproval*

The acquisition of words for different kinds of disapproval follows a similar course. Here again we need a serial record of the uses of a word in successive situations. From the half-dozen or so words of disapproval used by K in his second and third years we choose *dirty*.

dirty

1;9,3. His mother is washing his knees. She says, *Dirty little knees*; he replies, *duttie, duttie*.
She says, *Mummy make them clean*; he: *kee, kee*.
Mother: *Baby's knees were* . . . He: *duttie*.
Mother: *Mummy made them* . . . He: *kee*.

1;9,4. In the garden, he has fallen down. He comes over to his mother, rubs his hands on her dress, saying *duttie*.

1;9,15. He enjoys playing with garden-soil. Today, having run some between his fingers, he comes to his mother to have them wiped, saying, *duttie*.

1;11,14. In the garden. He comes up behind his mother and says *duttie* insistently. She looks up and finds his mouth and hands covered with soil.

1;11,23. In public gardens. Another child comes up to him; he holds out his hand in welcome. Then he retreats, saying, *duttie*. (The other child is certainly very dirty.)

2;4,0. Being wheeled in his pram, on which there happens to be a cardboard box. As they pass a garden, he says, *Throw it in there, make it dirty!*

As with *pretty* and *nice* there is imitation; not only of the adult word *dirty* as referring to a visual experience, but also of the orectic attitude which it expresses—disapproval, discomfort, even distress. The word has a declarative function for the child. But already in his first use of the word, at 1;9,4, it already has a manipulative function also—he is asking for his hands to be wiped. The final episode is a good example of transfer beyond the immediately experienced situation. The child uses the word manipulatively, demanding a change—which he knows would be disapproved, something wrong.

It is noteworthy that at this stage the orectic attitude is both aesthetic and ethical or, rather, that these attitudes are not yet differentiated. What is dirty is not only unpleasant, it may demand action, a course of conduct which will bring about an approved state of affairs. In the same way, a child's expression of approval is not only æsthetic—showing his pleasure—but also ethical, communicating his approval of a person's behaviour, actual or anticipated. When K says *nicie handies*, he is both demanding a course of conduct and approving it. When he says *Mummy, nice mummy*, this surely includes both his æsthetic satisfaction and also his approval of her as a person who behaves so satisfyingly towards him. We need to observe, in the further development of children, how they move towards differentiating the æsthetic from the ethical, with the aid of verbal symbolisation.

(iv) *The effect of contrast*

One important factor in the development of this discrimination is that a child is frequently presented with pairs of opposites. An instance is the first episode in the *dirty* series, at 1;9,3. The child's mother plays a sort of game with him, inviting him first to imitate her words *dirty* and *clean* and then to add them to her unfinished sentences. This gives each of the two words a special kind of verbal context—not only the sentence in which it occurs but also the presence of its opposite.

This presentation of pairs of opposites occurs as a means of emphasising disapproval rather than approval. To express approval, the most that is needed is the commendatory word—and even silence may express approval. But disapproval must be unmistakeable, and for this it may not be enough to use a derogatory word. The speaker will sometimes need to emphasise his disapproval by a positive indication of what by contrast would be approved.

In the everyday circumstances of an ordinary home, a child frequently experiences this kind of verbal contrast, so that often when he uses a word of disapproval he is aware of the contrasting, approved state of affairs. This is clear, for instance, in K's use of *duttie*. Other examples from his record illustrate the same development:

1;9,16. When his mother says, *He's a good little . . .*, he replies *Babba*. But when she says, *He's a naughty little . . .*, he remains silent or repeats, *Naughty*.
2;0,6. He playfully slaps his mother, saying, *Naughty! Naughty!* She pretends to cry, whereupon he 'loves' her

by putting his cheek to hers and saying in a comforting tone, *a* ... *a* ... *a*.

THE EMERGENCE OF ETHICAL ATTITUDES

As a child's verbal expressions of approval and disapproval become more clearly differentiated, we can observe the beginnings of the expression of ethical attitudes—that is, attitudes of approval or disapproval of people's behaviour.

So far the child has shown his attitude towards the conduct of others by such physical acts as pouting or smiling, slapping or caressing; or by the broad differentiation of *No!* or *Yes!* Gradually the finer verbal discrimination of ethical attitudes emerges as the product of a number of factors of the same kind as we find in other aspects of linguistic development.

First, even apart from language, a child's ethical attitudes will become somewhat more clearly defined in the course of his incessant everyday experiments in learning to live with others. He behaves in this way and that, and they respond: and he in his turn responds in different ways to the diversity of their behaviour towards him. As a result, he becomes aware of regular patterns of approval and disapproval of social behaviour; as he adopts and adapts ethical attitudes, he imitates forms of speech with which to express them. On the other hand, he will sometimes imitate a word in play and by using it, come to be aware of the attitude that other people express through it.

One special feature of ethical development must be recognised. When a child says such a word as *nice!* or *nasty!* he is not only expressing his own attitude, he is also declaratively inviting another person to express an attitude towards this attitude. For instance, when K at 1;11,23 encountered a dirty child, said *duttie* and retreated, he might well have evoked from his mother an expression of her disapproval of his attitude. A child's experiences of this kind must involve him in constant comparisons, the trying-out and weighing-up of attitudes, so that he comes to be more aware of the ethical patterns current in his immediate society and at the same time more aware of his own attitudes. He gradually gains insight into his own conduct.

Developments in this direction are particularly fostered by the child's expressions of approval or disapproval of people, whether directly towards them or indirectly about them.

THE EXPRESSION OF APPROVAL TOWARDS OTHERS

We may begin by looking back at the instance cited on page 63:

2;0,7. Patting his mother's face, he says, *Nice!* She asks, *What's nice?* He replies, *Mummy, nice mummy!*

We have seen this as an example of an orectic attitude in which the æsthetic and the ethical are closely intermingled or, it would perhaps be more accurate to say, undifferentiated. But not more than three weeks later we find the child speaking to his mother in a manner which much more clearly expresses an ethical attitude—an approval of her behaviour towards him:

2;2,27. A dialogue between him and his mother.
He: *Nice mummy.* She: *Darling baby.*
He: *Darling mummy!*
2;4,4. To his mother, spontaneously: *Own little mummy. Clean little mummy.*

The first instance, though imitative, is not simply so. His mother's word, *darling*, evokes from the child a similar word: but clearly this is declarative, expressing the child's warm approval of his mother and of the satisfying experiences which she brings him.

The second instance is particularly interesting as illustrating the emergence of the expression of an ethical attitude from a less differentiated orectic expression. The word *clean*—following as it does the word *own*—is hardly at all an expression of the child's approval of his mother's appearance. It is mainly an expression, once again, of his approval of her relationship towards him, as experienced in the ways she behaves towards him: it is ethical rather than æsthetic. Usages of this kind are, of course, common in childhood and indeed in everyday adult speech; when we say a person is 'clean-living' we are symbolising an ethical judgment—though this may have æsthetic overtones.

We must not omit to notice that such ethical expressions as *Darling mummy* and *Clean little mummy* are means by which the child invites the reciprocal approval of his mother towards him. The

LANGUAGE AND PERSONAL AND SOCIAL DEVELOPMENT 69

word supplements and replaces such approved acts as caressing and embracing; it is a means whereby the child invites responsive expressions or acts of affection towards himself. Utterances of this kind are among the chief means by which there is built up a network of ethical relationships between the child and those around him.

THE EXPRESSION OF APPROVAL ABOUT OTHERS

A somewhat different function is performed by a child's expressions of approval not *to* others but about them:

2;0,22. Picking up a block which he had lost the previous day; *Da find it. Kind Da!* 'Da' was a little girl who, while playing with him, had found the mislaid block.

This illustrates imitation at an early stage in the development of expressions of approval about others. No doubt someone had said *Kind Da!* when the little girl found the block.

2;2,3. *Dolly not broke. Daddy mend it. Clever daddy.*
2;4,13. *Roger good boy. Roger is K's good boy. K is mummy's good boy.*
2;4,17. *Doggie is K's little treasure.*
A little later. Mother: *What is doggie?* He: *Little friend.*

In all these instances the child is imitating an expression of approval that he has heard and adopting it with a declarative and ethical function. He uses the imitated word or phrase to express his own approval of the behaviour of the absent person towards himself. In doing this, in speaking for instance to his mother, the child is inviting her to share his approval, bringing her as it were into the circle of his approval of the absent person. He is inviting his mother's approval of his approval. In this way expressions of approval about others are even more effective than expressions of approval to others, in promoting the establishment of attitudes common to the child and those in his immediate society.

THE EXPRESSION OF DISAPPROVAL AND AVERSION

The rudiments of verbal ethical disapproval may also begin to emerge during a child's third year. They are likely to be more rudimentary than the expression of approval, for this reason—that the need to disapprove, to inhibit someone's intended or actual behaviour, is usually so urgent that a child will tend to revert to non-verbal means: forcibly restraining or pushing or slapping the other person.

The earliest instances, then, are often playful—as these, from the record of K. The first we have already cited as an axample of verbal contrast (page 66).

> 2;0,6. He playfully slaps his mother, saying, *Naughty, naughty!* She pretends to cry, whereupon he 'loves' her by putting his cheek to hers and saying in a comforting tone, *a ... a ... a.*
>
> 2;2,15. His mother is dressing him. He says *Coat!* She: *Dear me, I forgot.* He: *Silly old man!* (He has sometimes been called *silly old man* in play).
>
> 2;4,12. Father (in play): *Shall daddy spank K?* Child: *Spank K when he's naughty, not when he's good!*

As time goes on—and particularly if he meets other children with whom he comes into conflict—a child will use these imitated forms of speech not only playfully but in stark earnest. Ames, observing children in a nursery school, found instances of this already in three-year-olds:

> 2;6,0. A child, in response to a verbal attack by another child: *You bad boy!* (2).

The child is not only expressing disapproval—he is at the same time punishing his enemy with words that wound. It need hardly be said that a child's *bad* as early as this is still a long way from symbolising an objective judgment of behaviour. It is still an expressive act used as an ethical instrument; verbal punishment.

These expressions of disapproval are the rudiments of later objective judgments. We can observe the movement towards these as a child begins to express disapproval about third persons. For instance:

> 2;6,0. The child complains to his teacher about another child: *He's a bad boy!*

A still stronger impetus towards objective judgments is given when children join in an expression of common hostility towards a person:

2;6,0. One child to another, referring to a doll in a carriage; *Let's tumble her out. I like her to hurt herself!*
3;0,0. The children in chorus, to one who wants to enter their 'house'; *You can't come in!* (3).

In saying *He's a bad boy*, the child is asserting his own disapproval and inviting the hearer to take the same attitude towards the third person. The fact that sometimes he gets a positive, sometimes a negative, response means that his expressions of attitudes tend to be exploratory rather than fixed and final. The expression of common hostility—*You can't come in!*—works in the same direction towards objectivity, but in a somewhat different manner. Here the child begins by 'joining in' and then, as a result, discovers his conformity with the group—or, sometimes, his dissent from it. These are the beginnings of what come to be socially established and sanctioned patterns of disapproval and—in agreement or disagreement with these—the patterns of the child's own attitudes.

EXPRESSION OF SELF-ASSERTION AND SELF-AWARENESS

Closely associated with disapproval and hostility towards others is the child's self-assertion and his awareness of himself. Here again verbal symbolisation emerges and becomes more frequent as the child mixes with other children. But the rudiments may be observed earlier, at home in the family, as the child offers resistance and asserts himself against mother or father, sister or brother.

(i) *The inhibition of others' actions*

One important form of self-assertion is the child's attempt to inhibit, through speech, the act of another person towards himself. The self-assertion which, as we have seen at the end of Chapter 2, has first manifested itself by turning away—physical aversion—or by resistance or tantrums, and later by *No!*, is, as time goes on, supplemented and replaced by words or phrases which more specifically symbolise the child's attitude.

For a long time the child may continue to express disapproval of someone's intended act towards himself by *No!* or *Not!* In a situation in which he urgently needs to prevent an undesired action from taking place, he resorts to this well-tried verbal instrument rather than the untried word that he hears others use. But sooner or later, imitation has its effect and the child begins to use adult words and phrases.

Successive instances from the record of K illustrate this:

1;8,22. In reply to proposed actions by others: *Come to daddy?* He: *No!* Mother: *Baby have a drinky?* He: *No!*

2;2,18. Mother: *Play hunt-the-thimble?* He: *No! Booky!* She: *Play hide-and-seek?* He: *No! Booky!* When she then produces his picture-book he shows his satisfaction.

2;3,2. Mother, playing with him: *Smile for mummy!* He: *I don't want to!* This is the earliest recorded instance of his use of 'I'.

2;3,18. Father tossing him about. He: *Don't!*

2;4,10. He has just been given a new balloon. His mother happens to touch it. He: *Don't bust noony!*

2;5,0. Mother: *Have some apple?* He: *Yes!* She offers him stewed apple, whereupon he says: *Not that. Plain apple!*

2;7,6. His mother has been using the telephone. He: *No ring up, mummy.* She: *Why?* He: *'Cause K won't like it!*

3;0,0. In desperation, when his mother refuses to do something for him: *Don't tease, mummy, don't tease!*

An early instance recorded by Ames illustrates the incentive to expression provided by conflict with other children:

2;6,0. One child to another: *Don't be like that! You go down 'fore I hit you so hard!* (4).

(ii) *The assertion of personal ability and prowess*

Side by side with the inhibition of the behaviour of others towards himself, the child's growing self-assertion soon finds expression in insisting on his skill and achievement. This may occur even before the end of his second year:

1;10,22. At table he will not let his mother feed him. He takes the spoon and cries, *Self! Self!* many times.

1;10,25. Insists on putting on his shoes himself. He takes the shoes from his mother, saying *K* many times.

2;3,20. He: *I do this self.* Mother: *Who?* He: *K*.

2;3,25. During a meal. Mother: *Shall mummy help you?* He: *K manage.*

LANGUAGE AND PERSONAL AND SOCIAL DEVELOPMENT 73

Ames records a number of early instances from various children in her nursery class:

2;0,0.   Calling the teacher's attention to his activity: *Watch me! Look at this!*

2;6,0.   Speaking to teacher, announcing current, completed or intended activity: *I fix that, I make it go! I made a house! I want to climb! I can take my own coat off! Come here. Watch me! I climbed all by myself!* (5).

And one more instance from the record of K:

2;9,21. Calling attention to a feat of jumping: *Did you see that? Can you do that?*

(iii) *The expression of ownership*

In the course of his attempts to influence another's act towards himself the child begins to express his sense of ownership:

2;0,0.   Speaking to another child: *Mine! I want cup!*

2;3,2.   Late one night K received a present of a handsome wooden train. Next morning he awoke early and said: *Puffer. K want it!*

2;6,0.   To another child: *You can't have my dolly!*

Often, however, the child's growing awareness of himself is manifested by declarative expressions of ownership, where there is no question of influencing another's behaviour: *[culture impact]*

2;2,15. His mother is about to put on his shoes. She asks: *Whose shoes are these?* He replies: *K's shoes.* Then adds: *My shoes!*

2;2,17. On returning home from a visit. Seeing his cot: *Own cot!*

2;3,10. Seeing a picture of a child in leggings. *Leggings like K's.*

2;4,4.   His toy dog was with him in his pram. Catching sight of a dog in the street, he holds up his own dog: *K got own doggie!*

2;4,5.   Seeing the milk van at the door: *That's our milkman!*

2;10,21. He had been given a fine new toy dog. At bedtime, his mother said: *Which doggie will you take with you?* He: *My own old doggie what always do sleep with me!*

(iv) *The expression of self-awareness*

Finally we have to notice the expression of self-awareness which is not the inhibition of another's behaviour, nor insistence on personal prowess nor the assertion of ownership, but incidental in the course of making a statement in which the child is involved. He names himself, or says *I* or *mine*. Here and there, in the observations we have cited, instances have occurred. If now we gather these and some others together we may see more clearly the various ways in which this symbolisation of self may arise.

Some successive observations from K's third year:

2;3,2. In the course of play: *I see doggie, I see dolly.*
2;3,5. Mother: *What is your name?* He replies in full.
2;3,10. In the course of conversation: *K good boy!*
2;3,16. *Most sweet K. Dear little K. Dear little thing.*
2;4,4. To his mother, lovingly: *Own mummy. Own little mummy. Clean little mummy. K clean. Mummy clean.*
2;4,12. (Cited above, p. 70). Father (in play): *Shall daddy spank K?* Child: *Spank K when he's naughty, not when he's good!*
2;4,13. (Cited above, p. 69). *Roger good boy. Roger K's good boy. K mummy's good boy.*
2;5,16. Early in the morning he calls from his bed: *K all untidy.* His mother going to him finds his bedclothes tumbled.
2;9,2. Arranging his bed: *I'm going to bed in a minute, 'cause I'm very tired.*

It is evident that in the course of these varying ways of naming himself the child becomes more aware of himself. This, of course, is not to say that self-awareness coincides with the verbal symbolisation of self. Before he names himself a child may well have some concept of himself, perhaps symbolised non-verbally. In his daily life with others, as his awareness of social relationships and ethical attitudes grows, so his awareness of himself must also become clearer. And here, as so often in a child's development, language may help still further to clarify and define what is already symbolised non-verbally.

Our survey of a child's progress towards the symbolisation of modes of thought and feeling has shown that there are parallel processes in the progressive differentiation of his cognition of his environment, as also of his orectic attitudes towards this environment. We have seen that his conceptual thinking has its roots in his earliest perceptions; that specific concepts emerge in the course of his experiences, among which communication plays an increasingly dominant part, as he moves towards current modes of thought. So, too, his primitive orectic states of discomfort and comfort become differentiated into specific attitudes of disapproval and approval and, again largely through the influence of language, are modified in the direction of current æsthetic and ethical attitudes.

EVIDENCE FROM THE IMPAIRMENT OF LANGUAGE

The part that language plays in this cognitive and orectic development is made very clear by what we know of children whose language, from one cause or another, is impaired. The most cogent evidence comes from the study of children suffering from varying degrees of deafness. 'It has been shown', says Ewing, summarising much observation and research, 'that the linguistic development of most deaf children can and should be promoted by special training before the age of two years. Otherwise their social, emotional and intellectual development begins at once to be adversely affected' (6).

The general retardation of these children is not, of course, due only to the poverty of their language. The inevitable special orectic relationship between a deaf child and his family, the frustrations of the child in his everyday life, his comparative isolation from other children—all these conditions, unless ameliorated by the deliberate action of those about him, may contribute to his retardation. In his earlier years this retardation may not be obvious to the ordinary observer; it becomes more and more severe with the passage of time. We shall consider this in detail in our study of the later stages of children's development. In the meantime we may anticipate by noticing briefly its main features.

The cognitive retardation of many deaf children is seen in this, that although no less able than normal children in dealing with concrete situations, here and now, their comparative inferiority becomes more marked the greater the need for generalisation and abstraction (7). Their progress in conceptual thinking is slowed down by the poverty of the verbal instruments at their command, acquired by the normal child in the course of his communication with others.

The orectic immaturity of many deaf children consists in this, that they tend to be self-centred, solitary, irritable, aggressive and of uncertain temper. This, again, is without doubt largely due to the paucity of their language. The obstacles in the path of their recognition of approval and disapproval are obvious. Even those who are not so unfortunate as to be confined to signs and gestures, who learn something of the mother tongue by lip-reading and hearing aids, must be greatly hampered. Encountering words in specific concrete situations, with little or no aid from intonational patterns or verbal contexts, they tend to remain at the stage in which words relate to the situations themselves. They are slow in responding to the expression of orectic attitudes, still more to the symbolisation of them. At the same time they have only the crudest means of making known their own orectic attitudes. Thus their awareness of orectic attitudes tends to remain comparatively vague and undeveloped, among them the ethical attitudes so important in the development of personality.

But, as Ewing tells us, the development of many deaf children can be hastened if, as soon as their disability is ascertained, the right measures are taken—particularly the use of communication as linguistic as the circumstances will allow.

Recognition of the relation of language to the general retardation of deaf children points the way to understanding the backwardness of some with normal hearing. In recent years, increasing attention has been given to the plight of those children brought up in institutions who present a picture of immaturity somewhat similar to that of some deaf children. These are, for the most part, illegitimate children or children who are not receiving adequate care from their parents.

Their cognitive immaturity is evident if, in everyday observation and specific tests, we compare them with children who, although they have parents of the same economic, social and mental level, nevertheless have been fortunate enough to be placed in good foster-homes (8). Their orectic immaturity is equally evident. Bender has described them. 'Children who have been in institutions for the first two or three years of their lives without parents or other significant adults to visit them or take an interest in them, frequently show the most severe type of deprived, asocial psychopathic per-

LANGUAGE AND PERSONAL AND SOCIAL DEVELOPMENT

sonality deviation. These children do not develop a play pattern and cannot enter into group play with other children. They abuse other children near them as frustrating objects to the satisfaction of their primitive impulses' (9). The similarity of this picture with that of some deaf children is noteworthy.

It is evident that the linguistic retardation of many children in institutions must play some part in this. In Chapter 1 we saw that a comparative slowness in the development of speech may be observed as early as the first half-year of their lives—particularly in the range of their vocalic and consonantal speech-sounds. This retardation becomes progressively greater in comparison with children—matched in other respects—not in institutions; by the end of the third year there is likely to be a marked comparative paucity in the number and the range of vocabulary (10).

Now it might well be thought that the fundamental factor in the general retardation of these children is inborn cognitive disability and that this is the cause of their orectic and linguistic retardation. Certainly, it need hardly be said that cognitive ability does influence orectic and linguistic development—every step in a child's progress towards orectic and linguistic maturity presents him with problems to be solved, demanding the abilities to perceive and deal with relationships.

But everything we have considered in tracing the course of development goes to show that a fundamental factor in both cognitive and orectic growth is the constant and permeative effect of language. Where a child's hearing is impaired or where life in an institution is not conducive to easy and constant intercourse between a child and his elders, his linguistic development will be impeded, with marked effects of retardation of his cognitive and orectic progress.

There is an impressive accumulation of evidence of this. It is found that in the early stages of development—at any rate, in the first eighteen months—there is no regular relation between cognitive ability and the ability to produce speech-sounds, in variety and frequency. By the middle of the third year the correlation has become fairly high (11). What can we infer from this?

The answer would seem to be that a child of normal potential cognitive ability may, if his hearing is impaired or he lives in an institution, be slow in producing speech-sounds—because of the poverty of his communication with others, particularly adults. We judge his intelligence by his competence in solving problems; and so long as the solution of these demand little or no language, retardation in speech development may not affect cognitive development. But as time goes on a child's need to use language in the solution of problems becomes pressing; children with linguistic retardation will also tend to be cognitively retarded.

This is to put the relationships at their simplest; but the full picture is rather more complex. For a child's speech-sounds to become a means of communication, his cognitive powers must be brought into play; but at the same time there must be plentiful and frequent opportunities of communication. As we have so constantly seen, the transformation of a child's primary utterance into a means of communication and of symbolising his own behaviour depends to an enormous degree upon the response of others to his speech-sounds. It is here that the handicap of deaf children or those in institutions may be most severe. Where the pattern of everyday life is a routine in which the child's recurrent needs are met with such regularity that he is not incited to make his demands heard; and where, at other moments in his day, his utterance, manipulative and declarative, receives little or no response because his elders cannot attend to him—in such an environment his progress in linguistic communication must be slow. From this will follow cognitive and orectic immaturity.

The results of efforts made today to help such children bear witness to the truth of these generalisations. Particularly indicative are the results of changing the way of life of children in institutions, by removing them to foster-homes or by giving them, even while they remain in an institution, greater opportunities of easy intercourse with adults or older children. Since most of this work has been with children over the age of three, we leave the detailed discussion until later. We shall see that changes of this kind hasten the progress of these children, at first most noticeably in their social behaviour and orectic uses of language, later even in cognitive ability, as measured by verbal tests of intelligence (12). No doubt the process of accelerated progress here is again complex; as the child responds to warmer personal care and attention his social behaviour improves; with this, his language expands and at the same time penetrates more deeply into his life. His greater command of language promotes effectiveness and precision in his perception and his conceptual thinking, and at the same time fosters the more discriminative awareness of æsthetic and ethical attitudes.

What we witness as a dramatic change in the life of a deprived child is the normal growth of more fortunate children. We have seen how the transformation of their primitive utterance into the mother tongue enables them to co-operate more readily with others in coming to terms with their world, human and non-human. We have now to see how they move forward in their exploration of this world, both immediate and remote—not only what is immediately present to the senses but also what lies beyond, in time and in space. We have to see how language helps them to a deeper insight into what is going on around them and promotes an ability of supreme importance—the power of referring to the past and to the future.

5
Language and Exploration

At the end of Chapter 3 we left the child beginning to use semi-conventional forms such as *tee*, *pushie*, *goggie*, as means of directing his own and other people's attention to particular 'things', 'situations'. A sound-pattern used in this way is a kind of demonstrative act—a sort of pointing. It is of course a step beyond actual pointing and certainly it is a great deal more effective in communication; for not only does it draw the attention of another person but the manner in which it is spoken, its intonational character, expresses and symbolises the nature of the child's concern with the thing, the situation.

What the child must needs move on to now is the ability to draw attention to something which is not present; present neither for him nor for his listener; something beyond the actual here or now, or both. As he achieves this the child makes a further notable advance in the transformation of his speech from expression to a means of symbolisation (1).

We turn to the earlier stages of this development as they can be observed in infancy.

THE GROWTH OF REFERENCE TO WHAT IS ABSENT

When for the first time we notice a child saying a word which clearly relates to something absent, this may seem to us, the onlookers, a suddenly and completely new step. But here again, what has entered his life is not a new form of behaviour, but a more effective instrument for communication—he is now using an adopted word as he has already been using one of his own sound-groups. What is new is the word, and with it the additional power and effectiveness it gives to his ability to communicate, in drawing attention to what is absent.

Observation shows that, as in other aspects of linguistic development, there are a number of inter-related contributory factors. Of these the most important are the child's own rudimentary reference to what is absent, beginning far back in his history; the reinforcement of this by the constant attempts of others to direct his attention to what is absent; and the emergence of linguistic intercourse—speech in response to speech.

(a) *Rudimentary reference to the absent* is already implicit in a child's early utterance, in his manipulative use of discomfort-cries. When, for instance, a child cries *mama* as a means of bringing his absent mother to his side, he is, we may reasonably suppose, already in a rudimentary way also directing his own attention to her before she comes within reach of his sight or hearing. This direction towards something absent certainly gains in power, precision and effectiveness as the child, in communication with others, comes to substitute conventional, or semi-conventional, words for his own speech-forms.

Thus the first clear case of K's spontaneous reference to an absent thing by means of a semi-conventional word was at 1;4,17. At breakfast-time he was accustomed to have honey, for which his word for some time had been *ha*. This morning, no honey was on the table. Turning towards the cupboard in which the honey was kept, he said *ha!*—certainly a manipulative demand.

It is evident that it is a great gain for the child if he uses a semi-conventional word such as *ha* instead of a widely-ranging speech-form such as *mama* or *eh! eh!*—which might, on this occasion, be taken to refer to any one of a number of things in the cupboard. When he says *ha* he is more 'likely to be understood'—that is, a response from others is both more likely to occur and to be more appropriate to his need. Further, because its reference is narrower and more specific—that is, linked with this particular object, the honey—it becomes for the child, in his own inner speech, a more adequate means of referring to the absent honey. When now someone says *ha* or *honey* to him, there is a stronger tendency for him to direct his behaviour towards the honey, even though it is absent. This brings us to the second contributory factor—the manner in which the child is incited to refer to absent things by the remarks and behaviour of others.

(b) *Incitement by others*. In the course of ordinary family life, we are constantly speaking to the child about things that are absent, with the intention of directing his behaviour towards them. When at last we succeed, it is because we have managed, once again, to modify an already well-established pattern of behaviour—the child's response to a word or phrase referring wholly to the present situation.

Thus we saw in Chapter 2 how K was being taught, in play, to respond to the phrase *Baby, give mummy crustie!* There came a time when he responded appropriately to such a phrase when it involved an object not actually present to his senses.

1;1,5. The child was playing on the floor. His ball was in a corner of the room, where it had lain unheeded by him all day. His mother said, *Baby, where's ballie?* The child turned and crawled towards the ball. On the way there he halted at the coal-box, a favourite plaything. His mother repeated the question, whereupon he resumed his journey, seized the ball and looked up at her (2).

This is truly a remarkable event, the importance of which in a child's development can hardly be exaggerated. It is, however, mysterious only if we ignore what has led up to it. The question *Where's ballie?* has caused the child to perform an act, to engage in a series of movements culminating in grasping the ball. The detailed record of observations shows that this child, during at least four months before this episode, has regularly responded appropriately to the phrase when the ball was *present*. There can be little doubt that in the course of these occasions the word *ballie* has become linked with his experience of the ball when he has heard the word spoken and said it to himself. We can well believe that a connection has been established between his recall of the experience of the ball and his 'internalisation' of the word. Now, even when the ball is out of sight, the word uttered by his mother incites him to direct his behaviour towards it.

This development is fostered by another contributory factor, the growth of linguistic intercourse—the interchange of speech as a form of behaviour in itself, less tied to the actual present situation and ultimately independent of it. The child engages in communication freed from the dominance of what is present to his senses.

(c) *The emergence of linguistic intercourse.* Here again, observation shows that what may seem to be a new pattern of behaviour is in fact the development of earlier patterns. The child has now come to respond to speech by speech. Leading up to this there are, we find, two successive phases. First, the child learns to respond to speech by *acts*; then by *acts and speech* and, from this, by *speech alone*.

Response to speech by acts we have seen in such cases as *Baby, where's ballie?*—the child responding to speech by an action concerned with something not actually present to his senses. Sooner or later we find the child responding to speech by a pattern of behaviour which includes speech. K, for instance, had learnt to respond to *Peep-bo*, said by his mother, by covering his face with his hands and then withdrawing them. At 1;1,8 (three days after the episode of *Baby, where's ballie?*) he not only made the appropriate movements, but also said *eh-bo!*

Now, in ordinary circumstances, those about the child are constantly inciting him to respond in this way to speech by speech. At first, this will only happen when what is said is concerned with the present situation. For instance, at 1;5,10, K, pointing to the fire, said in a delighted tone, *Aha! fa!* When his mother, also pointing to the fire, asked, *What's that?* he replied, *fa!*

The child then learns to respond to speech by speech which refers to something absent, but with clues in the present situation. At 1;6,9, K's mother, standing by a drawer in which chocolate was kept, said, *I've got something nice for you!* to which he replied *gogga.* Finally, the child learns to respond to speech by speech when there is nothing in the present situation to support his reply. Five days after the last episode, K's mother said to him *What would baby like?* to which he replied, *gogga*. He has begun to respond to speech by speech, when the whole pattern of intercourse is relatively free from the present physical situation. The remark of the other person is itself sufficient to evoke his spoken response.

It is evident that in intercourse of this kind the child is being incited to direct his utterance towards what is absent. Having earlier learnt—as by *Baby, where's ballie?*—to direct his behaviour towards what is absent, he now learns to make a spoken reference towards what is absent. The step that he has taken is obviously of the greatest importance for his further development. It opens up for him the vast possibilities of conversation with others, in which there is reference to a universe beyond the immediate spatial and temporal present. The significance of this for the growth of his thought—and, indeed, of all his behaviour—can hardly be overestimated. But, as we have seen, it is not a sudden new creation in the child's life. Like his every other achievement, it arises from the conjunction of modes of behaviour already present in his earlier experience.

The beginning of reference to past and to future. From the growth of ability to symbolise the spatially absent there emerges the ability to symbolise what is temporally remote. As a child learns to converse with others about the 'there', he also learns to speak about the 'then' and the 'to-be'.

The rudiments of reference to the past are already to be found on occasions when a child's speech is directed towards what is spatially absent. For instance, when he says *ha!*, turning towards the cupboard in which honey is usually kept, this is likely to include some recall of a previous perception of the honey in the cupboard. To say *gogga*, while standing by the drawer where chocolate is kept, is likely to include some recall of a previous perception of chocolate in the drawer.

But in these cases the object which is recalled as having existed in the past also persists in the present. Mother has only to open the cupboard and there is the honey. What we have now to see is how a child comes to refer to what is past and gone; what can be brought into the present only through the power of thought.

There can be no doubt that, without any intervention by others, a child will, in some measure, recall the past—that he will 'turn round upon his own schemata', symbolising the past for himself, perhaps by non-verbal symbols. But there is also no doubt that the development of a child's verbal reference to the past is greatly aided by the fact that others so frequently speak to him about the past. It would seem likely that a child would be very much slower in communication concerning the past if we did not lead him in that direction.

It is interesting to notice that much of our reference to the past in talking to a child occurs in play with him—in a sort of game of question-and-answer. Take a typical instance, from the record of K at 1;8,22.

Adult	Child
Where's Da gone?	*goh!* (gone!)
Where?	Da
Yes, but where?	*cool!* (school!)

We enjoy this game of trying to get the child to give the right answer and feel that he is very clever when he succeeds. What a wonderful memory, he has, bless him! To remember that Da goes to school!

A more detached and critical person might point out that this interchange may be merely verbal, that the child is merely imitating words he has heard—*Da has gone to school*—without understanding them. There is surely some truth in this; but we must also recognise that purely verbal interchange, as a sort of game, is a factor in bringing about real linguistic intercourse. What it does is to accustom the child to utter patterns of speech whose only reference is to the past. Here, as everywhere, the child in learning language in intercourse with others, is provided with symbols which promote his thinking.

Thus in the growth of a child's reference to the past there is, once more, the convergence of factors springing from the child himself and his social environment. The child himself recalls and symbolises to himself past experiences. Others incite him to respond to and speak words which also recall the past. There comes a time when spontaneously he will speak about the past. With K, this first seems to have occurred at 2;0,20. On returning from a walk he said *mo-u-ka*. His father asked *motor-car?*, to which he replied *No!* When his father then asked *moo-cow?* he replied with satisfaction, *moo-ka!*

When the child says *mo-u-ka* he is repeating the word that he has uttered, either openly or to himself, on seeing the cow during his walk. The first reply of his father, *motor-car?* is not corroborative—it does not match his word or what it means for him. But when he obtains the reply *moo-cow?* he not only has the satisfaction of being understood, but his reference to the absent cow is also reinforced. It is in conversation of this kind, as we try to understand a child and work with him to achieve mutual comprehension, that we help him to refer more and more effectively to the past. Through linguistic intercourse, there is social reinforcement of his memory (3).

In somewhat similar fashion we promote his reference to the future. The main contributory factors are parallel to those that operate in the growth of reference to the past. First there is the child's own rudimentary reference to the future. Secondly there is incitement to make this reference, through linguistic intercourse with others. Finally there comes a time when he spontaneously refers to the future.

Here again we have space to cite only typical instances. A child is already making a rudimentary reference to the future when he is using a word manipulatively in order to secure something not actually present. When, for example, K at breakfast-time turned towards the cupboard containing honey and said *ha!*, he was looking forward to receiving the honey. More clearly still, some months later (at 1;8,24), as his mother was preparing to take him out, he said *gogga!*, asking for and anticipating the buying of chocolate.

Meanwhile, in intercourse with the child, others are constantly reinforcing his forward-looking reference. For instance, at 1;6,3, K began climbing upstairs at his usual bath-time. His mother asked, *Where are you going?* to which he replied *ba!* (bath). Anyone who has lived with children could give innumerable examples of this kind of question-and-answer, which, we notice, is exactly parallel to conversations referring to the past, such as *Where's Da gone?—Cool!*

There is one point worth mentioning here that perhaps has not received the attention it deserves. In our questions referring to the past, as compared with those referring to the future, there are differences in our intonation, probably also in our gestures and bodily attitudes. It may well be, that a child learns to respond to these differences—that he is led to make a backward or forward reference by these characteristics of utterances, as well as by the actual words used.

Finally there comes a time when a child makes a spontaneous reference to the future. Thus K at 2;1,23 was told a story by his mother and had it repeated a second and third time. Then he said, *K tell it now!*

In tracing the development of reference to the future we must notice that this is helped by the fact that, for a child, the future so often resembles the past. The child who anticipates chocolate when he says *gogga*, or his bath when he says *ba*, or says *K tell it now!* when he wishes to tell the story, is anticipating that the present situation will have the same sequel as a similar situation has had in the past. His imagination of the future is based upon his memory of the past—as is, indeed, all prediction throughout life.

What, most of all, fosters his forward-looking reference is the sort of response his attempts at this receive from us. It helps him if we reply by words or deeds or both. It helps him if our words show that we understand him; still more, if what we do satisfies him. If after he has said *gogga*, chocolate appears; or after *K tell it now!* he is allowed to tell the story, clearly his tendency to refer to the future is likely to be promoted. There is here, just as in the growth of reference to the past, social reinforcement of forward-looking reference.

The functions of questions. Perhaps the most powerful means of social reinforcement, in promoting his reference to what is present, to what is absent, to the past and to the future, is the question-and-answer which forms so large a part of our communication with him, from the time when we first begin to interchange speech with him.

Questioning is a form of behaviour, not always symbolised by an interrogative form of words. As Nathan Isaacs has said, 'For the psychologist, questions should before everything else be psychic *events*. His problems should be: What are their causes and functions? In what situations do they arise? What is their relation to these situations?' (4). This is particularly in point in describing the beginnings of questioning. The stages of development are certainly not simply marked by the appearance of interrogative words, Where? What? Why? and the rest. For at first a child often questions without using any interrogative form. Sometimes, on the other hand, he uses an interrogative word without asking a question. We cannot judge the development of questioning by the order of the acquisition of interrogative words—it is the activity of questioning, however expressed, which is our concern.

What is a question—what sort of behaviour is it, as we find it in everyday life? It is, of course, a form of instrumental language, an utterance by which we attempt to secure action from others. But the responsive action sought is of a special kind. The questioner needs to fill a gap in his knowledge or, at least, to test what he already supposes. This knowledge that the questioner seeks is either his goal in itself or a preliminary to action. Instead of thinking on his own—perceiving, remembering, imagining, reasoning—the questioner brings others into co-operation with him. He calls upon them to help him in exploring a situation, either to get to know more about the situation itself or as a means to further action.

Now it need hardly be said that the functions of questions, as we find them in adult life, are likely to be different, or present only in rudimentary forms, in infancy. Our present topic is precisely this, to trace the process by which the various functions of questions emerge in a child's linguistic behaviour.

Observations make it clear that questioning is a specialisation of tendencies already present in this linguistic behaviour. At an early stage, a child begins rudimentary questioning; he responds to the questions of others and to their incitement and encouragement of his own questioning. He asks questions about the immediate present situation; then the scope of his questioning is enlarged beyond the immediate situation to what is absent in time and space. Throughout all this, imitation and play are important factors.

The rudiments of questioning. As in so many other aspects of language development, a child begins his rudimentary questioning before he adopts conventional speech. Unfortunately, here again, because it is pre-conventional, this rudimentary questioning has received little attention. I have to cite my own observations.

> 1;6,3. K was looking at a picture-book with his mother. She asked *Where's eggie?* whereupon he pointed to a picture of an egg. Coming to a picture of a horse he looked up enquiringly at his mother, who said *Horse*. Coming then to a picture of a jug, he pointed to it and looked up at her. She remained silent. Then he said *eh...eh...eh!* urgently, pointing all the time until she answered, *Jug*.

LANGUAGE AND EXPLORATION

This observation, which we may reasonably take as typical of many children, is illuminating in a number of ways. We see the child's mother asking him questions to which he replies by simple pointing, without language. He then imitates her to the extent of looking at her interrogatively and this evokes her reply. When he tries again, however, his mother deliberately refuses to respond until he makes a *spoken* interrogation. By her manner and attitude, and in the urgency of his need to secure a response, she brings him to the point of utterance. His *eh* . . . *eh* . . . *eh!* is as yet hardly a question; it is, perhaps, no more than a demand that she shall reply, but it has the rudiments of questioning in it. It is manipulative, in that the child is using speech as a means of securing action from another person. The important development is this—that the action he hopes to secure is a *reply*, an act of speech. Only a linguistic response will satisfy him. The interchange with his mother is rudimentary question-and-answer, though still no more than a sort of game.

A further development is the child's use of speech as a means of securing a reply that he already expects. An instance is the episode cited in Chapter 2, page 45.

> 1;9,2. There are two low cupboards side by side, one of which is forbidden to him. He points to this cupboard saying *eh, eh* (a customary way with him of indicating a wish or request). When his mother replies *No!* he points to the permitted cupboard, again saying *eh, eh*. His mother replies *Yes!* All this episode is repeated about a dozen times. Later there is a similar episode in connection with a forbidden bottle and a permitted box.

Let us notice here the beginning of questioning as a substitute for physical, non-linguistic behaviour. Instead of opening the cupboard door, the child speaks. He calls upon his mother to help him in exploring the situation by symbolising it with him. The replies he obtains are satisfying in themselves because they fit into the pattern of the game; but they are also something more than this—potentially, a guide to further action. They are likely to influence his play with these cupboards in the future.

Throughout this development we see the three factors mentioned above—play, imitation and the co-operation of others. The rudimentary questioning is a form of play, enjoyed for its own sake. It is imitative play—the child asks questions in the manner in which he himself has been questioned. Most important of all is his mother's willingness to play this game with him; we see that she deliberately causes him to express his interrogation through speech. And when he utters his rudimentary question, she takes the trouble to make a verbal reply, even though a non-verbal reply might have sufficed—a nod or shake of the head. As always, the speed and efficacy of a child's linguistic development is immeasurably influenced by the adult co-operation that he receives.

The transition to conventional speech. Again, as throughout linguistic development, the growth of questioning from a child's primitive utterance is reinforced and facilitated by his adoption of conventional speech. In particular, as he comes to use questioning as an instrument for the symbolical exploration of his environment, he realises that one form of interrogation is specially valuable—questions directed to securing the names of things.

So we come to one of the most striking characteristics of children in their second and third years—their indefatigable concern with naming-questions. M. E. Smith, for instance, recording some three thousand questions of children of this age, found that one-fifth were directed to obtain the name of an object or person (5). William Stern, the pioneer of the modern study of children's language, saw this onset of naming-questions as one of the great moments in a child's life. The child discovers 'that every thing has a name'; that to every object there belongs a lasting symbol, by means of which we can indicate the object and communicate about it (6).

Stern appears to believe that children as early as the second year arrive at this formulated generalisation. This would seem to be too adult, too intellectualised, a view of cognitive development at this stage; but perhaps Stern means no more than that children behave 'as though' they had made this discovery—and this we can well accept.

There is no need to give examples of naming-questions. Anyone who has had anything to do with a young child will be only too familiar with them. Certainly at first, and often for a long time to come, a child will ask for the name of one thing after another, as a sort of game. Not infrequently he will know the name before he asks for it and will seem merely to be seeking the satisfaction of this affirmatory interchange. But what is learnt in play can subsequently be used as an instrument to satisfy other needs.

Questioning as exploration. Among these needs, none is more imperative than the child's desire to explore his environment; at first, what is immediately present; later, what is remote in place and time. Already, while he is playing the game of question-and-answer, he is learning that questioning is a means of exploration. Asking for names is a simple kind of exploration—the child builds up, with the help of others, a verbal universe which symbolises his environment. Even before he asks questions he will have begun to learn names by everyday trial-and-error—as we saw, for instance, K learning the names of animals. Then he begins to do it more directly by asking questions.

Some of these questions help him to extend the exploration of his environment beyond the immediate present situation. We have seen that before this, his reference to what is absent will have begun in the course of everyday interchange, in his attempts to satisfy his manipulative and declarative needs. Now he finds, that an instrument that more directly helps him to symbolise what is absent, is the question that asks *Where?*—although at first he may not use this interrogative word.

> 1;10,3. K asked his mother, *Daddy?* She replied, *Gone ta-ta*. He then asked, *Kah?* (Carrie?). His mother replied, *Kitchen*. She then said, *Where's mummy?* He replied, pointing to her, *eh, eh, eh!*

We see here several different forms of behaviour, already habitual to the child, combining to produce questioning that refers to what is absent. First, there is the interplay of imitation. For a long time past, the child has himself been asked Where-questions—beginning as early as 1;1,5 with *Where's ballie?* Now at 1;10,3 he imitates by asking Where-questions of his mother. His first two she answers; at his third, she imitates him, asking him in turn, *Where's mummy?* Secondly there is an interesting development of manipulative function. When the child asks *Where's daddy?* he has something of the same manipulative intention as when he said *ha!* for the unseen honey. But there is now this difference, that his request results, not in the production of his father, but in a verbal reply from his mother. As soon as a child receives such a verbal reply, his manipulative utterance begins to have the function of interrogation—a verbal demand which secures a verbal response. Finally, we see that there is still an element of play in this interchange. The child is obviously no less interested in the game of question-and-answer than in the whereabouts of his father or Carrie.

Clearly, the chief result of obtaining replies to his Where-questions is this, that the child finds that through these questions he can take the initiative in causing another person to refer to something within their common environment and yet beyond the immediate situation. By securing social co-operation of this kind he extends his area of reference, building up a structure of symbolisation of what is absent.

From beginnings such as these, there are two lines of development in the use of questions as a means of referring to what is absent. The child aids his own reference by addressing questions to himself, and he also asks questions to bring others into co-operation with him in referring to the absent.

Instances of K's communication with himself:

2;2,23. Looking through a picture-book, he finds the picture of a teddy bear. Shuts the book and says: *Ever can teddy bear be?* He repeats this many times.

2;3,5. Playing the game of hiding a pencil in a book: *Ever can you be, little pencil?*

2;4,18. Looking for his toy, 'Billy-boy': *Billy-boy, where Garkie put it? Where is it?*

2;4,19. Playing with his train, looking for the string: *Where's the string?* (7).

This kind of chatter, so characteristic of children throughout infancy, is not merely an accompaniment to action: the question the child asks himself is one element within the total action—the verbal part of the game (8). The words help to direct the child's perception and motor activity. The words also help to bring what the child cannot see into relation with what he can see—the absent in

LANGUAGE AND EXPLORATION

relation to the present. If we say that the child is 'thinking aloud', we must recognise that there is likely to be a two-way relation here between words and thought. On the one hand, the child utters words which he recalls internally from similar past experiences. On the other hand, the utterance of the words may be followed by 'internalisation' of them, so that the child is helped to think more effectively about what is absent—so that what is out of sight need not be out of mind.

If now we look at the questions asked of others we see an important line of development. The information received becomes, rather than an aid to an immediate physical activity, an incentive to further speech by the child.

Instances are:

2;5,0. Looking for a strip of felt, K asks his father, *Where is it?* When it is shown to him he says, *There it is.*

2;2,3. His mother has returned from a visit to a friend. He asks, *Auntie ya?* (Auntie there?). His mother replies, *Yes!* whereupon he says, *Want it auntie. Go ask her!*

2;7,9. He has been out to tea the previous day with his mother. Today she has been out alone. On her return he asks, *Has mummy been out to tea?* She replies, *Yes.*

The child's goal here may well be said to be knowledge as an end in itself. The question he asks has the intention of obtaining confirmation or denial of what he already supposes. The affirmatory answer he receives is sufficient in itself, giving him the knowledge he seeks. But if his mother's answer had been in the negative, he might have gone on with further questioning until a satisfying answer was reached.

With information-seeking interrogation of this kind we are at the beginning of that vast proliferation of questions so characteristic of this period in a child's life. In some children, as with K, it may begin as early as the middle of the third year; with others, later. Differences in the speed and the volume of this development are likely to be due to differences in temperament, intelligence, verbal ability and imitativeness and—running through all these—the extent of incitement and co-operation the child receives from those about him. There must be retardation in the development of a child's exploration of his world, present and absent, if he is not questioned and if his own questions remain unanswered. For a deaf child, or a child in an institution, this may mean a severe restriction of enterprise in reaching out beyond his immediate experience.

The differentiation of questions. In normally favourable conditions, a child's questions become more diverse in function and he acquires specific interrogative words. But since interrogative forms and functions do not at first always coincide, the course of development may not be simple and direct. As the child's interrogative needs become more specific, he may or may not express these by means of the conventional words. At the same time, in imitating conventional interrogative-words he may or may not use these with the conventional functions. The process by which he comes to use the interrogative forms of the mother tongue with their conventional functions may be long and arduous, in some cases extending over several years.

In general, the main features of this course of development are these. The child has interrogative needs which he has been expressing, though crudely and ineffectively, by the rudimentary means at his disposal. Meanwhile, others are constantly questioning him and each other; the child imitates the interrogative forms that he hears, sometimes as a kind of game sometimes as real questioning. Gradually he finds that specific kinds of interrogation bring specific kinds of response. For instance, What-questions supply names; Where-questions bring indications of location; and Who-did-this-questions and Why-questions bring information about the source or the goal of actions. He becomes more clearly aware of these various sequences of question and answer, and so learns to use specific forms of questioning to secure specific types of response.

Three kinds of interrogative behaviour may be distinguished. First, the child continues to play the game of question-and-answer; he asks what we may call 'pseudo-questions'—questions the answers to which he already knows and which he asks simply for the pleasure of the verbal interchange with someone. Secondly, he continues to ask questions to test the correctness of what he believes—a rudimentary form of testing a hypothesis. Finally, he asks questions by which he seeks real information—what he as yet does not know.

In actually observing a child, it is not always possible to draw clear lines of separation between these kinds of interrogative activity. Instances from the record of K will illustrate this.

(a) *Naming-questions*

2;6,17. With his mother he is playing the game of 'Counting', i.e., naming things. He says, *Could mummy count this and this?* She replies, *You count first.* He points and asks, *What is it?* She replies, *What?* whereupon he says, *Milk.* All this is repeated with one object after another.

If his mother had not been so persistent, one might well have thought that he really did not know the names of the various objects. On the other hand, there is little doubt that in the following instance we have a real question:

2;7,15. He points to word after word in a book of nursery-rhymes, asking each time, *What does this say?*

(b) *Where-questions*

Two observations on the same day—the first probably playful, the second probably really seeking information:

2;9,3. He says to his mother, *Do you know where R's bicycle is?* When she answers *No!* he continues, *R's bicycle is at Auntie M's.*

When his father awakens him in the morning he says, *Where's mummy?* His father replies, *In bed,* whereupon he says, *I want to say, Good morning.*

(c) *Questions concerning sources of actions*

A very important development in a child's life is the emergence of questions and answers concerned with the sources of actions. The child begins to ask Why-questions, and to answer questions of this kind with 'Because...' These exchanges might appear to imply that the child has begun to have clear ideas of causality. But here, no more than in other aspects of linguistic development, are children's words to be taken at their face value. Close observation of the circumstances in which these questions and answers occur, and of a child's linguistic and general development at the time, lead to the conclusion that what the child says is not so much an expression of an existing notion of cause-and-effect, as a means by which the growth of ideas of causality may be fostered.

A child approaches ideas of cause-and-effect by various kinds of questions that demand information, and it is the answers that he gets to his questions that do much to connect cause and effect for him.

Sometimes the question simply asks for an explanation of an action observed by the child:

> 2;9,8. His father goes to a drawer and opens it. K asks, *What do you want, daddy?*

But quite often the child has a glimmering of the answer and is asking for reinforcement and expansion of his knowledge:

> 2;9,9. Seeing his father putting on his spectacles, K asks, *What you putting those glasses on for?*

Taken by itself this might seem to be a genuine request for information. But in this case we happen to have a record of an earlier observation:

> 2;5,12. His father has his spectacles off. K says, *Daddy put glasses on.*

Since the child has seen his father putting on his spectacles he most probably has seen this followed by the reading of a book or newspaper. So that when he now asks why his father is putting on his glasses he has, we may suppose, at least some notion of the answer, 'To read . . .'. If this is so, the question has been directed to secure confirmation of what, to some extent, the child already supposes.

In many cases this function of a child's question is beyond doubt. For instance:

> 2;8,12. K, to his mother, *Who bought that frock?* She replies, *Mummy*, whereupon he says, *No, Lily!* (He has accompanied Lily, the maid, when she called for the dress.)

The child, in asking the question, already has his own answer to it. He has experienced a schema of events which, in recall, he can formulate in words. In putting a part of this as a question, he is seeking to have the rest of his inner formulation confirmed by someone else—it is a kind of game. But when his mother's reply does not, in fact, match his own inner statement, he supplies his own answer.

Often we deliberately make him do this. Instead of answering his request for information, we turn the question upon him, causing him to supply the answer, which he is perfectly able to do. For instance:

2;10,18. While eating soup: *Mummy, why do we use a spoon?* Mother: *Why?* K: *'Cause we can't drink it with our hands.*
2;9,0. His mother, referring to a projected excursion on Sunday: *Perhaps Lily will come too.* K: *Lily can't come.* Mother: *Why?* K: *'Cause of George.* (George is the young man who calls on Lily on Sundays!)

In these two instances the child has answered our Why-question with a Because-answer. But are we warranted in supposing that he has a clear awareness of cause-and-effect in these situations? It seems much more likely that in each case he is aware of a juxtaposition of events and can formulate this. It seems likely that he is not yet aware that we use a spoon *because* we don't drink soup with our hands: he is saying that these two things occur together—we don't drink soup with our hands, we use a spoon. Likewise when he says that Lily can't come because of George he is, surely, saying not that George is the cause of Lily's inability to come out, but rather that when George calls on Sundays, Lily stays at home.

This is in keeping with Piaget's contention that at first children are aware only of juxtaposition where later they recognise causality. More than anyone else, Piaget has made clear to us how much a child's progress in the development of ideas of causality depends upon his intercourse with other people. 'It is precisely to the extent that verbal-conceptual thought is transformed by its collective nature that it becomes capable of proof and search for truth, in contradistinction to the practical character of the acts of sensori-motor intelligence and their search for success or satisfaction' (9). But what Piaget does not, perhaps, sufficiently stress is that in a child's early questions his nebulous and inchoate ideas of causality are made more explicit by his imitation of the language which adults use to express causality.

The process of development here is similar to the growth of awareness of spatial relationships. By asking and answering Where-questions imitatively, in play, a child is led to enquire more and more specifically about the location of absent things and so to form for himself a patterned structure of objects in space. In the same way, his imitation of Why-questions and Because-answers, often in play, fosters his growing awareness of causal relationships.

In the course of the present chapter, what we have been witnessing is the progressive influence of language upon the child's schemata. While he is as yet poor in language, he already has some rudimentary symbolisation of the world about him; some dawning reference to what is absent, past or yet to come; some formulation of the linkage of certain events together. In our intercourse with him, the mother tongue helps him to become more clearly aware of spatial, temporal and even causal relationships by giving him the symbols for them—the linguistic forms by means of which we are accustomed to symbolise these relationships. Often it is his adoption, in imitation, of a verbal form that brings a structure of relationships into a relatively amorphous schema. If it is not true to say that words give birth to his ideas, at least this is true, that through words his ideas grow and ramify and become more clearly related to each other.

In his early questions a child may certainly be seeking information, but just as often—if not more frequently—practising the formulation of events that he can already tentatively make for himself. He is rapidly building up for himself a structure of knowledge, a system of symbolisation. He is incited to do this by others in their questions to him; he practises question-and-answer in play with them and by himself; and he often asks questions, the answers to which he already knows, seeking as it were social approval or rejection of his own answers. It may be said that he is experimenting all the time to discover what may or may not be admitted to his system of knowledge. At first this experimenting may be a half-blind groping by trial-and-error; gradually, through social co-operation, it becomes more clear-sighted and more immediately and effectively directed towards its goals.

PART TWO

Early Childhood

6

General Characteristics

THE earlier years of childhood, from about three to about seven are, for most children, a time during which they move beyond the family to wider societies of other children and adults. This enlargement of social environment continues a process which begins in the earliest months of life, as the close circle of mother and child expands to include father, brother and sister and later, perhaps, grandparents, aunts and cousins. The child then moves beyond the family circle and encounters people outside his home. School brings new adults and new children into his life—to father and mother is added teacher, to brother and sister many other boys and girls.

The wider society presents the child with greater possibilities of play and at the same time constrains him to perform new tasks. In the home and beyond, he now lives less to himself. If until now he has mostly played alone, now more and more he plays with others. In school he is led to undertake tasks in the presence of other children and his teacher, and in growing co-operation with them. Thus his cognitive and orectic growth continues to take its pattern under the constant influence of his social surroundings, in which other children and adults both make their specific contributions. Deprived of the society and co-operation of either, a child may grow deformed and stunted in thought and in feeling.

It is not that he plays with children and learns with adults. This is obviously too crude an antithesis. In play he learns and he learns by playing. Both directly and through the medium of language, he continues the exploration of his environment. In company with other children his play widens the range of his activities and, in a diversity of experiences, enriches his awareness and understanding of his world. At the same time the school undertakes, as its chief aim, to help him to carry out this exploration more precisely and systematically. So the systematisation of his behaviour, including his thoughts, feelings and impulses, goes on not only by his acceptance of tasks and rules, but also through the ordered play of the nursery class and infant school and the games of playground, street and home.

But the socialisation of the child is not simply an increase of conformity with current ways of living. While he is learning to live with others, his idiosyncratic individuality is also becoming more pronounced. While his thinking is being shaped in communication with others, he is also learning to think by and for himself. During this period we see, therefore, a changing balance in the pattern of relationships of language, social life and individual personality. Language fosters social intercourse, which in turn fosters language. Both affect the child's personal cognitive and orectic life, and this, again, influences his language and his intercourse with others.

To follow the course of a child's linguistic and general development during the present period, let us notice how language is related, first to his life with other children and then to his life with his elders.

WITH CHILDREN OF HIS OWN AGE

The wide diversity of a child's activities that we characterise as his play brings with it, as it grows in variety and complexity, a more varied and more flexible use of the mother tongue and this in turn helps to make his play more diverse and more fruitful for his general growth.

The main changes in the nature of children's play, as they pass from infancy to early childhood, have often been described—a multitude of observations combine to give us a clear picture of normal development. In the transitional period from infancy to early childhood much of children's play is still as solitary as in the preceding years; as time goes on, we see them engaged more and more in 'parallel' play—playing side by side with little or no concern for each other. Gradually there emerge the beginnings of group play and some rudimentary co-operation.

These changes in the social pattern of a child's play are due not only to the growth of common interests with other children. They also arise from, and in turn foster, a differentiation of the functions of his play for the child himself in relation to his world. It is exploratory, imaginative or constructive; solitary play or parallel play or group play may have any or all of these functions.

Thus a child's solitary play may continue to be exploratory when, as in his earlier months, he explores the resources of his own body or of his social and non-human environment. It is imaginative when he pretends, makes believe; when he plays out an imagined situation, corresponding more or less to actuality. Solitary play is, of course, often constructive as well—at its simplest when the infant puts one block on top of another, more elaborately when a year or two later he builds his blocks into a house. Parallel play or again group play may obviously be exploratory, imaginative or constructive.

The manner in which this growing complexity and variety of play bring about a corresponding growth in the mastery of language becomes clear from the observation of children. In solitary play, as we have already seen, a child often speaks to himself. He describes to himself what he is doing, he names the things he is playing with and the absent things he needs, he names relationships between things, he asks himself questions. We have seen that this talk is not so much egocentric as 'synpractic'—a help to the child in his play (page 92); and that as the child realises this, there will be an incentive for him to use language in this way more freely.

That a child often speaks to and for himself at this stage there can be no question; but it must be recognised that even when this occurs in solitary play it is still not always entirely non-social. The child's mother, or some other adult, or another child, will occasionally speak to him and even if he does not reply there will probably be some reinforcement of his own use of language as he plays. Thus, as Vigotsky has shown, 'synpractic' language—so important in the development of perceptual and conceptual thinking—is greatly promoted by the intervention of others in a child's solitary play (1).

The advent of parallel play is a further development in this direction. The child is playing side by side with other children, perhaps taking little notice of what they are doing and saying. But he cannot be altogether oblivious of them. They are doing some of the things he is doing, speaking to themselves while he is speaking to himself. They stimulate him to play and to speak. All this will happen more freely when he is in school. And not only because of the other children. Here in school is an adult who makes it her business to encourage children to talk while they play. As a result a child's personal use of language while he is absorbed in doing things is fostered.

When, then, he begins to play in a more social fashion—when in his play he is a member of a group and begins to seek the cooperation of others—obviously language will enter even more freely into what he is doing. His growing command of the mother tongue will help to make his group play more effectively imaginative, constructive and exploratory; and his play, at the same time, will provide an increasing and an even more powerful incentive to his use of language.

But not all of this will be evident as overt speech. As he grows up among other children he will tend to keep his 'synpractic' language to himself, and this inner speech will tend to play an increasingly important part in his cognitive and orectic life.

The retardation of a child whose social life is impoverished will therefore become particularly evident in early childhood. His play, his language and his cognitive and orectic development will all tend to remain at a more primitive level than that of children who enjoy a fuller social life. We have seen that even in his earliest months, life in an institution may hold back a child's linguistic development. This retardation may become more severe during the present period and contribute to immaturity, both cognitive and orectic. Linguistic and general retardation may also be the result of a restriction of a child's social environment even in his own natural home. Extreme examples of this are twins who because of their emotional bonds and common interests live much in each other's company.

A particularly striking instance is the systematic and experimental observation by Luria and Yudovich of a pair of identical twins. Up to the age of five the two boys played together in solitary fashion, having little or nothing to do with other children. Both their play and their language were immature. Their play was more limited in scope, less varied and more infantile than that of normal children of their age; their vocabulary was smaller and their general command of linguistic form more primitive. Within a few weeks after their admission to a kindergarten, both play and language were making rapid strides towards the normal.

At the same time the twins were given contrasting experimental treatment. The less well-developed of the two had regular lessons in the mother tongue. In a few months systematic tests showed that he was markedly in advance of his twin not only in language but also in cognitive ability and orectic maturity. This is only one illustration of the close relations between language and personal and social development in early childhood (2).

The observation of deaf children once again brings its corroborative evidence. Even when a deaf child is free to associate with other children he will find it difficult to approach them and they to accept him; but frequently, as Ewing points out, deaf children are restricted in their freedom to mix with other children because their parents are reluctant to expose them to the possible risks of playing in the street, the park or the playground. It is not surprising then that the play of deaf children tends to develop slowly—that it is usually much more solitary than that of normal children of the same age. Thus the primary impairment of their language is further aggravated and this, says Ewing, may have a markedly adverse effect upon their use of symbols in general—even non-linguistic symbols (3). For what may most help the development of a deaf child who is retarded in acquiring language is the ability to use other symbols, such as signs and gestures, in his own thinking; and the ability to grasp these symbols—as also pictures and diagrams—when shown to him by others. If the very impairment of language itself retards his mastery of these other symbols, then he is still further handicapped.

These instances of the effects of social deprivation combine to show by contrast that among the favourable conditions for progressive development during early childhood one of the most powerful is this: that a child has plenty of opportunity to play in the company of others of his own age, and that while he plays he is speaking, hearing others speak and being spoken to.

INTERCOURSE WITH ADULTS AND OLDER CHILDREN

Association with his elders has obviously also a distinctive contribution to make to his general development and to his linguistic growth in particular. Intervening in his play they may stimulate and guide him, helping to make what he does richer and more fruitful. Without this help and by his own initiative, a child will no doubt gradually progress in exploring, understanding and mastering his world. His elders accelerate his progress by 'bringing him up'—that is, by deliberately and specifically carrying him forward towards adolescence and adult life. By suggestion, injunction, exhortation and question-and-answer they stimulate him to act in new ways to find himself in new situations; they lead him to see how to approach problems that arise in these situations.

Inseparable from this is the function of adults and older children in promoting a child's linguistic development. Playing with other children of his own age will of course improve his ability to communicate with them. His elders can do something more—they can help him to move more readily and rapidly towards the current forms and usages of adult language.

Deaf children often communicate with each other by signs and gestures—a language of their own—while they are deficient in language of a wider currency. Twins who are retarded in the mother tongue often have a private language intelligible only to themselves; the strong bonds between them and the satisfaction they find in their companionship weaken the incentives to communicate with other people. Children in institutions who have no difficulty in understanding each other may be restricted in their command of the mother tongue where their life with adults and older children is restricted.

But in normal conditions the full development of a child as he passes from infancy depends upon free and fruitful communication both with his contemporaries and with his elders. Only so will he progress in his mastery of the mother tongue and in his cognitive as well as in his orectic development. Let us now look at each of these three aspects of his growth, noticing how they are interrelated during this period of early childhood.

THE GROWING MASTERY OF FORM AND USAGE

From the beginning of the modern systematic study of children, constant attempts have been made to measure their progressive mastery of the forms and usages of the mother tongue. But there are serious obstacles to the establishment of general norms of development at successive ages. Differences in environment mean great differences in attainment and there are obvious difficulties in recording the speech of young children which will provide valid and reliable measurements. The most one can hope to do is to describe the broad successive stages in the mastery of linguistic forms and usages, from the data provided by the available studies of phonetic, syntactic and lexical development.

In general, details of the command of phonetic form are given as measures of 'articulation', in which no distinction is made between enunciation and pronunciation; that is, between precision of utterance and the child's mastery of the repertory of phonemes used in his social environment. Intonation appears to be neglected. With these qualifications, probably the best survey of speech in early childhood is that of Templin, who systematically observed and tested 480 children of 'normal intelligence' between the ages of three and eight. The three-year-olds attained, in accuracy of articulation, a mean score approximately 50 per cent of that of the eight-year-olds, who—as had also been shown by previous observers —normally produced nearly all sounds 'correctly' (4).

In measuring the development of syntactic form, Templin observed the length of utterance, the complexity of sentence structure, grammatical correctness and the proportionate use of the parts of speech. In the two former of these, children's progress during the period is summarised in the general statement that there is a steady increase in the length and complexity of sentence. As to grammatical correctness, Templin found that the speech of the three-year-olds was about 50 per cent correct, as compared with the 75 per cent attainment of the eight-year-olds. And on the use of parts of speech, she comes to the conclusion that 'after the age of three, the parts of speech ... show little change. This is in agreement with other studies.'

As to the measurement of vocabulary, this, as has often been pointed out, is peculiarly fraught with difficulty (5). What is a word and how do we judge a child's comprehension? The most that can be done is to take samples, as representative as possible, of his utterance and response to language. This Templin did, attempting to estimate the vocabulary of use and of comprehension, together with the 'basic vocabulary', that is, the number of words apparently understood, from lists made up by taking systematic samples at intervals throughout a standard dictionary. Recognising, however, the uncertainty of any measures of vocabulary, she commits herself in the end to no more than the very general statement that normally there is a steady growth of vocabulary.

Taken by themselves these facts may be interesting but they tell us very little about children's development. They begin to have significance when we see them in relation to social life. This is the outstanding value of Templin's work. First, she was able to confirm her expectation that there are some positive correlations of attainment in the three aspects of linguistic form. She found that the correlation was greater between phonetic and syntactic growth than between these, taken together, and lexical growth; and that, in general, the relationships become smaller as the children grow older (6). This would suggest that during this period, children's personal cognitive and orectic characteristics are finding more individual expression; that they will be more alike in the phonetic aspects of their language—since these are susceptible of direct training in school—than in semantic growth, which is much more dependent upon individual cognitive and orectic disposition and the influences of general social environment.

Equally illuminating are her comparisons between different groups of the children studied and between these children and children in the past. As to sex differences, while confirming the conclusions of earlier workers that girls tend to excel in articulation and boys in the knowledge of words, Templin found that in general the linguistic differences were smaller than had usually been stated. She offers the interesting suggestion that during the last twenty-five years the differences may have become smaller owing to the trend towards a single standard of child care and training in the upbringing of boys and girls.

In comparing upper and lower socio-economic levels, Templin was again able to confirm previous conclusions: she found the performance of the upper group consistently better than that of the lower, with statistically significant differences for nearly all the measures of attainment in linguistic growth. But, as she cautiously adds, the differences in measures of intellectual ability were also statistically significant.

Her most striking generalisation is in the comparison between children past and present. Having used many of the criteria and methods of measurement of previous workers, Templin concludes that 'there is a tendency for children of the same age to use more language than they did twenty-five years ago. . . . This would seem to reflect an increased amount of adult language in the child's environment, whether as a result of increased viewing of T.V., more inclusion in family activities, general permissiveness towards the child's behaviour, or other factors.' This surely is a very interesting instance of the importance of a child's elders in accelerating his progress in the mother tongue.

What also emerges very clearly from her results is the manner in which innate capacity and environmental conditions combine to produce the progressive mastery of linguistic form during this period. There are, we can hardly doubt, innate differences of intelligence in children. There are also, we must suppose, differences of innate linguistic capacity, as between children and perhaps as between the sexes. Acting upon these inborn potentialities is the constant influence of social environment. Sex differences are diminished because boys and girls are now brought up more uniformly than in the past. Having more interests in common they can converse more freely with each other and with adults about the same things.

Again, differences corresponding to social and economic conditions, have in the past been due, among other things, to the fact that—compared with the lower levels—adults in the upper levels have tended to be more highly literate and able to give their children a more varied and wider linguistic experience. But during the last twenty-five years there has been at all levels an increasing penetration of adult language into children's experience because of freer association between them and their parents, not least through the admission of children to adult ways of thought and communication in the cinema and by radio and television. As a result children are now, by and large, further advanced towards adult language than at the same age twenty-five years ago.

It is clear that what we are witnessing during this period of transition from infancy to childhood is what we have seen from the beginning of linguistic development. The acquisition of the linguistic forms of the mother tongue is not simply the acquisition of a system of utterance; it is the mastery of a means of communication—the use of forms to achieve functions. It is true that form and function do not always grow at the same pace. Children use words in advance of a concomitant command of their functions; they also attempt communication for which they have as yet only inadequate linguistic means. But in the main, the development of language is the growth of a complex skill—a hierarchy of habits—constantly adapted to the task of communication with others and with oneself. How well these others co-operate with the child must always be a most powerful determinant throughout the course of his linguistic development.

We now go on to consider the manner in which the growing command of language is related to cognitive and orectic growth during this period of early childhood. The relationships become more complex; to understand them demands a close attention to the facts, as far as these can be ascertained.

LANGUAGE AND COGNITIVE DEVELOPMENT

During infancy a child's primitive speech and his rudimentary command of the mother tongue may, together with non-linguistic symbolisation, be relatively adequate for his needs in communication with others and in his own thinking—in his perceptual and conceptual development, the growth of his powers of reasoning and the enlargement of his knowledge. But as he passes from infancy to childhood the possibilities of his further development depend more and more upon his mastery of language as a more sensitive, more refined and more finely-adjusted instrument of communication and thought.

This is because his social environment becomes increasingly linguistic. He enters school: and education, in a modern society, is largely the verbalisation of behaviour. We, his educators, encourage, incite and train the child to verbalise his experiences—to use words to supplement and then supersede physical acts. The centre of school education—traditionally, and today more than ever—is the fuller development of ability to manipulate verbal symbols. In school the 'intelligent' child is the child with aptitude for this kind of education. When we test intelligence by means of the usual individual and group tests—whether 'verbal' or 'non-verbal'—we are testing, in Burt's phrase, scholastic aptitude; that is, a child's potentialities and attainment in the mental skills that demand the manipulation of verbal symbols. We do all we can to foster his cognitive development through language.

But our best teachers do not forget that this can be successful only if a child's language, from the first intimately bound up with the rest of his behaviour, is not too soon and too crudely divorced from it. They still heed Pestalozzi's warning about the dangers of empty verbalism for all children and they recognise that the dangers are greater for some children than for others.

For it is clear that children vary considerably in the speed and effectiveness with which they come to verbalise their behaviour, alone or with others. There is evidence that some children manage their cognitive tasks more efficiently without rather than with the aid of language. These children, indeed, may acquire skill in verbalised thinking only if this is allowed to grow slowly out of a comparatively prolonged period of physical manipulation in which there is a minimum of verbalisation. By contrast, other children begin very early and progress very rapidly in verbalised behaviour. Such individual differences are, we may take it, the combined results of relative innate capacity and a relatively favourable environment.

Many teachers of young children take account of these differences and are careful not to allow an undue insistence upon language to stultify rather than foster their education. But there is a corresponding possible danger of going too far in this direction. The education of young children in the spirit of Pestalozzi may fail to recognise that his war against verbalism was a battle for the true place of language in the development of every human being. 'What is the end of language for man?' he asks: and replies, 'The final end of language is obviously to lead our race from vague sense impressions to clear ideas' (7).

Our task here is to study precisely this; to see how the increasing impact of language upon a child, as he moves forward from infancy, is related to his advance towards 'clear ideas'.

We take up the story where we left it in Chapter 5, with the child exploring his world perceptually and conceptually, with and without the aid of language. We now have to trace, in the course of his early childhood, his wider and deeper exploration of his environment—non-social and social, immediate and remote—with the aid of his increasing command of verbal symbolisation. We see language becoming for him a means of dealing with relationships of greater and greater complexity as he perceives; as he advances in his conceptual thinking; as he remembers, imagines and reasons.

To guide us we have evidence of three kinds. First there is the comparative study of different groups of children who in the ordinary course of their lives have, in varying degrees, been open to the impact of language upon their behaviour. Secondly we have the results of the controlled observation of children who have been experimentally required to perform tasks in which language has entered to a greater or a lesser extent. Finally we have the more or less systematic records of individual children. From all this evidence we can derive a picture of the general relation between linguistic and cognitive development in early childhood.

EVIDENCE FROM THE COMPARISON OF GROUPS

As children pass from infancy to early childhood, we begin to be able to measure their cognitive abilities with greater precision. 'Intelligence' tests, though by no means wholly trustworthy, enable us to compare groups of children with somewhat greater certainty than at an earlier age.

The differences corresponding to different social and economic levels have long been known. The conclusion reached by Templin, that children in the higher levels are more advanced not only in language but also in cognitive ability, is only one confirmation of what has been repeatedly found from the very beginning of the testing of intelligence. Binet himself was quite clear about this and hoped that the tests he devised with Simon took account of the effects of social and economic conditions, but he was never quite happy that he had succeeded. At once other workers such as Stern, Yerkes and Terman confirmed his misgivings; and from that day to this a succession of investigators have closely studied the relations between socio-economic level and cognitive ability (8).

Using revisions of Binet's own tests, Goodenough tested 380 children under four and a half years, Terman and Merrill 831 under five and a half years. The two independent investigations produce strikingly identical curves of decrease of children's I.Q.s corresponding to six grades of their fathers' occupations, from 'professional' to 'unskilled' (9).

But how can we say that language has anything to do with these differences? The answer can only be by way of inference from the known facts. All that we have seen of development in infancy suggests that his parents' education will continue to be an important influence on a child's cognitive growth. Investigations as soon as children can be measured with standardised tests confirm this; for instance, the work of Van Alstyne and of Bayley and Jones with children of three years of age, giving high correlations between measures of their 'intelligence' and of the education of their parents. In summarising this and other work, Jones points out that the correlations may reflect hereditary as well as environmental influences. This is evident; but all we are concerned with here is to establish the reality of these environmental influences on children, including the linguistic competence of their elders (10).

Today this is being brought home to us with growing emphasis from our concern with the welfare of handicapped children, whose disabilities we are no longer willing to accept without question as ineradicable. Many of these children are at an early age placed in institutions where, as we have seen, even in infancy their cognitive and linguistic development may be retarded. As they grow up into early childhood their retardation, in comparison with the development of children living an ordinary family life, becomes more marked. But a great deal of recent work has shown that the adverse effects of living in an institution may be ameliorated if the children are brought into a way of life less impersonal, more like that of an ordinary home.

Skeels and Harms investigated the cognitive development of some two hundred children, of mothers of low intelligence or fathers of lower-grade occupations, or both, who from infancy had been brought up not in institutions but in adoptive homes; these children were found to have 'attained a mental level which equals or exceeds that of the population as a whole.' Skeels and Dye arranged for some two-year-old orphanage children of very low I.Q.s to be given individual attention by older girls and adults. After two years their average I.Q.s had risen considerably while that of a comparable group left in the orphanage nursery without special attention had *fallen* by the same amount. Kirk studied eighty-one mentally retarded children, from three to six years old, in four groups: living at home either with or without special experimental attention; living in an institution either with or without this experimental attention. The average I.Q.s of the two experimental groups increased; that of the non-experimental home group remained unchanged; that of the non-experimental institution group decreased.

To remove a child from an institution or give him greater individual care while he is there may ameliorate his handicap, but the effects of institutional life in infancy are likely to persist for some time. Some evidence of this comes from a careful investigation by Goldfarb in comparing fifteen children who up to the age of three had lived in an institution with fifteen children who up to that age had lived in foster-homes. The two groups were closely matched; but, if anything, the mothers of the institution children were of a higher occupational grade than those of the foster-home children.

At age three both groups were given standardised tests. In motor co-ordination there was no difference, but the institution children were below the normal in linguistic attainment and in verbal and non-verbal tests of cognition, while the foster-home children were within the normal ranges. The institution children were then placed in foster-homes and seven months later the two groups were again tested. The institution children now responded more readily to the person giving the tests, but were still below normal in language and cognitive ability, as compared with the normal achievement of the foster-home children.

From these investigations and others one thing is certain: that what matters most for the progress of a deprived or retarded child is not simply whether he is living with his natural parents, or is adopted, or in a foster-home, or in an institution—but the quality of the attention he receives from his elders wherever he is (11).

Coming still closer to the problem are investigations which differentiate the results of comparing groups by means of tests into which language enters to a smaller or greater extent. There are so-called 'performance' tests, presented with little or no verbal symbolisation; diagrammatic tests, in the presentation of which there may be some verbal symbolisation; and purely verbal tests. It is evident that the extent of verbal symbolisation in presenting a test is not in itself a measure of a child's use of language in solving it—this is a ques-

GENERAL CHARACTERISTICS

tion we shall consider shortly. But confining ourselves for the moment to differences of presentation, we can take note of the general trend of the results of comparing groups of children from different social and economic levels. Herrick has summarised nine investigations between 1911 and 1947, including some with children under seven. 'In general', he says, 'test items which are essentially linguistic or scholastic in nature show comparatively large differences in favour of children from high socio-economic backgrounds, while test items which are primarily perceptual or "practical" in nature show either smaller differences or differences in favour of children from the lower socio-economic backgrounds' (12).

A similar pattern appears in testing deaf children. In general they do as well as children with normal hearing, if not better, when given performance tests. Kendall, for instance, comparing 370 deaf children under five and a half years with 324 normal children 'balanced for socio-economic status' found no significant differences in test score. On the other hand, when it comes to purely verbal tests there is, as we should expect, a statistically significant inferiority of the deaf children, as Oléron, for instance, showed from an elaborate investigation of deaf children between the ages of four and seven (13). But many of these children were also inferior in diagrammatic tests, even when these were presented without the use of language. Why is this? Emmett has shown by factorial analysis that for normal children there is a verbal factor in the solution of these tests; deaf children may obviously be handicapped by their inferior command of language. There is even some evidence that this handicap may extend to the solution of performance tests (14).

THE GENERAL PICTURE OF NORMAL DEVELOPMENT

We are now able to form a picture of the place of language in the development of perceptual and conceptual thinking in early childhood. First, we have seen in Chapter 2 how language may enter into early perceptual behaviour. Perception is exploration. From the beginning it is an intrinsic part of the physical acts by which the child takes hold of and familiarises himself with his world. Perception is never merely the passive registration of something out there in the environment—the combining of impressions received through the sense-organs. Perception is activity; when a person is perceiving he is engaged in coming to grips with—'comprehending'—his environment. By the time we reach adult life we have learnt to limit the direct exploration of our world by physically getting hold of it; we have learnt to supplement and replace immediate physical exploration by the use of symbols—above all, language. The perception of children is obviously much more immediately physical than ours; they perceive not only as we do, through vision, hearing, taste, smell and touch but, much more than we do, through the physical manipulation of things.

Language enables them to perceive more discriminately what is before them. 'The development of discriminatory sensitivity in children is inextricably bound up with improvement in their speech in the course of their upbringing' says Ananiev (15).

Secondly, language may help children as they progressively undertake tasks which demand motor adjustment. There is much evidence that many children who are inferior in linguistic skills also tend to be inferior in motor skills, and Goodenough and Brian have demonstrated that precise verbal instructions can help children of four to acquire new perceptuo-motor skills (16).

All this, however, does not mean that in infancy and early childhood language is essential for the effective and skilful performance of perceptuo-motor tasks. For, as we have seen, deaf children are sometimes superior to normal children in solving problems in performance tests: and the evidence from the observation of children in general suggests that where the situation is open to direct perception and physical manipulation, the tasks may be successfully carried out without verbal symbolisation (17). This is the more likely to happen where, from one cause or another, a child does not readily resort to language. Because of his innate constitution or some acquired defect or an unfavourable social environment he may accustom himself to manipulate his world directly or with non-verbal symbols. As a result, in simple performance tests he may be quicker and more effective than children of higher linguistic attainment who are still fumbling with the more complex instrument of language that they have not yet learnt to use efficiently.

But as the tasks become more complex, involving increasingly abstract relationships, the possibility of effective non-linguistic thinking and manipulation becomes more remote. There is a pre-

GENERAL CHARACTERISTICS

mium on the use of language in solving problems, even those predominantly perceptual and motor in nature.

For as we have so constantly seen, a society such as ours presents a child with an environment permeated by language. Everything leads him to use language and demands that he shall use it. As a result, there is a constant tendency, which becomes more pressing as the tasks become more complex, for verbal symbolisation to be an aid to perception and motor skill, and for the lack of it to be a hindrance to his success. The relationships here may well be circular. Speech itself involves perceptual and motor skills. A child who by nature or upbringing has good perceptual and motor co-ordination will learn to speak more readily and this skill in language will in turn help him in dealing with the perceptual and motor tasks in performance tests. Conversely, a child by nature or upbringing inferior in perceptual and motor co-ordination, and so in learning to articulate speech, may be deprived of some of the aid that verbal symbolisation might bring to the performance of perceptual and motor tasks.

We now have to look more closely at this; to observe how, during this period of early childhood, language may enter into the perception of things and the manipulation of relations between them. We shall review some of the investigations that have been designed to elucidate the functions of language in the performance of these tasks.

7
The Growth of Reasoning

LANGUAGE IN THE PERFORMANCE OF A TASK

A NUMBER of investigations have been designed with the intention of observing the extent to which language may influence the performance of a given task. In Chapter 2 we cited the experiments of Shipinova and Surina in support of the view that already in infancy a specific phonetic pattern may foster a child's perception of relationships in a particular situation and in transfer to a somewhat similar situation. In early childhood more elaborate experiments become possible, providing more cogent evidence.

Pyles carried out an interesting investigation with children between two and seven years of age. These were presented with three different sets of shapes made of papier-mâché: a set of five 'nonsense-shapes' unnamed, a set of five other nonsense-shapes with nonsense names, such as 'Mobie', and a set of five shapes of familiar animals. In each set one shape—always the same one—hid a toy; the test was to find this. A child was deemed to be successful in each set when, in four successive trials, his first choice was the shape hiding the toy. Taking the median number of trials needed by the children to achieve successful recognition with the three kinds of shapes, we have:

> Nonsense shapes unnamed: 69 trials
> Nonsense shapes named: 37 trials
> Animal shapes: 5 trials

THE GROWTH OF REASONING

It is obvious that the presence of a name greatly facilitates the task; the more so where, as with the animals, the name already exists for the child (1).

Now, as children grow, they become more and more capable of recognising relationships between data in a given situation. But it is clear that this growing ability is due not only to the accumulation of experiences of the perception of things, but often also to the use of language in symbolising the data. Thus Weir and Stevenson investigated the ability of children to choose correctly-drawn pictures of animals from among a mixture of these with incorrectly drawn pictures. At each year of age the children were divided into two matched groups; for one of these the instruction was to name the animal before choosing a picture. At every age from three onwards, those who were required to name the animal were the more successful in choosing correct pictures (2).

LANGUAGE IN TRANSFER TO A NEW SITUATION

What is the place of language when a child is required to transfer his recognition of relationships to a relatively new situation? This has been studied in 'transposition' experiments in which children are presented with a new situation which offers some variations of a pattern of relations which they have already experienced. Kuenne, for example, devised an experiment in which forty-four children of age 2;6 to 5;10, mental age 3;0 to 6;11, were confronted with two wooden squares of different size, and learnt by repeated trials that a toy consistently lay concealed under the smaller. They were then tested with a pair of squares of nearly the same size as the original—'the near test'; and with a pair of much smaller squares—'the far test'.

Kuenne noted what use the children made of speech during these tests. She classified them into four groups: those who (1) made no comment on size; (2) commented on size-difference without connecting this with the solution; (3) stated the principle of solution in response to questioning at the end of the experiment; (4) spontaneously enunciated the principle during the experiment.

As might be expected, groups 1 and 2 were the younger children, those of mental-age groups three and four years. Now while all the children were equally successful in the near test, the far test revealed striking differences. Not one of the three-year mental-age group was successful in this, as against 100 per cent of the six-year group, with intermediate percentages for the four-year and five-year groups.

Kuenne infers from this that transposition to a situation not very different from a past situation may well take place without the use of language, but that language becomes more necessary as the difference increases. For now the child not only has to name the data—in this case two squares and a toy—but also needs the aid of language to deal with the relations between them (3).

Crucial confirmatory evidence of these inferences, from experiments with deaf children, is given by Oléron in the investigation cited on page 115. Using Kuenne's squares as a transposition test with children from five to seven, he found increasing success with age even when there was no overt use of language. But he also found, in corroboration of much work by other investigators, that the comparative retardation of the deaf children behind normal children progressively increased as the transposition tests became more complex and the relationships more abstract; in particular, that there is a strong connection—'une liaison forte'—between the enunciation of a principle and the performance of a corresponding task (4).

What part precisely does language play in this process of dealing with a new situation which has affinities with previous experience? To this question we can bring once again the illuminating contribution of Piaget. For him, as we saw in Chapter 2, the first two years of life are the pre-symbolic, sensori-motor, stage of behaviour. Following upon this, as the child begins to internalise symbols he enters upon the 'pre-operational stage' which, says Piaget, normally continues until the age of seven. At this pre-operational stage the child can use symbols—overt or inner, linguistic or non-linguistic—in dealing with a familiar situation. But his behaviour remains pre-operational so long as he cannot use symbols as a means of relating a new situation to past situations. He will advance to this stage of 'concrete operations'—normally after the age of seven—when he is able to deal with the new situation by consciously assimilating it to his past experiences and adapting these to the new situation. And in order to do this he must, in Piaget's terms, have 'concepts of conservation and reversibility'; and for these concepts, some symbols—more particularly verbal and numerical—are necessary.

What Piaget means by these terms becomes clear from his experiments, now well known to teachers. A child is shown two exactly similar bottles containing equal quantities of a liquid or of beads. Piaget finds that often 'when a child aged four to six pours liquid or beads from one glass bottle into another of a different shape, he still believes that the actual quantity in the recipient bottle is increased or diminished in the process.'

The child needs to revert to the earlier situation, to conserve his judgment of the original quantity of the liquid and yet transfer this to the shape of the new container. In Bartlett's terms, which Piaget also uses, the child needs to be able to carry forward his earlier schema and yet modify it in transfer to the new situation. It is in order to do this, says Piaget, that the child needs a concept of conservation and a concept of reversibility (5).

It would be pointless to repeat the common criticism of Piaget that stages of cognitive development do not, in all children alike, correspond to successive slices of chronological age. It is evident, for instance, even from the few investigations we have just cited, that some children much younger than seven are capable of some 'concrete operations' in Piaget's sense. But this criticism is really beside the mark. We must agree with Isaacs that Piaget regards his stages, not as chronological periods, but as successive phases of cognitive development (6). For Piaget himself shows that only certain children are incapable of concrete operations in early childhood; but—and this is the great value of his investigations—it is precisely the mistakes that these children made that help us to understand normal development.

Where we have to join issue with Piaget is in his apparent insistence that a child can never deal adequately with a new situation unless he has symbolised these concepts of conservation and transitivity. For from the work we have cited—particularly that of Oléron—it is evident that sometimes children are capable of successful transposition without verbal symbols of the processes involved. On the other hand, it is equally clear from the same work that as the situations become more complex, children become increasingly unable to deal with them unless they have verbal—or numerical—symbolisations of the processes of conservation and reversibility.

Here, then, is the contribution made by Piaget. He has added to our understanding of the general trend of development by showing how, for the elaboration and refinement of reasoning, concepts of conservation and reversibility may be helpful, and how language may promote these concepts. He has reminded us that in dealing with a new situation, a child performs dual, complementary, tasks. He assimilates the present to the past and he accommodates the past to the present. Piaget has brought detailed evidence and close analysis to show that it is through the verbal symbolisation of perceived relations to be carried forward into new situations that children normally advance in abstract reasoning. He has shown that there is normally a regular succession in which each advance in non-verbal problem-solving is followed by verbal symbolisation, by means of which a child is better able to reason.

In this his view converges with that of the followers of Pavlov. In their terms, a non-verbal situation is a 'first signal system'; in cognitive development this is supplemented, even superseded, by 'the second signal system', language. The delay between the ability to perform an action and ability to give a verbal account of it constitutes a 'retardation of the transition to the second signal system' (7). For them, as for Piaget, language aids reasoning by enabling the child to symbolise the past and so bring it into relation with a new situation.

Where they would seem to differ from him is in their view that the use of language is more general before the age of seven than he believes and also in emphasising that the absence of overt speech does not necessarily mean the absence of verbal symbolisation in performing a task. If a concrete problem, says Luria, 'is presented to a child of five-and-a-half to six years, it is at once subjected to verbal analysis and fitted into certain cortical systems formed with the aid of speech. . . . It is important to note that this is so even when the experiment is concerned with relatively simple, perceptible connections; when speech does not replace the signals presented and is not mentioned in the subject's verbal report after the experiment.'

They also, perhaps, go further than Piaget in emphasising the effects of training children to use language in performing tasks.

They bring evidence to show that children between three and seven learn most readily when they are helped by a combination of direct demonstration and verbal instructions (8).

Recognising, then, that language must play an important part in a great deal of cognitive behaviour in early childhood, we must now observe more closely a child's attempts to deal with a new situation. The child, we say, is 'learning to think' about what he is doing. As Bartlett has emphasised, he is acquiring a skill—the ability 'to spot and use directional properties of information.' The effective thinker, says Bartlett, is the person who can readily recognise which features of a situation will best enable him to deal with it.

Speaking of adults, Bartlett points out that while language and other symbols are the usual aids in our abilities to deal with situations, the roots of these abilities lie in behaviour which does not employ symbols. 'All the essential responses which these [abilities] require are found in lower bodily skills. Thinking takes them over and exercises them, not with overt bodily movements but with signs and symbols' (9).

Now a child confronted with a new situation has to exercise skill in dealing with a mixture of the familiar and the unfamiliar. To deal with the familiar he must bring the past up to the present—Piaget's 'conservation'. To deal with the unfamiliar he must project himself beyond his present experience—Piaget's 'reversibility'. In more everyday terms, he must remember and imagine.

It is a commonplace of psychology that there is no hard-and-fast distinction between these two forms of mental behaviour. Bartlett expresses this in terms of schemata. 'The processes', he says, 'by which recall of the past is accomplished are precisely those which we use in anticipation of the future.' Both remembering and imagining are constructive; the difference is that in remembering, a man 'constructs on the basis of one schema'; in imagining he 'freely builds together events, incidents and experiences that have gone to the making of several different schemata' (10).

LANGUAGE AND REMEMBERING

Nothing is more certain about children than that the past strongly persists in all that they do. As Hildreth says, in a summary of many observations, it appears to be a law of children's perception, thinking and problem-solving, that what has previously been learned tends to persist—change is resisted (11).

What is the place of language in this conservation of the past? First, it is clear that the effects of a past situation may be carried forward into the present without verbal symbolisation. In Bartlett's terms, transposition may occur by carrying forward unsymbolised schemata and transitivity without the verbal symbolisation of 'schèmes antérieurs'. Thus Bussmann, using Piaget's methods in studying about a hundred children between two and eight, concluded that transposition to a new task often took place without symbolisation of past or present situations (12). And transposition experiments with deaf children, by Oléron and others, also point in the same direction.

But what difference does it make if there *is* symbolisation by language? There are two possible effects, which may conflict with each other and yet may combine to help a child in dealing with a new situation. By enabling him to symbolise the past, language reinforces a child's conservation of a past experience. The presence of the word, by keeping the past situation more vividly in the mind of the child, may thus conflict with his attempt to adapt himself to the new situation. But this very symbolisation of the past may also be a help towards adaptation, in this way: that by enabling the child to keep the past situation in his mind, he may be helped to bring it more clearly into relation with the new situation, to incorporate the past into the present. Symbolisation of the past may therefore help to free the child from the dominance of the past.

This dual effect of language in transposition to a new situation is seen very clearly in the close analysis which the study of deaf children makes possible. Chulliat and Oléron, for instance, in experiments with children between the ages of five and twelve, of varying degrees of deafness, conclude that they are often hampered in transposition to new tasks by paucity of the language that would enable them to organise 'schemes' of their past experiences. One characteristic of these children is particularly illuminating—the comparative inflexibility of their behaviour in dealing with a novel situation. They are shackled to their past. Presented with practical tasks, the solution of which demands relating things to each other, the children show a much lower level of initiative than those with normal hearing. They have difficulty in organising the data; typically they use trial-and-error with little critical reflection and considerable perseveration (13). Ewing, drawing upon his own wide experience of deaf children, and surveying the results of much recent research, says, 'There are indications that sub-normal linguistic experience causes a lack of intellectual flexibility' (14).

We may conclude that the greater flexibility of children with normal hearing—the free incorporation of the past into the present—is made possible by an adequate command of language. And this is already evident in early childhood. One piece of evidence may be cited. Bryan has analysed the performances of two hundred children of five and six years of age in the Stanford-Binet Test, observing in particular the manner in which the verbal or non-verbal presentation of problems affects the children's ability to deal with them. She concludes that what the Test measures at this stage is largely retentivity and adds: 'The power to retain complex groups or series of impressions undoubtedly depends upon the ability to organise one's impressions through verbalisation. Memory ability and verbal ability, as they develop in the young child, may thus be thought of as co-operating and combining to form the matrix for the later development of the higher intellectual powers collectively termed intelligence' (15).

LANGUAGE AND IMAGINATION

The flexibility which promotes the development of higher intellectual powers is largely the ability to look beyond, to transcend, what is actually present to the senses. Confronted with a problem, the solution the child is called upon to find is something new, something not already here and now. In Bartlett's terms, the child has to build together freely schemata of events, incidents and experiences. In everyday terms, the child has to imagine.

In doing this he can proceed only by using symbols, alike for past events and experiences, for what is actually present, and for their combination into something new. This symbolisation is, of course, not always verbal. There may be symbolisation by means of physical acts and by non-verbal imagery. Our task here is to see how language enters into the imaginative process and the part it plays in this.

The development of the diverse forms of imaginative symbolisation may perhaps be seen most clearly in children's play—particularly in make-believe, whether this is solitary, parallel, or group play. In solitary make-believe play, for a long time it is obviously physical activity which predominates. The child in 'acting out' a supposed situation is using his present behaviour as a means of symbolising the absent situation. The upturned chair on the floor is a high-powered sports car; as he drives it, the child is combining the revival of past experiences with his behaviour in the present situation to produce an imagined pattern of action.

But even here—in this relatively simple make-believe—the child's behaviour can hardly be exclusively physical. We can assume that there will often be some non-verbal imagery—that memories of past sense-impressions, particularly visual and kinæsthetic, will act as symbols which help to make possible an imaginative re-combination.

But clearly also in most cases, from a very early age language will enter into and foster imaginative play. We have seen the beginnings of this in the manner in which children, even in their second year, talk to themselves and ask themselves questions while playing alone (16).

The importance of imaginative play in a child's cognitive development is that it readily expands into exploratory and constructive play which, as it presents him with successive problems, demands the exercise of reasoning. Well-known to observers of children, this has been the subject of the systematic study and cogent analysis of such workers as Piaget and Susan Isaacs. She says, 'Imaginative play at its most active may be looked upon as the prototype of "mental experiment" in the sense of Rignano and Mach'. She points out that as a child plays, he explores his environment and he experiments. For instance, in playing with water, he explores its physical properties and is confronted with problems which he may try to solve (17).

In the growth of this exploratory and experimental play, language may play a part of ever-increasing importance. While the playing child speaks to himself, he verbalises his own acts, and so aids his perception, helps his recall of relevant past experience, helps his imaginative constructions, his anticipations and predictions and so fosters his conceptual and generalising thinking in the direction of reasoning. In saying this, we of course recognise that the extent of verbalising may differ from one kind of solitary play to another and from child to child. And it is clear that the effects of language are immeasurably reinforced as a child comes to play with others—particularly if adults take interest in what he doing. Language then helps to make play more imaginative, more constructive and a greater stimulus to reasoning.

First, language opens the way to a wider range of play, by helping the child to learn new games. As we noticed in the last chapter, even children of four learning a game may be helped by verbal instructions (18). Even nonsense-words may help in this way, by providing symbolic aids to memory; but soon actual words become more effective (19). It is evident that while a child in solitary play may help himself by using verbal symbols devised by himself, the effect is greater if the words have meaning derived from social intercourse.

Language, and the greater diversity of play, have one consequence of particular importance in the growth of thinking: the emergence of real problems. To Susan Isaacs, observing the children at the Malting House School, no influence seemed so potent in the growth of reasoning as the challenge of problems felt to be real problems. Here, more than anywhere else, adults play a special part: the parent or the teacher with skill and discretion may heighten the child's awareness of a problem in the course of his play. As Nielsen has shown, a child cannot very well benefit from the help of others until the problem has become real for him (20). The pattern of development, then, seems to be this: social language opens the way to more diverse and more social play; real problems emerge; these incite the child to co-operate with others in problem-solving and so his conceptual thinking is helped forward.

All this is corroborated by observation of children retarded in language. The twins observed by Luria and Yudovich are particularly in point. Brought into the company of other children, their play, as we have seen in Chapter 6, page 104, became less stereotyped and restricted to the immediate situation. The effects were, however, much greater in Twin A—originally the more physically inactive and retarded of the two—who was given special training in language. He achieved significant advances over his brother. His play became more imaginative, he was able to pretend, to make-believe, to play a game, to follow a pattern of action, while as yet Twin B was incapable of any of these (21).

Similar evidence is provided by the study of deaf children. Not only are they, as we have already noticed, often prevented by parents from free play, but even when they do play with other children, their defective language hampers participation. It is this restriction of experience in their play which, as much as anything else, results in that comparative rigidity and inflexibility in problem-solving shown, for instance, in the work of Chulliat and Oléron.

As a child moves from concrete problem-solving towards abstract reasoning and needs to grasp and use spatial, temporal and causal relationships, language becomes increasingly indispensable. He may, perhaps, be able to 'carry' spatial relationships in his mind without using words for them; but as these relationships become more complex, verbalising them will obviously become a valuable aid in dealing with them. Still more will this be so as he needs to deal with temporal relationships. These demand imaginative constructions based upon past experience, often a difficult task. The slowness with which some children achieve a grasp of temporal relationships is indeed a measure of their difficulty in freeing their imaginative thinking from the grip of the past and the actual present. And here again no means of symbolisation is so powerful an aid as language, with all the resources it brings to symbolise the passage of time and the relations of past, present and future.

The importance of language when a child needs to deal with causal relationships is even more obvious. While some awareness of cause-and-effect may begin to dawn in a child's performance of an actual task, he can hardly move forward until he can symbolise causal relationships and so carry them in his mind to meet new situations. This symbolisation may, here again, be non-verbal; the child may, for instance, carry in his mind a picture of events which are related as cause and effect. But a picture of this kind is likely to be restrictive, too closely connected with particular events to be of use in 'mental experiment'—Piaget's 'psychological operations'. To free the child from the stranglehold of particular cases, to enable him to explore new combinations of relationships, nothing can help him so much as language.

Everything, then, points to the importance of linguistic intercourse in promoting problem-solving and so of reasoning. And of all the forms of intercourse, probably none is so great an aid to a child as questions, particularly to and from adults.

QUESTIONS DURING THIS PERIOD

This is the time in a child's life when questioning is at its height. From the beginning of the period both the volume and the diversity of questions increase; a decline does not set in until after the end of the period, usually at about the age of nine. Comparative studies show that, in general, during this period of prolific questioning far more questions are asked of adults than of other children; and that the better the economic and social conditions at home, the greater the number of questions (22). It is evident that the more adults encourage a child to ask questions, and the more they answer him in a satisfying fashion, the more will he be stimulated to think.

How then do the functions of questions develop during this period and how are they related to cognitive development? Evidence from systematic records is surprisingly scanty. Fahey, reviewing in 1942 the available work, had to say, 'the literature reveals little of value bearing upon the nature of the question', and since then the situation has not improved (23). We have to content ourselves with what partial studies can contribute to a tentative and somewhat hypothetical picture of growth.

The general pattern of development is hardly in doubt. At the beginning of the period, children's questions are still largely concerned with what is immediately present to the senses, what can be directly perceived and handled. By asking, the child acquires names for objects and for the relationships between them; he 'comes to terms' with the perceived world, with an order largely determined by the society in which he lives.

With the growing need to deal with relationships beyond those which can be immediately perceived—spatial, temporal and causal—a child's awareness of his failure to solve a problem often impels him to seek aid through questions. As Nathan Isaacs says: 'Children do tend, at a quite early age—often between four and five, sometimes earlier—to develop some degree of concern about the truth, sufficiency or clearness of their knowledge, because they frequently stumble into situations which force just this concern upon them'(23).

When, impelled by this concern, a child asks a question, the answer will often draw his attention to relationships not open to his immediate perception. Clearly, the answer is more likely to be enlightening, leading to a recognition of relationships relevant to the solution of the problem, if it comes from an adult rather than from another child.

Now this advance in the scope of a child's questioning is not a sudden new step; it arises by a process of change from those earlier questions which a child has been accustomed to address to himself, at a moment of check in the performance of a task. We saw, for instance, that K, at 2;4,19, when playing with his train and searching for a string by which to draw it, said to himself, *Where's the string?* (page 92).

The change from such self-addressed questions to questions asked of others arises from a complexity of factors which are inherent in and emerge from a child's general growth. First, there is the challenge of problems that cannot be immediately solved by physical manipulation, by finding, for instance, a piece of string. The problem is now of a kind that impels the child to 'cast about' in his own mind. Secondly, the child has by now become accustomed to receive answers that help him—he has the repeated experience of using questions as a means of bringing others to his aid. Thirdly, his growing mastery of conventional language enables him to direct his questions with increasing precision: words like When? Where? How? Why? enable him to pin-point his difficulties.

As a result, the development of most children during the present period is marked by the incessant spate of questions which is so familiar to parents and teachers. If they are sometimes wearisome, to the limit of our endurance, it is partly because we feel that often they become an end in themselves, a persistence in ever-increasing volume of the game of question-and-answer, the beginnings of which we saw in the previous period (page 90). The child is not so much seeking information as continuing to enjoy the to-and-fro of question-and-answer—verbal tennis.

Perhaps this must be accepted as one of the penalties of an active concern for the development of a child. Perhaps the child will be led to some 'mitigation and remorse of voice' if we are as careful as may be to give him real rather than perfunctory answers; if we indicate that while we do not altogether object to a game, we give a warmer welcome to real questions.

The justification for such a tolerant attitude lies in this: that here, as throughout a child's growth, we cannot draw a hard-and-fast line between the playful and the real. Through play a child learns to deal with reality; through the fluent intercourse that comes from verbal play, a child is more readily able to ask real questions. And of the importance of these real questions for a child's cognitive growth there can be no doubt, as Nathan Isaacs has demonstrated with great cogency and insight. Through questions the child is made aware of relationships—temporal and causal—that lie beyond the possibility of direct perception. His questions become a means of bringing memory and imagination to bear upon a problem.

A sharp light is thrown on all this by the contrast between deaf and blind children. Deaf or partially hearing children naturally ask fewer questions than normal children and this aggravates the retardation of their powers of reasoning. But blind or partially sighted children often ask more questions than normal children. By means of language their perception through touch, hearing and taste is sharpened and enhanced and so the development of their reasoning is frequently more rapid than that of normal children (24).

It is evident that the extent to which a child's questions are brought to bear upon his cognitive growth depends both on his personal characteristics and on his relations with his social environment. Whether he asks a question, if he does, whether he asks at once or delays while seeking his own solution; how long the delay, how relevant and how persistent his own attempts at a solution—all these obviously depend upon his innate powers, his interests, his temperament, his past experience and the measure of encouragement and co-operation he receives from others.

QUESTIONS ADDRESSED TO THE CHILD

A major means of our co-operation with a child lies in the questions we ask him. They may be one of the chief ways in which we initiate him into our ways of thinking. But how far this happens depends very much on the nature of our questions. Broadly speaking, these may be of three kinds. First, there are questions by which we genuinely seek information: *Where have you been? Why have you done this?* Secondly, there are those questions the answers to which we already know; their intention is to lead the child to discover the answer for himself: *Why is this so? What should you do now?* Through questions of this kind we make the child more aware of the world around him, his physical and social environment. They may stimulate his curiosity, challenge him with problems, lead him to see the gaps in his knowledge and understanding, and suggest to him means by which, in his own thinking, the gaps may be filled and the problems solved.

The third kind of question is that so intensively used by Piaget in his studies of children. We ask *Why . . . ?* not because we are concerned with the answer itself, nor in order to stimulate the child's thinking, but as a means of obtaining insight into the workings of his mind and the processes of his thinking. And here, as Nathan Isaacs has pointed out, there is a constant danger that we may be misled by the child's answer. 'It is a complete error to equate the situation in which we ask children Why-questions with that in which they ask us' (25).

When we ask a question of this kind, the child realises that we know the answer—the problem to him is to find the answer that will satisfy us. As a result, what we are likely to get from him is not so much an active exploration, an exercise of thinking, as a reversion, a harking-back, to knowledge that he already has. As a means, therefore, of reminding him of what he knows, such a question may serve its purpose; but it may be a poor means of obtaining insight into the forward-looking working of his mind, and useless as a means of stimulating him to think for himself.

It is clear that, at home or in school, if our questions are to lead the child forward, they must, as far as possible, arise out of situations which challenge his thinking and must be felt by him as aids in meeting the challenge. Otherwise our questions, instead of stimulating him to think, may evoke only perfunctory answers. Instead of attending to the problem implied by a question, the child may merely cast about for a reply, a form of words, which he hopes will satisfy the adult. For the child the real problem then becomes, *What does my questioner want me to say?*

Throughout early childhood, the interchange of question-and-answer between a child and his elders may exercise a continued influence upon his cognitive development; but not, of course, always by his conformity with them. He may know what they expect and refuse to satisfy them or, even with good will, be unable to do so. This constant potential duality of a child's responses is clearly inseparable from the ambivalence of his ethical relationships with his elders. In passing now to the consideration of ethical development during early childhood we shall, as always, attempt to identify the nature of its inter-action with the development of language.

8

Ethical Development

ETHICAL education during early childhood continues—and in a more marked manner—a dual process the beginnings of which may be traced in infancy. The child becomes more aware of himself and others; as his life becomes more social, his individuality becomes more marked.

This duality of a person as an ethical being is generally recognised as fundamental in the development of personality. It is, for instance, the theme of one of the most widely accepted definitions of personality. 'Personality', says Allport, 'is the dynamic organisation within the individual of those psycho-physical systems that determine his unique adjustments to his environment' (1). This definition not only recognises the individual and social duality of a person—it also reminds us that a person's ethical life is not an independent entity that stands apart from his cognitive and orectic experience and behaviour. The psychophysical systems whose 'dynamic organisation' constitutes personality include both the problem-solving skills that we have described in the last two chapters as well as the personal and social patterns of conduct by which a child is able to live and grow in his society.

The child is confronted with ethical problems—within himself and in his relations with others—which demand the exercise of cognitive skills. The factors that we have seen at work when he attempts to deal with inanimate things also operate in his dealings with himself and with other people. He has to learn to choose between one course of conduct and another. He has to learn to bring his past experience to bear upon the present situation, to carry schemata of past conduct forward to the present problem, assimilating the present to the past and accommodating the past to the present. He has to learn to anticipate, to predict, the outcome of a course of conduct.

So far there is similarity. But when we come to look at the place of language in ethical development, important differences appear. First, there is a difference of emphasis upon rules—or, as we term them in ethical behaviour—principles. In a child's ethical education we aim at the inculcation of principles of conduct, formulated as precepts. In his dealings with non-human problems, as we have seen, a child's awareness of rules may or may not be a factor in his success. When we guide a child towards the solution of these problems, we are not always particularly concerned to make sure that he can formulate the rules. It is far otherwise in ethical education. Precept as well as practice—both are important: not only right conduct, but the principles of right conduct. In ethical education the verbal formulation of principles is not merely a means to an end—it is an end in itself.

A second function of language in ethical development is that speech, in itself, is a mode of ethical behaviour—a means of bringing about changes in other people's conduct. It is not only a child's physical acts towards others that matter; equally important is what he says to them and about them. His expressions of approval and disapproval become a form of ethical conduct—as powerful a means of ethical action upon others as his physical behaviour towards them.

In Chapters 2 and 4 we have observed the progress in infancy of the intervention of language into ethical development. Now in the period of early childhood we see a vast and complex proliferation of the earlier rudimentary growth. The several functions of language in ethical development become more clearly differentiated. The child is moving towards the time when language may serve him in his personal and social life in a diversity of ways. It will become a means of symbolising his attitudes to other people, of formulating principles of conduct towards them, of symbolising and so enhancing his awareness of himself and of debating problems of conduct within and for himself as an individual.

In this period of early childhood these diverse functions of language are as yet, of course, still in process of emerging. To describe them in detail we need systematic observations which, here again, are too sparse to give us more than a sketch of the main features of development. For general guidance in this still largely uncharted field we are above all indebted to two men: Freud for his picture of the genesis of human personality and Piaget for his formulation of the stages in the growth of children's moral judgment.

FREUD ON THE GENESIS OF ETHICAL DEVELOPMENT

With an eye that ranges over the whole of human behaviour, Freud surveys in a wide view the general development of ethical conduct and the emergence of personality. He presents us with a picture of development that has permeated all modern discussion of man as an ethical being. Out of the fundamental instinctive id—the child unconscious of the forces that impel his behaviour—there emerges some awareness of himself as he is, the ego; and some awareness of himself as he might be, the super-ego or ego-ideal.

What is the place of language in this remarkable process by which a child, as he grows, is becoming aware of himself; in Bartlett's phrase, 'turns upon' his own schemata, begins to see himself as he is and as he would become?

The answer is graphically expressed by Freud in picturesque terms, misleading only if his imagery is taken too literally. From the id there emerges the ego, as a child experiences the impact of his physical and social environment. From the ego there emerges the ego-ideal, as the child 'identifies' himself with figures in his social environment—parents, teachers, other children.

These successive emergent transformations occur under the influence of language. Out of the id the ego takes shape as a child becomes aware of his hitherto unconscious strivings, as he symbolises them in language and so gradually forms a verbalised picture of his actual self, his ego. While this is going on, the ego-ideal also begins to emerge. The child gradually forms for himself a picture of an ideal self, fashioned from the constant orectic interplay between himself and all those who influence his behaviour—who approve or diaspprove of him and of whom he approves and disapproves. Freud calls this growth in the pattern of an ideal self the identification of the child with his parents, but makes it clear that identification is ambivalent and that the term parent embraces all those who excite the child's emulation or hostility.

Freud also calls upon us to recognise that the growth of the ego-ideal is not a wholly conscious process. The ego-ideal is in constant change. Its roots are in a child's unconscious strivings; it arises, says Freud, from 'the pre-history of every person'. As time goes on this emergence becomes a conscious process through language, in communication with others and within the child himself. 'That which prompted the person to form an ego-ideal... was the influence of parental criticism, conveyed to him by the medium of the voice, reinforced, as time went on, by those who trained and taught the child and by all the other persons of his environment.' Gradually the pattern of ideal behaviour becomes internalised, so that 'as the child was once compelled to obey its parents, so the ego submits to the categorical imperative pronounced by its super-ego'. The relationship between the ego and the ego-ideal is expressed by Freud in the somewhat cryptic statement that the ego-ideal becomes an object for the ego, and the ego an object for the ego-ideal. This means that, on the one hand, the ego-ideal is the goal towards which the ego strives; on the other hand, the child's ego is constantly measuring his actual behaviour against the standards of his ego-ideal (2).

It need hardly be said that while insisting upon the importance of language in promoting awareness of the ego and the super-ego, Freud also emphasises the unconscious dynamic organisation of personality. At best, awareness of the self is likely to be only partial. Some aspects of personality will be symbolised by words, some by non-verbal imagery, some not at all.

But in the complexity of social relationships which shape a child's personality, his verbal symbolisations of himself—his names—are of paramount importance. I, John Smith, a boy, a naughty boy, Tom's brother. Each of these names symbolise for him an aspect of his personal life, an intricate combination of ego and ego-ideal; and each has deep roots and wide ramifications in the organisation of his personality.

No less important are his verbalisations of ethical attitudes, his own and others', and his formulations of rules of conduct. For light on the development of these we turn to Piaget.

PIAGET ON THE DEVELOPMENT OF ETHICAL JUDGMENT

Early in the course of his investigations into the thought and language of children, Piaget gave his attention to the emergence of criteria of ethical behaviour. *The Moral Judgment of the Child*, 1932, has the merits and weaknesses of much of his work. The evidence he brings is sometimes too scanty, his conclusions too sweeping, his stages of development too rigid. Yet here as elsewhere he excels in offering highly stimulating hypotheses to be tested by the further observation and investigation of children.

In the development of moral judgment he sees four stages. Up to the age of about three, the child is in the pre-verbal stage of behaviour determined by 'motor rule'; he behaves in regular ways imposed on him by others, without formulating principles of conduct. With the advent of language there begins the stage of 'coercive rule'; in this period from about three to about seven the child accepts rules with 'unilateral respect' for the authority of his elders—older children as well as adults. After about seven, rational principles of conduct begin to emerge; the growth of moral judgment is guided by 'mutuality' and a growing sense of equality with others. Finally, after the age of about twelve, the child begins to develop an 'autonomy of moral judgment', based upon 'principles of equity'.

What we have to question—here as in Piaget's account of the growth of reasoning—is his linkage of stages with ages. While there is no doubt, as actual observations by other workers have shown (3), that these are broadly the successive phases in the development of moral judgment, they certainly vary not only in strength but also in incidence from child to child.

Secondly, Piaget asserts that 'before the appearance of language there is nothing that allows us to affirm the existence of norms of conduct... the child's feelings do not tend to regulate themselves from within.' This would seem to deny the existence of pre-verbal schemata of ethical behaviour, but in fact Piaget does not mean to go quite so far. He says, in fact, that already in the pre-linguistic stage the child is unconsciously striving towards a 'functional equilibrium' between himself and his social environment. In his everyday conduct with others and in his games, a child develops 'schemata of motor adaptation'; the 'motor rule' is the result of the 'ritualisation' of these schemata. Then, through continued social intercourse and communication by language, the unconscious functional equilibrium becomes transformed into norms of conduct (4).

Finally we have to notice that since Piaget is mainly concerned with one aspect of the development of ethical behaviour—the emergence of moral judgments—he tends to minimise the functions of the rudiments of language which are closely interwoven with the beginnings of ethical growth. This is in contrast to his account of the growth of reasoning. It is, however, not the least merit of his work that he constantly reminds us that moral judgment is inseparable from reasoning. He presents us with a conspectus of ethical development as a unified whole, in which cognitive development is integrated, stage by stage, with the growth of moral judgment.

It will be seen that Piaget is at one with Freud. Piaget's account of the transition in moral judgment—from unverbalised regularities of behaviour to the awareness of rules and then to the formulation of principles—is one aspect of the transition, in the growth of personality, from id to ego and ego-ideal. But in one respect Piaget comes closer than Freud to the facts of ethical development in childhood. He reminds us that an important stage in this development is a period in which a child's relationships with others is marked by mutuality, and that it is out of this, that autonomy of ethical behaviour and judgment ultimately emerges.

THE FUNCTIONS OF LANGUAGE

We now have to look at the place of language in this ethical development. As a child passes into early childhood, the two main influences on his ethical behaviour become progressively more powerful—the expansion of his social life and his growing mastery of the mother tongue.

If there is a restriction of either of these, a child's ethical development may suffer. Normally, however, early childhood is a period in which a child's ethical experience is greatly enriched. At home, in the family circle, as a child becomes more capable of understanding what is said to him and in his hearing, he becomes more aware of the finer shades of affection and hostility, submission and self-assertion, between father and mother, brother and sister. This is augmented by a widening range of vicarious experience, as they talk of other people, real and imaginary. Bossard has shown, in a highly illuminating study, how fruitful a source of ethical education family table-talk may be; and, more recently, Bernstein has cogently indicated how the language of the home, reflecting parental occupations and interests, may in its very structure and vocabulary powerfully influence children's ethical behaviour (5). It must not, however, be forgotten that in almost every home television also makes its own vivid impact, whose relationship to the 'culture' of the family we cannot as yet estimate.

When a child's life begins to move more freely beyond the home, when he enters school, there is a further expansion of the range and diversity of his ethical experience. He perceives, and he himself engages in, new modes of co-operation and conflict. He speaks and is spoken to. He hears children talking to each other and the teacher talking to them and sometimes there is the rapt half-hour of listening to a story. We have seen how the extension of a child's life beyond the family circle may foster his cognitive development. Concurrent with this, and indeed inseparable from it, is his ethical development as an individual personality and as a member of a group.

But his emotional ties with his home are, of course, only loosened —certainly not severed. The patterns of feeling engendered within the family circle are carried over into the wider world of school and out-of-school play. 'Feelings of jealousy, rivalry, hostility, comradeship shown to schoolmates can only be understood in terms of the child's previous responses to his family' (6).

The loosening of a child's bonds with his home brings with it, in some measure, the decreasing ethical importance of parents and elders as, instead, other children become more important ethically for him. If a child has adequate opportunities of living and playing with other children, the intensity of his feeling towards his elders may be relaxed. Susan Isaacs concludes that towards the age of seven 'the adult becomes to a far smaller extent the arbiter of the child's happiness. . . . A morality of equals begins to take the place of a morality based upon the parent-child relation' (7).

ETHICAL DEVELOPMENT

All this long and complicated process is summed up in the picturesque phrase of Freud's—the emergence of the ego and the super-ego. In competition and co-operation with other children, a child becomes aware of himself and moves towards standards of conduct for himself. His attitudes range between the two poles that McDougall called self-assertion and submission—from resistance and aggression to co-operation and docile acceptance. For the emergence of these attitudes and their expression and symbolisation in speech there must be constant and intimate interplay with others; and towards the children and the adults that the child encounters in his widening experience, his ethical behaviour will be as ambivalent as towards the members of his family. And although at this time of his life his relationships with other children will mostly arise in playing with them, the attitudes which are engendered will be as powerful an influence on his ethical attitudes as in his 'real' encounters with his family.

The modes of expression will vary. They may be gestures and other bodily acts, tantrums, tears, laughter—or words. Imaginative dramatic play will often be the means of acting out and so symbolising a widening range of ethical experience. He lives, as Wordsworth pictures him, as if his whole vocation were endless imitation. In playing many parts, in taking now this role now that, in identifying himself with a diversity of persons, he becomes more aware of himself as a person. And here his growing command of language begins to take on the function whose importance G. H. Mead has so strongly emphasised, that 'it provides a form of behaviour in which the individual may become an object to himself.' The child forms a picture of himself as he is—an ego; a picture of himself as he may become—an ego-ideal (8).

For some children—especially those whose life with others is restricted—much of this may happen even in their solitary play. But so intense may be the need for another person with whom to engage in ethical interplay, that it may give birth to an imaginary companion on whom affection may be lavished and hostility and anger vented. Not only in communication with others but often in communion with himself—sometimes with an imaginary other self—a child's personality may take shape.

A detailed account of the place of language in these developments in early childhood is hardly possible because, as we have said, of the paucity of systematic studies. But general patterns can be made out. The earlier broad expressive functions of speech become differentiated and specialised, so that by the end of the period a child will normally be using language more discriminatively in symbolising a diversity of ethical relationships with others and so will be using language as a means of acting upon them. As these symbolisations become internalised, the relationships and attitudes themselves become the objects of attitudes. The child comes to approve or disapprove of the relationships between people; and to approve or disapprove of attitudes within these relationships.

THE GENERAL DIFFERENTIATION OF APPROVAL AND DISAPPROVAL

Approval and disapproval have different patterns of growth. The most striking characteristic of this period is the abundant flowering of the verbal means of self-assertion, aggression and hostility. Compared with this the verbal expressions of goodwill and co-operation are usually meagre and less diversified.

In the course of a child's daily experience of the alternation of conflict and co-operation with others he finds that to achieve an equilibrium in his life with them he must sometimes submit, sometimes assert himself. For submission and co-operation—at any rate at the beginning of the period—words are often hardly necessary; the child need only acquiesce and join in the common task or game. As Susan Isaacs puts it, 'The happiest days of children are those which have no history' (9).

But at those moments when a child is impelled to be self-assertive, aggressive and hostile, he finds that direct action—snatching, hitting, pushing—is less and less rewarding. It is disapproved of by those in authority; more than this, the child becomes aware that direct action is progressively a much cruder means of communication than language and often a much less effective means of acting upon other persons. The rough-and-tumble of social life engenders a powerful incentive to the use and differentiation of the verbal expression of disapproval.

Towards the end of the period a new element normally appears in the pattern of development—an access of the verbal differentia-

ETHICAL DEVELOPMENT

tion of approval. As a child begins to engage more positively in co-operation with others, he finds that language helps him to establish companionship and goodwill and to join more effectively in common activities.

THE EXPRESSION OF APPROVAL TOWARDS OTHERS

We saw in Chapter 4 the beginnings of differentiation of æsthetic and ethical approval from earlier undifferentiated orectic approval. A word such as *clean*, which has expressed a broadly favourable orectic attitude, comes to express sometimes æsthetic, sometimes ethical, approval—that is, the approval of behaviour. Side by side with the use of familiar words in a more distinctively ethical sense, the child begins to adopt new forms of speech such as *Darling mummy* which, from the first, symbolise attitudes which are entirely, or almost entirely, ethical.

All this is continued into early childhood. The child's vocabulary increases; he symbolises finer shades of ethical approval towards others. As to which comes first, the non-verbal discrimination of attitudes, or the words to symbolise them—again, as elsewhere, there is no regular development. Sometimes the child finds words to express what he already feels, sometimes his imitation of words makes him aware of differences of attitudes. What is certain is that the words, once used, help him more and more to symbolise the finer shades more fully. Susan Isaacs, in her daily observation of children, has recorded instances which illustrate this (10):

3;10 and 4;1. Cecil and George climbing on the window-sill together. Cecil: *I love you.* George: *And I love you.* Cecil: *Do you? Why?*

4;4. Dan had not seen Priscilla for some weeks. When she came home he greeted her with great delight. They walked arm-in-arm. He said: *We'll talk to each other, won't we, because we like each other.*

4;10. Dan is very friendly to Jessica just now, calling her *My lovely Jessica*. This may be because Jessica brought him some beads.

5;0. While the children were knocking nails into a wooden floor, Mrs I. put her foot on a board to help. Dan: *Oh, thank*

> *you, Mrs I., for standing on it—that makes it much better!*
>
> 7;2. Mrs I. helped Priscilla with her sewing. Priscilla hugged her, saying: *Oh, I do love you. Do you know why? It's because you've done my buttonholing so nicely!*

It will be recognised that all these remarks are essentially ethical in function, in that they express approval of a person's behaviour—in this case, towards the speaker himself. They are approval of conduct, expressions of appreciation, the rudiments from which there will ultimately develop moral judgments. There is a clear development in the course of these half-dozen observations of different children during a period of some three years. At first we have nothing more than the child's simple approval of the other person. Then justification of this is brought in—in terms of cause-and-effect: 'Because we like each other'; 'Thank you, for standing on it'; 'I love you because you've done my buttonholing so nicely.' At which point in this development, mere juxtaposition becomes an awareness of causality, we cannot say; as we saw in Chapter 5, we must agree with Piaget that ideas of causality become clarified only in the course of communication with other people. What is very evident is that when the child uses a causal form-of-words such as 'Because...', he is—whether he realises this or not—seeking a further response from the other person, testing how far his own attitude is reflected back to him from his listener. In this way, two closely-connected changes take place: the child becomes more clearly aware of cause-and-effect in ethical relationships and at the same time is moving towards objective ethical judgments. At present his judgments are still subjective—they manifest the child's satisfaction at behaviour towards himself; in process of time they will be transformed into objective ethical statements, judgments of approval of specific modes of conduct in general.

In the meantime these remarks of the child have two functions. They are declarative of his ethical attitudes—they promote and foster an orectic rapport, predominantly ethical, between the speaker and the person addressed. In expressing an attitude towards another, the child is inviting approval towards himself. A particularly interesting form of this invitation of approval is the reversion to infantile speech by children who have outgrown it. A not uncommon cause of this is the birth of a brother or sister; the child seeks in this way to recapture his mother's love that he fears lost (11).

A second function of these remarks of the child is that in themselves they are modes of ethical behaviour—supplementing and replacing such primary non-linguistic acts as embracing, caressing and smiling—rewards offered to the other person for his behaviour to the child, thus inviting the continuance or repetition of the desired behaviour. At this stage the two functions of language are closely interwoven—the symbolisation of attitudes and the use of language to cause others to act in an approved fashion. These functions persist and become differentiated in the child's language throughout his life; they will enter into the complex patterns of language and mental behaviour that we call moral judgments. These will come to have the two functions usually distinguished in ethical terminology: 'positive', formulating moral principles, and 'normative', demanding conduct in conformity with principles.

THE EXPRESSIONS OF APPROVAL ABOUT OTHERS

Expressions of approval not towards, but about, others have somewhat different functions, the rudimentary forms of which also appear in infancy, as we have seen in Chapter 4. The child invites his listener to share with him a favourable attitude about a third person: and because this brings the child's own attitude to the test of the listener's response, it helps him to move more rapidly towards the establishment of common attitudes and so towards objective ethical judgments.

Our instances are again from Susan Isaacs:

3;4. Jessica told her mother, *Mrs I. is my friend*.
3;9. Dan, speaking to Miss B: *I wish Cecil would come. I like Cecil*.
4;1. When Martin fell down and hurt himself, Paul said, *He is a brave boy*, because he did not cry.
4;9. Dan said to Harold, *I like you and I'm going to kiss you*, and kissed Harold's hand. Harold said, *He's a dear little thing*, and the others agreed.
5;6. Jane was teasing Conrad and Dan took his part against her, saying, *I like him very much indeed—I adore him* (12).

In all these instances the child is symbolising, in a declarative fashion, his approval of the behaviour of the third person; and to the extent that this receives assent or dissent from his listener, he is establishing for himself attitudes common to himself and to others in his society. Sometimes he addresses his elders, sometimes his contemporaries; and as time goes on different patterns of attitudes emerge, corresponding to the various societies of which the child is a member: the family; the child and his teachers; the child and his contemporaries in general; the child participating in a game with its special rules. There are, of course, attitudes common to all these societies; but often, too, marked divergencies in attitudes from one society to another.

THE EXPRESSION OF HOSTILITY TOWARDS OTHERS

In Chapter 4 we saw the development of the child's use of words to prohibit or show disapproval of the action or intended action of another person. To his undifferentiated *No!* the child adds expressions of disapproval in which his attitude is more fully symbolised—*You bad boy!* The progress of further differentiation during the period of early childhood is illustrated in these instances:

3;11. Mrs I. insisted on Paul's resting longer than he wished. He said angrily, *I'll send you away and cut you up and eat you!*

4;2. When Mrs I. said *Darling* to Dan, Benjie said to Cecil: *I don't like you, Cecil. I'll get a gun and shoot you dead!*

4;11. Angry with Mrs I., Dan struck at her with a towel. When she took this away, he said, *I shan't sit next to you, bang fool beast of an I!*

5;1. When Mrs I. refused to do something for him, Harold said, *If you don't, I'll kill you and throw you on the roof.*

5;3. When Mrs I. asked him to do something for himself, Harold said, *You horrid Mrs I!*

5;3. When Dan's mother showed affection for her son, Frank said to Mrs I., *Naughty Mrs I., dirty Mrs I. We'll spit in your face!*

5;4. Frank, seeing some visitors, shouted to them, *You dirty creature!*

5;11. Conrad accidentally broke his glass. He said to Miss D.

ETHICAL DEVELOPMENT

who was not even near him, *It's* your *fault, you made me break it, you horrid thing!* (13).

The most striking change here is the emergence of threats as a form of expressing hostility. Mere disapproval of the type of *You bad boy!* still, of course, persists—*You horrid Mrs I! You dirty creature!* But now the child is rapidly learning through imitation to exhibit his hostility more specifically, by symbolising imaginary physical action, what he would do to inflict pain upon the offender.

The stages in the development in the symbolisation of hostility towards others are now seen to be:

(i) Bodily non-linguistic acts such as crying, tantrums. These acts are expressive of the child's state, but not efficiently communicative. His mother, for instance, will recognise that he is angry but may not know why.

(ii) *No!* and *Not!*—the verbal expression and symbolisation of negation. This is communicative to the extent that the listener is made aware that the child wishes to inhibit intended or actual behaviour.

(iii) Ethical disapproval of behaviour: a statement such as *You bad boy* has a twofold communicative effect. It declares the speaker's orectic state—anger, hostility, frustration—and at the same time is intended to cause pain, to inflict punishment. It is hardly as yet an ethical judgment.

(iv) Ethical disapproval made more explicit. A statement such as *If you don't I'll kill you and throw you on the roof* has a threefold communicative effect. It indicates which action the child disapproves of; it symbolises the child's orectic attitude towards his listener; it describes the (imaginary) punishment.

It is evident that here again, as in the expression of approval, the child can only progress towards the formulation of moral judgments by loosening his ethical statements from their egocentric bonds—by making them more objective. A step in this direction is taken with the development of the expression of disapproval of a third person.

THE EXPRESSION OF HOSTILITY TOWARDS A THIRD PERSON

In Chapter 4 we brought the child to the point where his disapproval of a third person is expressed in a phrase that has the outward form of an ethical judgment—*He's a bad boy!* We suggested there that at this stage such a phrase is probably no more of an objective ethical judgment than *You bad boy!*; that both are still patterns of speech imitated and adopted by the child and used simply to express disapproval. But there is an important difference in the functions of these two phrases in the development of ethical judgments. Expressions of hostility about third persons lead more rapidly towards objective judgments than expressions of hostility addressed *to* persons. For, in speaking about a third person, the child is inviting listeners to support his disapproval and so is testing his attitude against theirs. And as they agree or disagree with him he becomes aware of their attitudes and standards. This brings him to look at his own attitudes—to persist in them or change them—and so to become aware of his own standards.

To illustrate the earlier stages of this process we can group together a number of observations, again from Susan Isaacs:

(i) The child continues to express disapproval, which is ethical only to the extent that it is a reflection on a person's behaviour:

4;3.   Dan, after a quarrel with Tommy, *Tommy is silly.*
5;2.   Harold, when Mrs I. was singing nursery rhymes to children, *Silly Mrs I., silly tunes!*—because the tunes were different from those on his gramophone at home.

(ii) The child launches out into more elaborate patterns of speech, which are still no more than expressions of disapproval sometimes coupled with threats of imaginary action:

4;9.   Dan, after Jessica had torn a card which had been sent to all the children: *I'll get a policeman to put her in prison. I'll kill her, because I hate her!*
4;11. Dan, angry with Mrs I., said to his mother, *I hate her, she's a beast!*
5;4.   Paul, when Frank had refused him Plasticine, speaking to Mrs I., *I am very disappointed with him. I am very angry with him!*

(iii) The beginnings of self-justification—the child 'explains' his disapproval; that is, he relates it, though not explicitly, to a general principle and thereby seeks support for his attitude of disapproval:

ETHICAL DEVELOPMENT

4;11.   Dan hit Jessica with a towel while she was taking her coat off. When Mrs I. took the towel from him he said, *Well, she was going to take her coat off and she shouldn't!*

4;11.   Frank said to Dan, *I'll bite you.* Dan cried. Frank, to Mrs I., *I only meant to tease.*

(iv) The child explicitly seeks support for his disapproval of a third person:

4;4.   Lena to Mrs I.: *I don't like Dan. He pushed me down. I hate him.* Then, with a smile, *And I hope you do, too.* She seemed disappointed when Mrs I. said, *No, I don't.*

5;4.   Theobald: *Christopher shan't come in, shall he?* Paul: *Yes.* Theobald: *No, he is too nasty!* Paul: *I like him.* (14).

The importance of language throughout all this, and especially in the later stages, is clear. In the absense of verbal symbolisation, progress towards objective ethical standards would obviously be far more difficult. Words enable the child not only to express his disapproval, but to communicate the grounds for it and to receive a reply which makes him aware of his interlocutor's attitude.

CO-OPERATION IN HOSTILITY

A further and probably more powerful move in the same direction is the growth of co-operation in the expression of hostility towards some object of common dislike. Sporadic beginnings of this, as we saw in Chapter 4, may occur even as early as the third year. It will obviously become more frequent as children mix with each other, for instance, in a nursery school; particularly if they are of different ages. The younger will take fire from their elders, and join in a chorus of common disapproval, hostility and aggression.

Here again we are in debt to Susan Isaacs for cogent observations made in her Malting House School; the expression of common hostility towards strangers, adults in authority, or younger children. The age in each case is that of the eldest child mentioned.

(i) To strangers:

5;1.   A visitor came into the schoolroom and Harold led the other children in clustering round her and saying with laughter, *Silly lady, silly lady!*

5;4. Martin (3;0) a new boy, came dressed in a sailor suit, which interested the others greatly. They laughed at him. Tommy (3;0) said he was 'a sailor'; the others 'a silly sailor'. Dan (3;9) and Frank (5;4) said, *Shall we hit him?*

(ii) To those in authority:

4;11. Robert (4;6) and Frank (4;11) were digging in the garden and found some worms. Mrs I. was digging near them. Frank to Robert: *Shall we put a worm down her back so that it will bite her?*

5;1. Paul (3;11) and Harold (5;1), seeing Mrs I. in a dress they had not seen before: *It's a silly dress, a wretched dress.* Paul: *Wretched Mrs I.*

6;6. Priscilla (6;6) instigated Christopher (5;5) to join her in hurting Jessica (3;5). Mrs I. interfered, showing some anger: *You shan't do those things to Jessica!* All the children —including Jessica herself—then joined against Mrs I. They said, *You're a beast. Now we shan't come to tea with you when you ask us!*

(iii) To younger children:

5;0. When the children were playing at giants, Paul (3;11) and Theobald (5;0) said, *This giant is going to kill Dan* (3;9); but later they were friendly to him.

5;4. The children were drawing and painting. Dan (5;4) and Jessica (4;0) expressed great scorn at Phineas's (3;7) picture, sniggering at it behind their hands and saying, *That's not a nice picture.*

Susan Isaacs observed that orectic co-operation of this kind is usually fleeting, although the emotion, while it lasts, is often fiercer than individual hostility (15). But even if this heightening of feeling is only momentary, it is still likely to foster the lasting co-operation that becomes characteristic of the later years of childhood, and so contribute to the establishment of common ethical attitudes and, ultimately, objective judgments.

In everyday conflicts and co-operation a child will often move in swift alternation from one role to another. Now he is a member of a

ETHICAL DEVELOPMENT

group united against someone, now he himself the object of group hostility. Now he will conform and acquiesce, now he will assert his individuality. This close social interplay will tend to sharpen his awareness of himself and the growth of his idiosyncratic personality.

THE EXPRESSION OF INDIVIDUALITY AND OF SELF-AWARENESS

The growth of self-assertion manifests itself in a diversity of forms of behaviour. A child sometimes becomes more possessive, showing an increasing sense of ownership. Exhibitionism may become more blatant while, at the same time, the child seems more critical of his own prowess and achievement. This self-criticism may soon embrace the rightness of his own conduct, so that he demands and even inflicts punishment upon himself. All this strengthens his growing tendency to stand away from and look at himself.

Much of this, no doubt, may be independent of language—the direct results of competition and co-operation with others. Language will help a child to symbolise the diverse modes of his self-assertion with greater precision and so to communicate them more effectively as well as to become more clearly aware of them himself.

(i) Possessiveness

3;0. One child to another: *Don't touch my cup and dishes, Solveig dear.*

3;3. James, a visitor, had a toy engine. Tommy took it away, saying, *You shan't have it!*

3;8. Teacher had lent Dan a pair of scissors. Some time after he had put them down, she took them up. Immediately he screamed, *These are my scissors! I want them now!*

3;10. Cecil, standing with his own stick in his hand, saw another child with a similar stick. Trying to take it, he shouted, *That's mine!*

5;0. Dan, speaking of the tricycle which Tommy had lent him, *Tommy lent it to me while he was ill—I wish he was dead, then I could have it always.*

5;1 and 3;11. Harold and Paul often say to other children, *You are not to talk about Humpty-Dumpty*, referring to a rhyme or story they have at home (16).

(ii) Exhibitionism

This is, perhaps, the form of self-assertion which is least hostile to others, though it may, of course, be somewhat discomfiting to their self-esteem.

3;0. They were acting 'Jack and the Beanstalk.' Tommy, the smallest child, climbing up: *Here is another giant!*
3;0. Martin, walking round the garden with sticks: *I am a man! I am a man!*
3;6. *Look what I made. I made a whale. Lookit his tail wiggling!*
4;0. *See, I ride with my hands off. Ain't I smart?*
5;8. Dan, admiring his own painting. *You'd hardly think I'd done that, would you? You'd think a grown-up had done it, wouldn't you? You come and look, Jane and Mrs I.!* (17).

(iii) Adverse self-criticism and self-punishment

Not very often during this period does a child express criticism of himself. I have been able to find only a single instance throughout the entire records of Ames and Susan Isaacs:

4;0. Surveying his own painting: *I can't do this very good!*

A child may be well aware of his shortcomings but deterred from giving voice to it for fear of exciting derision. Children at this time are too deeply engaged in the need to be a respected and accepted member of the group to risk inviting humiliation. As a result the consciousness of guilt, the recognition of misconduct, will often be expressed by belligerence, anger and defiance:

4;1. Benjie, having broken a water-jug before he could be prevented, was very defiant, shouting, *I'll hit you in the face; I'll not come to school any more!*

But we may also witness the beginnings of the expression of shame and contrition, perhaps with the expectation of arousing sympathy and securing forgiveness:

3;7. Phineas accidentally broke his cup when drinking cocoa a few days ago. He at once said, *Now I can't have any cocoa* and since then he has steadily refused to have any,

ETHICAL DEVELOPMENT

  although he has been repeatedly offered it in another cup.
3;11. Paul, having wet his trousers, *I'm so ashamed of myself!* He could not be comforted for a long time.
5;8. After school yesterday, Christopher accidentally hit Dan's finger with a hammer. He had run away when the adults had approached him after the accident; he said, *They won't blame me, will they?* All today, he tended to go off by himself into the far part of the garden, staying the real one on his cycle (18).

The impetus given to the child's ethical development by his increasing use of language to express and symbolise shame and guilt is evident. When he has behaved wrongly and is aware of this, language enables him more readily to come to terms with others and with himself. Instead of confining himself to non-linguistic manifestations of what he feels—striking other people, tantrums, refusal to obey, withdrawing from the group, sulking—he speaks. Others then are made aware of his trouble and can intervene, sometimes by reinforcing his disapproval of himself, sometimes by condoning his misdemeanour, sometimes by expressing sympathy with him, sometimes by helping him to recognise—when there has been an 'accident'—that he is not to blame. The variety of responses he receives helps him to discriminate among the ethical attitudes current in his immediate society. So he symbolises and establishes criteria for his own conduct; in Freud's terms, there is the emergence of his superego.

(iv) Projection in play

In his ethical development—as in other aspects of his growth—imaginative play affords a child one means of learning to deal with reality. His playthings, and sometimes his playfellows, are occasionally made the objects of ethical attitudes which themselves are largely, if not entirely, make-believe.

We see the beginnings of this in infancy when an inanimate plaything is for the time being given a shadowy personal life, and is treated by the child as though it could experience feelings like his own. He speaks to it in language that on occasion has been addressed to himself.

2;3,18. K. at lunch-time, 'fed' his toy balloons with soup, saying, *Noonies hungry*. When it was time for his afternoon nap, he said, *Noonies sleepy. Noonies in beddy-byes*, and took the balloons with him to bed.

2;4,23. Of his toy dog: *Wants to go to beddy-byes with K. Goggie so sleepy*.

2;5,14. Having been told that he was going to see some swans: *Would Goggie like to see some swans?*

2;9,14. *Just taking this dolly's 'jamas off . . . he's awfully tired*.

When a plaything conforms to or resists his intentions, a child will sometimes express his approval or disapproval. Then, as he becomes accustomed to the verbal expression and symbolisation of ethical attitudes, his praise—or more often reproof—becomes more explicit. At the same time as the plaything is the object of his attitude, he will be putting himself in its place, speaking to it as he has been spoken to:

2;4,19. K, addressing his train, which seemed to be falling over: *Sit up, puffer train, be good!*

3;1. Penelope and Dan (3;4), playing with a small statuette of a boy, put him to bed. Suddenly Penelope uncovered him and said in a shocked tone, *Oh, look what he's done— he's wet his bed, the naughty, naughty baby!*

4;2. Alfred and Herbert (2;11) were making mice run up and down in the mice-box. When they couldn't make them do this they said, *Aren't they naughty mice?* Mrs I.: *Are they?* The children: *They won't do what we want, so aren't they naughty?*

4;2. Lena and Phineas (4;0) were poking a stick into a hole in the wall. When it came out covered with dust and cobwebs, they said in awed tones, *Isn't it a naughty wall?* Questioned about this, Lena replied gravely, *Muck— isn't it a naughty wall?*

6;1. Priscilla and Dan (4;4) were playing house with Jessica (3;0) as the 'baby'. They sat her down in a chair and said in the severest tones, *You're a naughty little girl!*

6;5. Priscilla who had been playing with her doll, told Mrs I. that it had been a 'horrid little beast' and 'fiddling about in the pram all the time.' Later she prepared the doll for bed and said to it, *Go straight to bed and don't fiddle about and do such horrid things* (19).

To speak of all this as animism is to obscure rather than elucidate the child's behaviour. It may well be that in some societies life has really been imputed to such inanimate things as mountains, streams and trees. It is true that children—and indeed adults—sometimes give causal explanations in animistic terms. But with the children here the essential characteristic is not the imputation of life and behaviour to inanimate things; it is rather that these things—as also living creatures such as the mouse and Jessica—are made the objects of the children's attitudes of approval or disapproval. It is clear from such observations as those we have just quoted that when a child says that the doll or the wall or the mouse or Jessica is naughty he is saying that he doesn't like what is happening—and that the fault is not his. He is projecting his feeling of frustration on to an external object, in the same way as K at 2;9,14 projected his tiredness on to his doll or at 2;5,14 projected on to his toy dog his own wish to see the swans.

Sometimes, no doubt, the expression of attitude is make-believe, as with the doll at 3;1 and Jessica at 6;1. Sometimes, no doubt, it is in earnest, as with the mice at 4;2 and the wall at 4;2. But whether make-believe or earnest, the element of projection in the act of expression has its place in the child's ethical development. His sympathy with an imagined wish (to see the swans) or his disapproval of an imagined misdeed is a projection of his own wish or guilt. In putting the doll or the toy dog in place of himself he is also putting himself in the place of an elder, approving or disapproving. He may even—as Stern and Piaget pointed out—have heard his parents using animistic or anthropomorphic terms in speaking of inanimate things or animals (20). In expressing his sympathy with his toy dog the child is seeing himself as an object of sympathy. His disapproval of the doll, reproving it for an imagined offence, is seeing himself as an object of reproof. This verbally-expressed projection is part of the process in which he objectifies his attitudes and in doing so becomes more aware of them and of criteria for them. Here again he is building up a pattern of social conduct and at the same time a pattern of his own personality—his ego subject to the sanctions of a parent-self, his super-ego.

IMAGINARY COMPANIONS

One of the most striking manifestations of this need for the projection of attitudes is the imaginary companion—at once the imagined object of a child's ethical behaviour and the embodiment of the child himself as the object of other people's ethical behaviour towards him.

Imaginary companions are often mentioned in observations of children, but systematic studies are rare. One of the most comprehensive is that of Ames and Learned in 1946, summarising the literature up to that time and also systematically observing 210 children, about one-fifth of whom were found to have imaginary companions.

Ames and Learned concluded that in general a child who has an imaginary companion tends to be above the average in intelligence, highly verbal and without brother or sister. They were also able to trace a fairly regular pattern of development. A child will often begin with an animal as an imaginary playmate—a real or toy animal or even an imaginary animal. After this, often in the latter part of the third year, an imaginary human companion may appear and persist for a considerable period—sometimes older, sometimes younger than the child himself (21).

Susan Isaacs narrates the development of Eleanor who, at the age of three, pretended from time to time that she was the 'little mother' of her teddy bear. Later, during a period of some months, she pretended that she was 'Dinkie'—in real life a neighbour's cat. She would curl up in a chair as a sleepy cat, crawl on all fours and come to her mother to be stroked.

Two months after this had ceased, 'an imaginary person called Bisseker appeared. He used to run beside the pram and was variously a man, a boy or a little girl. We still (two years later) have him with us and a whole history has been evolved about him. He is now definitely a boy, aged thirteen, with a sister and a crowd of friends. But for nearly a year now Eleanor has said that "of course he is only pretend"' (22).

An imaginary companion is the overt symbolisation, in speech and action, of social relationships and ethical attitudes. It would also seem likely that sometimes a child who has no imaginary companion may yet symbolise these relationships and attitudes internally, carrying on silent imagined conversations in imagined situations within himself. In this way he forms verbalised pictures of himself and other persons and of their relations with each other and with himself. The verbalisation helps him to see these pictures more clearly and bring them more readily into relation with everyday verbal communication between himself and others, and among others in his hearing. All this makes its contribution to the formulation of ethical attitudes and of general principles of conduct.

EVIDENCE FROM THE IMPAIRMENT OF LANGUAGE

In Chapter 4 we have seen that already in infancy impairment of language may contribute not only to cognitive but also to orectic immaturity. As a child moves into early childhood these adverse effects, as compared with the normal development of children, may become more severe.

(i) *Deafness*

The orectic immaturity of children with impaired hearing may retard their ethical development, both in the formation of a stable personality and in their relations with other people. It is the common experience of those who have to deal with deaf and hard-of-hearing children that they are liable to neurotic troubles and difficulties of personal relationships. Minski, a psychiatrist working with these children, finds that neurotic disturbances are evident before the age of seven. Ewing concludes from a survey of many studies of deaf children that they have difficulty in forming socially desirable habits. These generalisations are supported by the results of using ratings of personality traits to compare children with impaired and with normal hearing. Pintner, summarising much of this work, while advising caution against exaggerating the differences, yet concludes that they certainly exist. The children with impaired hearing find it a little more difficult to adjust to their environment, they are a little more emotionally unstable, slightly more introverted and less dominant, a little less mature in judgment and social competence. And these traits arise not so much from severity of deafness as from a child's social upbringing (23).

The distortions become more marked with the passage of years because they reflect the diverse aspects of the child's difficulty in adjusting himself to others, both directly and through the medium of language. In the home, as Ewing and Minski point out, there is likely to be emotional tension between the child and other members of his family; parents may feel guilty, brothers and sisters are impatient, the child himself frustrated because of failure to make himself understood. He is cut off from free conversation with others and isolated from the overheard casual conversation among others which, as Bossard has emphasised, normally plays so large a part in a child's social development.

His play with other children is also likely to be restricted. In the preceding chapter we noticed some of the probable cognitive effects of this—when a deaf child's parents are afraid to allow him the full freedoms open to ordinary children and when other children do not readily accept him as one of themselves. One result of these restrictions in the life of a deaf child is likely to be a certain lack of confidence, sometimes compensated for by aggressiveness.

The paucity of a deaf child's language may also mean an impoverishment of his imaginative life. Heider and Heider, closely observing deaf children between the ages of four and seven, found that their imaginative play with other children tended to be limited to what was possible in physical action. A serious effect of this was that their 'role play'—the playing of parts—was severely restricted; the kind of play which, as we have seen, may contribute so much to personal and social development (24). It would also seem likely that deaf children may not so readily as hearing children have their imaginary companions; or quite so freely carry on internal conversations with themselves. One notable piece of evidence does point to some poverty in the inner imaginative life of deaf children. Kendall, in a study of a large number of such children under the age of five, found that they were relatively immature in their free drawings. Up to the age of three, there were no clear differences between the scribbling of these children and that of comparable hearing children. But at ages four and five while 90 per cent of the hearing children were making representative drawings, only 25 per cent of the deaf children had advanced as far as this (25).

The restriction and rigidity of his personal and social life at home, in school, in the playground and in the street, have their due effects upon his ethical development. Instead of the constant delicate adjustments, from which emerge the refinements and differentiation of ethical attitudes and behaviour, the deaf child's links with the world of men are both more tenuous and cruder. He cannot readily make his wants known nor grasp the intentions of others. And since, like all children, he must depend upon language for the more precise symbolisation of ethical attitudes and standards, here again he may suffer a heavy disability. The finer shades of meaning may elude him so that he is constrained to guide his conduct by narrow, fixed and formal rules which impede the free growth of his ethical life (26).

The importance of language is so great in personal and social development that its recognition has led to an apparently paradoxical effect on the practice of many teachers of the deaf. While maintaining and even emphasising that for a child's future as a member of society he must speak and lip-read the mother tongue as far as this is possible for him, they nevertheless are deeply committed to the practice of teaching and encouraging deaf children to use manual sign-language for immediate everyday intercourse with their schoolfellows. Only in this way, the teachers believe, can the children be helped to overcome the disabilities of personal and ethical development which the impairment of language will impose upon them (27).

(ii) *The effects of living in an institution*

We have seen in Chapter 6 that life in an institution may retard both cognitive and linguistic development; that the linguistic retardation may in part be due to the cognitive immaturity; and that, reciprocally, the impairment of language may adversely affect cognitive development. How far is this paralleled in ethical development in early childhood?

To this question no simple answer can be given. Little systematic work in this field has been published and what is available only tends to bring out the complexity of the problem, quite apart from the constant difficulty of estimating personal and social maturity.

A child is admitted to an institution usually because of home conditions which already will have had adverse effects upon his personal and social development. He may be an orphan, or illegitimate, or the child of divorced parents, or come from a home where there is constant emotional tension or where there are other seriously harmful conditions. As a result his personal and social development may be retarded and distorted and his linguistic development impaired—this, in its turn, further slowing down his progress towards ethical maturity.

Transfer to an institution may further disrupt and inhibit his ethical development, both immediately and progressively. The immediate effect may well be a shock of nostalgia and fear of the unknown, and a feeling of insecurity at being suddenly cut adrift from the warm familiarity of home, bad though this may seem to us, looking in from the outside. Then, as the days pass in the institution and the rapid alternations, excitements and uncertainties of his home life are replaced by a vapid and unstimulating routine, the child's ethical attitudes and behaviour may become narrow and rigid, with lack of confidence and enterprise in encountering new social situations (28). Already in infancy, as we saw in Chapter 4, the result is often a picture of personality remarkably like that of a child with impaired hearing.

As this resemblance becomes more marked with the passage of time in an institution, there would seem to be support for the inference that the children there, like the deaf, may suffer from some deprivation of the two important experiences mentioned by Bossard—things said to a child or said casually in his hearing. But when we look for specific evidence that ethical development in early childhood is affected in this way, we are confronted with the difficulty of isolating linguistic immaturity from the complexity of concurrent factors. We have to rely upon the indications given in studies which compare children living in institutions with those living at home; or studies of the effects of transferring children from an institution to another environment.

Pringle and Tanner have made a comparative study of eighteen children living at home in 'an impoverished and unstimulating' environment with the same number living in residential nurseries. The groups were of the same mean age (four-and-a-half years) and with mean I.Q.s not significantly different. The residential children were found to be somewhat retarded in linguistic skills; and 'in so far as they lacked the ability for verbalising phantasy and for using speech in making social relationships, to that extent their general emotional and social development may become adversely affected' (29). The similarity with the imaginative and social immaturity of some deaf children, as we have just described it, is striking.

Among studies of the effects of transferring children from an institution, one of the most careful is the work of Goldfarb, whose account of the effects of institutional life upon cognitive development is summarised in Chapter 6. He compared fifteen children who up to the age of three had lived in foster-homes, with fifteen, equated for sex and age, who until that age had lived in institutions and who —judging by the 'occupational status' of their mothers—were, if anything superior in heredity to the foster-home children. Nevertheless the institution children were more immature in some aspects of personal development, particularly in their friendliness to strange adults.

These children, it will be remembered, were placed in foster-homes and seven months later again compared with those who had lived in foster-homes since early infancy. The former institution children were no longer inferior in their friendliness to adults but, strikingly enough, their relative social immaturity in some other respects was even more marked than before. Inferences from this limited study must be made with caution, but it would seem that the inhibiting effects of life in an institution during infancy persist into early childhood and even—as indeed Goldfarb concludes from some other work—into adolescence (30).

The place of language as a causative factor cannot, of course, be determined; but it would be very difficult to maintain that this can ever be entirely absent. What appears to be more direct evidence comes from a study of adolescent children by Haggerty, who analysed some of the language patterns of a hundred fourteen-year-old children who had spent a prolonged period in a hospital or other institution. He found that not only were they retarded by as much as two years behind normal children in their command of linguistic forms, but also that their use of these and their traits of personality resembled those of schizophrenics. He ventures the striking suggestion 'that language impairment may contribute to the development of schizophrenia rather than just being one of its symptoms' (31).

This remains a hypothesis to be tested by further studies. Haggerty is speaking of fourteen-year-olds, and it may well be that some children living in institutions until adolescence become schizoid or even schizophrenic. In early childhood the effects are likely to be less overt, at any rate; and as yet more open to change. But the severity of the effects of continued life in an institution bring home to us very forcibly the close inter-action between linguistic and cognitive and orectic development, relationships which become more intimate and intricate with the passage from early to later childhood.

PART THREE

Later Childhood

9

General and Linguistic Characteristics

IF we call the period from about seven to about twelve the stage of later childhood it must be with a full recognition that this is a time of transition, when children are moving forward to adolescence. And now, even more than in the preceding years, children of a particular age, while having much in common, will be marked off from one another by a multiplicity of individual variations. These diversities emerge as the result of a double process, in which while the influences of the home diminish, life beyond the home—at school and with other children—operates with increasing strength upon the growing child. Thus as the children move towards adolescence, their individual profiles—the patterns of their cognitive abilities and orectic idiosyncrasies—become more distinctive (1).

Allowing for these individual variations, it yet remains possible to draw a broad picture of the main features of development—physical, linguistic, cognitive and orectic—at this time. Physical development is in general steady during the period and rather less interrupted by illness than in earlier years. There is usually an acceleration of competence in bodily skills and a growing desire to achieve greater mastery of them: in the broader skills of games, athletics and dancing as well as in the finer skills of craftsmanship and æsthetic creation.

These skills, as well as language, cognitive abilities and ethical behaviour, are more and more powerfully influenced by a child's growing awareness of himself as a person and as a member of different groups. In particular, his individuality is asserted and shaped in close fellowship with others more or less of the same age. In this contemporary society he is tied to the present, the demands of his everyday life, here and now; at the same time he is constantly drawn towards the future, not only by the influence of his elders but concurrently in forward movement with his contemporaries. It need hardly be said that his behaviour is a complex pattern of conformity and resistance to these social forces that impinge upon his individuality.

It is in these ways, through his membership of two societies—the actual present and the potential future—that a child's personality is shaped. At the same time as he is incited to greater effort in emulation or competition with his contemporaries, he is impelled by the urgency of the need to feel grown-up. And if he is inhibited by self-criticism, it may be both from measuring himself against his contemporaries and from a sharpening awareness of adult achievement.

The effects of this double reference, to the present and the future, are seen very clearly both in ethical and in cognitive development.

ETHICAL DEVELOPMENT

The main trend of growth in later childhood is well described by Piaget as the period in which, as we have seen, the 'coercive rule' of adult authority gives way to a 'principle of mutuality'. Attempting to investigate the growth of moral judgments at this stage of their development he was confronted with the problem which must have daunted many others—how to make a systematic survey of everyday ethical behaviour, relating this to the characteristics of language during this period. It occurred to him that a game such as marbles would evoke patterns of social conduct—under formulated codes, the rules of the game—sufficiently representative of children's everyday ethical behaviour at this stage of their development. Using his customary 'clinical method' of questioning the children and discussing their answers with them, he was able to demonstrate that they felt that the rules exist in and for themselves, deriving their authority not from parents or teachers but from the sanctions of the group: and that behaviour in the game is governed by mutual and reciprocal adjustment. He tested the validity of this generalisation in children's conduct by asking them to offer judgments on various ethical situations presented in the form of stories. He found support for his general hypothesis in this, that there was a tendency for the judgments to move towards principles of mutuality and reciprocity as the children grew towards adolescence (2).

In his work on cognitive development Piaget has shown the close relationship of the forms and functions of children's language to the characteristics of their thinking; his study of moral judgment goes no further than suggesting connections of the most general kind between language and ethical conduct. A more detailed understanding of these relationships—for English-speaking children, at any rate—has now been made possible by the pioneer work of I. and P. Opie. Observations recorded by and from the children themselves, show that they have a language of their own which is not only a means of symbolising their attitudes and formulating their behaviour, but also an instrument of their individual and social development.

The language, the attitudes and the conduct are all diverse manifestations of children's need at this time to live in company with one another.

Most children urgently seek the support of their contemporaries. To be one of a group, to behave in accordance with a heritage of custom transmitted from the older to the younger children, is a way of life in which a child learns that conformity with others is a source of strength. It gives him the security within which he can find himself and assert himself. More particularly is this so when, in the later part of this period, the group becomes limited to one sex. Now, more than at any other time, boys will be boys and girls girls.

Of course the fact that a child recognises the authority of the group for the rules of his conduct does not mean that he always conforms. He rebels, he asserts himself, he risks disapproval and ostracism—sometimes he suffers, sometimes prevails. It is the same ambivalent pattern of conformity and resistance which hitherto has marked his behaviour under adult sanctions and prohibitions. But now the child's growing adherence to a contemporary group brings with it a change in his responses to adult authority. As in earlier years, he may still usually have no choice but to conform; as before, he sometimes secretly rebels and sometimes openly resists. But where the younger child has often had to fight single-handed against the adult oppressor, the older child is strengthened by a consciousness of group support. He may now seek to justify his refusal to accept adult authority by an appeal to the conduct of other children. The earlier expression of personal feelings and desires is reinforced by a resort to social sanctions: 'Other boys don't—why must I?' And where open defiance of adult authority is not possible, it may now find an outlet in covert group misbehaviour.

Through this complex pattern of conformity with and rebellion against the authority of the group and the authority of his elders, the child is establishing himself as an individual personality. As a member of a contemporary group he finds his place among his equals—as a follower or leader according to his temperament. As a member of a sex-group his life takes on a more distinctive sex pattern. As a child among adults, while in many respects he remains a child, he is moving towards adolescence. No simple statement can adequately describe the stage he has now reached in his ethical development.

COGNITIVE DEVELOPMENT

A child's cognitive development, inseparable from his ethical growth, must of course be subject to the same social influences. The most favourable conditions for cognitive growth at this stage are that the features of his thinking and the nature of his knowledge shall be shaped by the experiences he shares with other children, while yet he remains free to exercise his independent initiative. A similar duality may mark his relations with adults: the urgency to find things out for himself and the necessity to follow adult guidance and seek adult help when in difficulty. These factors will combine with some natural maturation of cognitive abilities to produce characteristic forms of reasoning, the details of which are becoming familiar to us from the continued work of Piaget and others.

As we have seen, he finds that this period of later childhood is predominantly a stage in which thinking is increasingly 'operational', but is as yet concrete in nature and insufficiently formal. It is operational in that the child is, to some extent, able to analyse and re-synthesise a situation that confronts him. He can go so far as to classify things in accordance with specific criteria; he can manage some serial relationships among things; and, whether classifying or serially ordering things, he can often take account of more than one criterion at a time.

In saying that all this thinking still tends to be concrete in nature, Piaget does not mean that the child's reasoning is necessarily confined to what is present to his senses. In memory and in imagination the child can transport himself in time and space. But his thinking remains concrete so long as it is bound to the actual features of a situation—present or absent—rather than free to explore and deal with new and abstract relationships or to entertain a hypothesis and reason from it. His thinking is hardly as yet systematised, so that he rarely if ever tests a train of reasoning by applying the touchstone of generally valid principles (3).

Here again, in his cognitive as in his ethical development, the child's behaviour has a double reference. To think too abstractly while his contemporaries are still immersed in the concrete, is to invite a certain degree of ostracism—a highly intelligent child has sometimes to subdue and even to conceal the forward march of his mind in order to remain at one with his fellows. At the same time this very forwardness is rewarded by the approval of his elders and the promise of future success—and also, to some extent, by the admiration of his contemporaries. Thus the balance between the assertion of individuality and the need for social acceptance is just as delicate in a child's cognitive as in his ethical behaviour. To consider them separately as we do here is only to bring home more strongly that they are but two different manifestations of his life at this time. Again and again, while he is closely bound to his physical and social environment he must be learning to free himself from their trammels. Through constant social interchange and in the unceasing exploration of what he perceives for himself and what is presented to him by others, he must be moving towards principles of wider validity in thought and in conduct.

We now have to consider the place of language in all this—how it continues to reflect, and also to provide an instrument for, a child's growth as an individual personality and as a social being. To see this more clearly we must first look briefly at the characteristics of language itself at this stage.

LINGUISTIC DEVELOPMENT

The most striking development in this period is the manner in which the two social forces acting upon the child—his elders and his contemporaries—tend to make him a member of two linguistic communities. He has to acquire the adult terminology necessary for his education in school, and also something of a special language for everyday communication with his fellows. As he moves from the narrower circle of the home to wider societies, those special characteristics of his language which have been fashioned by the socio-economic culture of his family tend to be submerged in certain uniformities—the language of school; the language of the group; even the language of his sex (4). His increasing mastery of the resources of the mother tongue is shown in the further differentiation of its functions for him rather than in his acquisition of new syntactic forms. Templin's evidence, as we have seen, bears out the common observation that already at the beginning of the period many children have explored the entire range of the phonetic and syntactic forms of the mother tongue (5); and there can be little doubt that by the end of the period this is true of nearly all children.

The increasing differentiation of functions is also seen in an extension of vocabulary and in the use of words more discriminately expressive of orectic attitudes and with greater precision of cognitive reference. This development reflects and reinforces a child's adhesion to his contemporaries, his relations with his adults and the emergence of his personal individuality.

The force of attraction towards adult language is evident in a characteristic eagerness to show familiarity with adult vocabulary and locutions—'long words' and complex constructions, often used tentatively and experimentally. It is obvious that this is a necessary and valuable part of growing up—however bizarre, amusing and even irritating to adults some of its manifestations may be. For now, even more than in his earlier years, it is by the adoption of language which for the adult symbolises modes of thinking—particularly abstract thinking—that a child is helped to move towards these adult ways of thought. And where indeed a child's elders are not much given to abstract thinking and do not often use language that symbolises thinking of this kind, the child's progress towards abstract thinking may be slowed down. It is now that the effects envisaged by Bernstein are most likely to appear; the cognitive differences, due to the nature of communication in the family circle, will have their effects upon the symbolisation of attitudes and so upon ethical conduct (6).

Now, more than in the earlier years, while the children continue to be influenced by their elders at home and in school, there is rarely simple acceptance and conformity. Ambivalence now becomes more marked, resistance more violent. In extreme cases this resistance may take the form of an allergy to changes in linguistic habits —particularly those changes which consist in learning to read and write; an allergy which may be one of the causes of backwardness in school (7).

GROUP LANGUAGE

More normally, a child's resistance to adult influence finds expression in conformity with his contemporary group and gains strength from this conformity. He acquires and enjoys a sub-language—a group lingo—which, like their games, is transmitted from elder to younger children by oral tradition.

A mine of information on this is the work of I. and P. Opie (8). In the sub-languages which they have recorded directly from children—instead of indirectly through adult memories of childhood—we find adherence to the contemporary group combined with a constant pull towards adult language and behaviour. Group influence is seen in the flowering of a special vocabulary, rich in slang and words foreign to the adult language and in a wealth of rhymes, alliteration and other kinds of verbal play. At the same time the pull towards adult ways is seen in another characteristic of the sub-language—a 'secret' repertory of words forbidden to the child by his elders but which he knows, or suspects, they themselves use. Children tend to see the prohibition of swearing and scatological expressions as instances of the adult conspiracy to prevent, or at any rate postpone, their initiation into the freedoms of adult life. Thus the use of 'forbidden' words becomes one of the ways in which a child asserts his independence of his elders and his allegiance to his contemporaries and lays siege to the barriers that exclude him from the adult way of life.

But the child's use of this language is all the time influenced by the fact that he is still a child, and knows it. By his wilful rejection of adult prohibitions he may assert that he is growing up, but because he must still recognise adult authority his resistance to it must be 'secret'. So most of his use of prohibited language will be confined to his talk with his contemporaries, out of hearing of his elders. In this form of self-assertion the child finds support and encouragement from his contemporaries; daring, in conformity with them, what he would hardly dare to do alone.

To say that a child has a language in conformity with his fellows is not to say that he sinks his individuality. On the contrary; as his linguistic resources are enriched, the personal language of each child tends to take on characteristic idiosyncrasies. As in conflict and co-operation with his fellows the features of his personality emerge with growing clarity, so his language—in such features as intonation and choice of words—will also begin to have something of an individual style. In a similar fashion, a child's increasing acquisition of the language of the school will also make it more possible for him to express his individuality. For since the constant effect of education is to give scope to the cognitive abilities and practical skills of each child, his individuality will be promoted by and reflected in specific linguistic features, marking off each child more distinctly from his fellows.

VERBAL PLAY DURING THIS PERIOD

Side by side with these instrumental functions of language, there still persists during this period an enjoyment of verbal utterance in and for itself, as a form of play: more complicated and sophisticated manifestations of the behaviour which we first see in early infancy as babbling. It is more sophisticated because it is now social play, a verbal game, something done in company with others. This is an extension of the social element which is present in babbling almost from the beginning. As we have seen, as soon as a child imitates heard speech, he tends to bring this into his babbling. Now, with the growth of his membership of a contemporary group, a child's verbal play becomes highly socialised, tied to the conventions of the group. The personal element may still remain strong—the child may begin to be more self-consciously something of an artist and craftsman in words. Such a departure from convention will not always meet with disapproval. Sometimes it will be applauded as a novel contribution to the linguistic resources of the group; so that the child's assertion of his individuality will be reinforced by his contemporaries' recognition of his achievement.

The wealth of observations gathered together by the Opies has shown that the verbal play of children is worthy of attention as an important feature of their linguistic development. The conventions of this verbal play arise both from oral tradition handed down from past generations of children and from the impact of striking events in current adult life—again the double reference which permeates the whole of a child's life during this period. From the many examples given by the Opies we cite one instance.

In 1855, if not earlier, this well-known rhyme was popular among schoolboys:

> When I was young and had no sense
> I bought a fiddle for eighteen pence;
> The only tune that I could play
> Was *Over the Hills and Far Away*.

In 1891 Lottie Collins made a tremendous hit with her song *Ta-ra-ra-boom-de-ay*. Immediately, children were singing

> Lottie Collins, she had no sense
> She bought a piano for eighteen pence,
> And all she played on it all day
> Was *Ta-ra-ra-boom-de-ay*.

and other more daring versions.

Today, the Opies tell us, this has become:

> Charlie Chaplin has no sense
> He bought a fiddle for eighteen pence;
> And all the tunes that he could play
> Was *Ta-ra-ra-boom-de-ay* (9).

This is as good an example as could be found of Bartlett's account of the changes that occur in the transmission of a verbal tradition in a social group (10). A closely-knit society of children maintains a well-established verbal culture transmitted from older to younger and yet changing from time to time under the impact of changes in current adult life. The conventional rhymes are schemata established in the individual members of the group by the influence of their leaders—usually the older children—upon the rest. When a new event, such as the advent of Charlie Chaplin, demands expression, it is recorded in a rhyme which is a modification of an existing schema.

This instance also illustrates two characteristic features of children's sub-languages: a delight in rhymes and the enjoyment of parody. Rhymes give pleasure in themselves, they can readily be remembered and, above all, they have a certain social force—they can be chanted in chorus. Parody is one expression of the irreverence which is gaining strength throughout this period and onwards into adolescence; cocking snooks at the grown-ups, but as yet more playfully than seriously and as yet under cover of secrecy.

Pleasure in the playful exploration of the manipulation of words is also seen in other characteristic features of children's sub-languages. Nonsense rhymes flourish; instance these, recorded of children of twelve:

> The sausage is a cunning bird
> With features long and wavy;
> It swims about in the frying pan
> And makes its nest in the gravy.
>
> The elephant is a pretty bird
> It flits from bough to bough
> It builds its nest in a rhubarb tree
> And whistles like a cow.

Puns and riddles, however well-known to the children themselves, bear unending repetition:

> Why did the coal scuttle? Because it saw the kitchen sink.
> What kinds of fish do you wear on your shoes? Soles and eels.
> (10)

It must be recognised that verbal games often have something aggressive about them. They may express irreverence towards elders. Or they may be ways of scoring off other children, expressing the need for individual self-assertion that tends to be present even in children's most co-operative group life. To this extent verbal play is a form of conduct towards others and so a factor in ethical development.

We must also recognise that these games, like verbal play from the beginning of babbling onwards, have their due effect in promoting a child's command over language, by making him more aware of its formal patterns and of the finer shades and subtleties of meaning. Thus the rhymes, the puns and the parodies which to adults may seem merely silly and tiresome, may have a place in children's linguistic development, playing their part in cognitive and orectic growth.

After this brief survey of the main features of later childhood, let us go on to consider them in closer detail.

10

Language and Concrete Thinking

THE GENERAL CHARACTER OF CONCRETE THINKING

ONE of the most salient features of the transition to later childhood is the manner in which social influences are brought to bear upon cognitive development—upon a child's growing knowledge and the growing power and complexity of his ability to reason. And the chief means by which these social influences are made effective is language.

No doubt a child's cognitive development owes something to his individual characteristics: something, no doubt, to the maturation of his latent potentialities; to his immediate and direct experience of his world, to a sharpened awareness of its possibilities. But above all his cognitive powers are awakened and developed by his life with others—his contemporaries and his adult elders—and through his constant communication with them.

This pattern of development has, of course, its beginnings in infancy and early childhood. What makes it emerge with greater distinctness in the period of later childhood is this; that now the child is so much more powerfully and consciously a social being. His contemporaries take notice of his mental powers and express their approval or disapproval; his elders constantly make him aware of their assessment of his intellectual maturity.

His play with other children presents him with frequent problems and with sharp incentives to solve them both by his own initiative and in co-operation with others. He is stimulated to compete with these others in making his own contribution to common undertakings. At the same time he is constantly stimulated by the example and the demands of adults. The movement of his mind, the modes of his thinking, are moulded by the behaviour of others—what he perceives, what he remembers, what he imagines, how and what he infers.

Thus while children's cognitive processes during this period have common characteristics, each child, of course, has a mind of his own. Since it is the product of divergent forces, his cognitive development, particularly the growth of his reasoning, does not follow a direct line towards adult modes of thinking. It frequently traces a winding path. In advancing it sometimes retreats.

Our main guide to the understanding of cognitive development during this period must be the work of Piaget—modified, it is true, by the qualifications of other workers. We have seen that he specifies this period of later childhood as the stage of concrete operations—meaning by this that the child can deal with the observable features of a situation, whether actually present to his senses or imagined by him. The child is able to classify things in groups, in accordance with one quality or another—for instance, size, colour or shape. He can arrange things in series—for instance according to size or weight. He can also group or serialise things by taking account of more than one quality at a time, for instance by size and shape. Piaget summarises these operations as classification, seriation and multiplication. It is for these that the child needs to be capable of the two fundamental operations of conservation and reversibility, which Piaget regards as complementary: 'Conservation has to be conceived as the result of operational reversibility' (1).

The nature of concrete thinking is brought out more clearly by contrasting it with what develops from it—the ability to engage in formal operations. Concrete thinking is confined to carrying out, in thought, actions that could be undertaken if the situation were actually present: 'Concrete ideas' says Piaget, 'are internalised actions' (2). But to engage in formal thinking, a child must be able to move beyond a situation, to embrace it in a wider context of abstract relationships, expressed in propositions. He must be able to entertain and proceed from hypotheses and to think systematically; and his reasoning as a whole must have a structure. This stage, says Piaget, is not normally reached before the age of about twelve.

Other workers who have repeated Piaget's experiments—for instance, those summarised by Lunzer (3)—have been able to confirm his general conclusions. In doing so they have emphasised two features of cognitive development which are rather less evident, though certainly present, in Piaget's account. First, it must be understood that 'concrete thinking' is not simply a stage of general development. A child of a given age may vary between intuitive, concrete and formal thinking, according to his past experience and the nature of the situation confronting him. Further, it is clear that by the use of carefully devised methods, children can be helped to advance in their concrete thinking and even to engage in formal thinking during this period of later childhood. Piaget indeed strongly emphasises the function of social life as an essential factor in determining the modes of a child's thought, without however discussing the possibilities of deliberate education as a means of promoting cognitive development.

LANGUAGE AND CONCRETE THINKING

We have now to ask what precisely is the place of language in concrete thinking. Here there is no doubt that we come to a serious gap in Piaget's work and in that of most of those who have followed him (4). And this is all the more surprising and regrettable when we remember that Piaget has been a pioneer in leading us to a fuller understanding of the relations between children's language and their thinking. Moreover, in considering the nature and genesis of concrete thinking he maintains in the strongest possible terms that it owes its very existence to the child's life with others: 'Operational grouping presupposes social life' (5).

As a child spends more and more of an ordinary day in playing with others or in the classroom, it is evident that language must play an even more important part in his concrete thinking than in his earlier intuitive thinking. Sometimes, no doubt, he may be faced by a problem in the absence of any intervention by other people, and may deal with it entirely on his own initiative. But most problems are now brought to him by the acts of others—and mostly through the medium of language.

This, of course, is particularly true of the very situations on which

Piaget's account of children's concrete thinking is based. In speaking to the child, the experimenter uses language in a number of ways: he draws the child's attention to the situation—the lemonade in the glasses or the string of beads: he names some of its features; he describes a change in the situation—'You see, I have now poured the lemonade'; he states the problem; in doing this he indicates and names relationships—'Are there more brown beads or more wooden beads?' and at the same time he invites the child to formulate a solution. What the child is called upon to do—whether he physically manipulates the objects in front of him or performs an operation in his mind—is to make a statement in words.

Something of the same kind, though not so systematic, happens again and again in the course of a child's everyday life: and it would be strange if such highly a verbalised interchange were not accompanied by considerable verbalisation in his concrete thinking. Piaget is, of course, well aware of this: he says that concrete ideas are internalised actions. From this one would have expected him to consider the precise functions of language as one of the chief means of internalisation in this process of concrete thinking. But although he discusses in detail the place of language at the earlier stages—the sensori-motor and the intuitive—and again at the subsequent stage of formal thinking, on language in concrete thinking he speaks only in the most general terms.

LANGUAGE AS A HINDRANCE TO CONCRETE THINKING

For us here it is necessary to do what we can to go more closely into these relationships. Everything that we have seen so far of children's development suggests that while verbalisation must play a large part in their thinking, it is likely both to hinder and to promote mental operations at this stage.

Now the general emphasis of Piaget and of others who follow him is on the hindrance that language may exert at this time. They point out that because a child is now so constantly in conversation with other children, because in school so much of his education must be through words, spoken and written, and because usually he is so quick and eager to conquer new fields of language, there is a danger that his use of words may run ahead of his understanding. Now more than ever before there is the risk of an empty verbalism. Instead of thought through language the child may become adept in manipulating verbal and numerical forms that replace thought and even hinder its development.

Piaget himself puts it in this way, that language comes to the child carrying an already prepared system of ideas, classifications and relations: from this collection the child borrows only as much as suits him, remaining 'superbly unaware' of everything that is beyond his mental level. Following Piaget, Lunzer speaks of the inadequacy of the learning process where accommodation to a new situation has not been integrated with existing schemata; such behaviour, he says, is all too familiar in school, amounting to no more than the mechanical repetition of 'steps' given out by the teacher (6).

It is understandable that today this is of great concern, particularly in the teaching of arithmetic, because of the imperative need to extend mathematical education to more people. The understanding of the nature of number at the primary stage is seen to be the indispensable basis of mathematical thinking later. With this in mind, such workers as Stern, Cuisenaire and Dienes have devised apparatus to help a child to arrive at concepts of number—quantitative thinking—through the actual manipulation of things instead of the rote manipulation of number-words. Unfortunately, their recognition of the danger of premature verbalism has sometimes been misinterpretated to mean that the use of language should be excluded from a child's induction into concrete thinking. Peel, for instance, makes a statement which, unless it is taken in the context of his review of work on children's thinking, lends itself to this kind of misconception. He says that since language and number are 'artificial', it is essential to ensure that 'activity and construction form the basis of primary education, not only to close the gap between actual thinking levels and the stereotyped use of language, but also to provide a naturally developed, surely based foundation for the more abstract formal thinking of adolescence' (7).

The validity of the general principle expressed here can hardly be gainsaid. The manipulation of words and figures as things in themselves may impose a severe check upon progress towards the goal of all reasoning—the power to solve problems. The argument is that if a child is to advance in ability to deal adequately with more complex and increasingly unfamiliar situations, he must be led to apprehend concepts which relate these situations to others in his experience. But in order to perceive relationships between situations he must be practised in grasping the relationships that are latent within a situation—the various ways in which the concrete features of a situation are related to each other. This in turn rests upon his ability to organise things, to classify them or arrange them in a serial order according to one or more criteria. And this ability may be hindered if a child is encouraged in a pre-occupation with words and numbers as objects in themselves instead of the concepts that these symbolise. To substitute for concrete thinking the manipulation of linguistic terms may well prevent, or at best seriously hinder, the development of insight into abstract relationships of wider generality.

Now there is no doubt that this emphasis on the need for first-hand experience in the solving of problems through concrete thinking is supremely justified by the evidence and that it has far-reaching implications for the education of primary-school children. Yet in itself it throws light upon only one part of the picture of cognitive development at this stage.

LANGUAGE AS AN AID TO CONCRETE THINKING

We must now turn to the other and somewhat neglected part of the picture and consider the ways in which language may actually promote concrete thinking and may even be indispensable in its development. Of direct evidence of this there is very little. Certainly, if we look closely at the observations and conclusions of Piaget and the other workers whom we have mentioned, we find occasional pointers in this direction. These can be supplemented by gleanings from work not inspired by Piaget; but, all in all, we are once again in the position of having to attempt broad generalisations in the absence of adequate specific detailed evidence.

Since up to this period language has played so important a part in promoting cognitive development, it is unlikely that now it would suddenly become a hindrance and never be an aid. If in early childhood a child's conversation with himself helps him in what he is doing, does this no longer happen in later childhood when he is thinking concretely and moving towards formal thinking? If in early childhood, conversations with others promote reasoning, does this no longer happen in later childhood? Certainly, when he plays alone he will often continue to speak to himself—and probably silently as well as overtly; and more than ever he will talk to others about what he is doing. What we have to ask is whether language, used individually or socially, has no positive functions in helping a child in his concrete thinking and in his advance from this to abstract thinking.

One important consideration here is that now when a child is alone his speech is likely to be silent, 'internalised', more often than hitherto. Of this silent speech we can, of course, hardly have direct evidence; but it is an inference that many workers of different schools of thought are ready to make. In U.S.S.R. there has been a wide acceptance of Vigotsky's emphasis on the directing function of egocentric language when it becomes inner speech—an emphasis that Piaget himself now endorses. Luria, in the statement we have previously cited, sees this function of language continuing into later childhood and, indeed, into adult life. When a child, he says, is faced with a problem he will always tend to find his bearings by calling to aid the abstracting and generalising, analysing and synthesising functions of language; and we can assume that this happens even when the child himself does not mention it in telling us how he dealt with the situation. In U.S.A. the same view, though differently expressed, finds an equally wide currency, especially in terms of the hypothesis of Osgood that internal speech may act as a mediating process in dealing with a situation. Cofer, in a review of the work in this field, concludes that in problem-solving a child or an adult may be unable to report on the mediational processes, verbal or other, that may occur (8).

When we turn from a child's solitary play to his attempts to solve a problem in the company of others, the question of language in concrete thinking moves from inference to certainty. Not only in the clatter of talk when he is with other children; even more when an adult presents a problem to him. There is a wide range of possibilities here. The adult may merely bring the concrete problem to the child and remain silent. Often he will say something to draw attention to the problem. Sometimes he will go as far as telling the child what he is required to do and he may even interject remarks or ask questions while the child is trying to solve the problem.

LANGUAGE AND CONCRETE THINKING

In all these cases there will be verbalisation by the child, overt and internal. If the adult remains silent, the child will tend to ask questions. When the adult speaks the child will tend to verbalise silently while he listens.

Much of this may not appear in the special situations devised by Piaget and his followers, when the experimenter puts an artificial restraint upon his own utterance and perhaps that of the child. But this is certainly not the state of affairs in the ordinary everyday problems that a child encounters in the company of other people.

Russian workers, who tend to see education as the guidance of a child by an adult, have given much attention to the place of language in these circumstances. Galperin, for instance, in reporting investigations on this, begins by saying that in the development of any mental operation there are five levels, a higher level always assuming the existence of all the lower ones. There is the preliminary conception of the task; the mastery of action using objects themselves; mastering the action on the plane of audible speech; the transference of the action to the mental plane and finally the consolidation of the mental action in itself and with other acts.

But having set out this clear-cut scheme of development in which language comes after the non-linguistic exploration of a situation, Galperin proceeds to make an illuminating comment on what actually happens at this earliest level when the child is obtaining 'the preliminary conception of the task.' He describes an experiment in which two alternative methods of procedure were compared. In the first method, 'after the teacher's preliminary explanations, the child immediately proceeds to make himself familiar with the material by his own efforts, though under the teacher's direction.' In the second method, 'the child does not himself perform any action for a long time, but takes an active part in the teacher's explanation by prompting his next operation or naming its result.'

The investigators, Galperin tells us, expected that the first method, which appears to be more 'active', would give the better results; but in fact it was the second that proved 'rather more productive.' He asks why this is so, and surmises 'that the second method frees the child from the task of performing the act physically and at the same time organises his orienting activity, his attention' (9).

No doubt this conclusion must be accepted with caution, particularly because of the difficulty of estimating what is 'rather more productive.' But this, at any rate, seems clear and is, indeed, in line with common experience: that a child attempting to grasp the nature of a task before he puts his hand to it, may benefit from language in two ways—from explanation by another person and from his own verbalisation.

The investigators reported by Galperin were surprised at the apparent discrepancy between their observations and the Pavlovian general principle that in a child's cognitive development, the ability to deal with concrete experience must lag behind the use of 'the second signal system'—language. To this we can add that their conclusions, and the observations of everyday life, also appear to be out of line with the stages of development pictured by Piaget. It is important to recognise the nature of these discrepancies. Pavlov and Piaget alike are concerned to emphasise a broad general principle of the genesis and sequence of development in human thinking, that this is the way children tend to grow, irrespective of special conditions in their environment. But in a child's casual everyday experience, still more in school, deliberate instruction brings language into concrete thinking at an early stage, if not at the very beginning.

Take for instance an investigation reported by Ascoli, a follower of Piaget, who tested the ability of children between the ages of five and fourteen to classify named objects according to various criteria. The name of an object was mentioned to the child, who was required to name something similar and justify the choice. As was to be expected, the younger children were generally successful where the named object had distinctive 'external' characteristics such as form and colour but often failed where the only criterion was the function of the object—for instance, 'Give me the name of something which is like a lady's dress.'

When, however, these younger children were successful in naming an object functionally similar and were asked to justify the choice, there was often an illuminating result. They invoked characteristics such as form and colour which were in fact irrelevant. Only by the age of ten were the majority capable of verbalising the true basis of this choice. Ascoli concludes: 'There is a clear diminution between the possibility of evoking an object similar in function and the capacity to express the similarity' (10).

This of course bears out the common view—of Pavlov, Piaget and others—that a child's ability to perform an appropriate action is usually in advance of his ability to explain what he is doing. In this case the child has chosen 'intuitively'—that is, without having put the criterion of choice into words for himself. Pressed to do so he resorts to a pattern of explanation which up to this moment has been valid for many situations. Piaget's 'clinical method', used here by Ascoli, reveals the gap between performance and explanation.

But—and this is a crucial point—in everyday life, at home or in school, we do not simply use the clinical method, questioning a child and letting the matter rest there. Parent or teacher, by further questions, by discussion and illustrations, would usually help him to become aware of the functional similarity; and so help him forward in his ability to grasp this kind of similarity in the future.

How this may happen has been clearly shown, not only by the Russian investigators who have deliberately set themselves to instruct children but also by those workers who, repeating the tests of Piaget, have indicated the possibilities of helping children to move forward in their thinking.

Churchill, for instance, investigated the effects of freely talking to children while they were 'playing' with specially devised apparatus. Having tested some five-year-old children in their ability to perform certain concrete tasks—for instance, the recognition of the unchanging quantity of a group of beads in glasses of different dimensions—she then divided them into two groups matched in ability. One group received no special attention beyond that which normally occurs in an infant school; the other—the experimental—group was given a variety of apparatus which demanded grouping and ordering; and in play periods during three months the investigator sat with them chatting as they played, and guiding their attempts. When both groups were then tested with tasks of classifying and ordering things, the experimental group were clearly in advance of the control group. 'Experiences in play periods with materials that lend themselves to grouping and ordering, counting and comparing ... may bring the children to the formulation of the basic concepts sooner than is the case for the children who do not have these experiences.'

Churchill also brings some evidence of the possibility of promoting children's conceptual thinking by asking them questions. Of sixteen children shown a group of beads in glasses of varying size and asked whether the quantity remained unchanged, eleven answered Yes or No without making any attempt to count. Asked then how they could find out, three of these eleven replied that one could count, and three others responded by counting. Now although it is true that when a child of this age counts he may still have an imperfect grasp of the cardinal function of a number as symbolising a class of objects—and therefore he may still have an inadequate grasp of 'conservation' —yet there can be no doubt that counting may be made to hasten his advance towards this.

A similar picture is presented in a study by Blair Hood of 120 children between the ages of five and eight-and-a-half. In giving them a series of Piaget problems, Hood found that those who were under verbal guidance could be helped to reach a stage of reasoning ability beyond their usual powers. But with some of the younger and less able children this advance might only be temporary, so that Hood agrees with Piaget that in general children progress to higher levels of reasoning 'by the normal process of intellectual maturation'.

In saying this Hood also emphasises the importance of language in promoting maturation. Confronted with a problem a child is often guided in his thinking by the very existence and arrangement of the material before him, on the table; and as he attempts a solution the pattern of action becomes internalised and symbolised. Words may hasten this; so that the processes of solving the problem give meaning to the words which, in turn, become an instrument of more effective reasoning (11). It can hardly be doubted that, if while all this is going on, the child also hears and speaks the relevant words, his progress in reasoning will be hastened; this is exactly what normally happens in everyday life at home or in school.

THE SPECIFIC FUNCTIONS OF LANGUAGE IN CONCRETE THINKING

Having seen in broad outline, that language may promote children's progress in reasoning, we now have to ask how this may occur in each of the diverse processes that go to make up concrete thinking and the transition to more formal thinking.

Let us picture the situation in which the child finds himself when confronted with a problem which engages his concrete thinking. He is required to classify things, or place them in a serial order, with respect to one or more criteria; or he has to make a judgment of relative quantity, as in the 'beads in glasses' problem. In the performance of any of these tasks language may play an important part.

MOTIVATION AND COMMUNICATION

First of all, language has an influence upon the strength of the incentive that moves a child to undertake to solve a problem—the extent to which his interest is engaged, how far the problem is real for him. The intervention of others, vital as we have seen it to be in infancy and in earlier childhood, is now more closely channelled through language, which may evoke and direct incentive. In school and in the playground a child is increasingly led to see a problem in a situation by the suggestions of others (12). These come partly from their manner and attitude in face of the situation; but, more and more, from what they say to him. As the sanctions of his contemporaries become of increasing importance for a child, their words may be of almost inescapable power in deterring him from action or inciting him to it. If, asserting himself, he resists, he may be called upon to justify himself, and so his words may lead him to become aware of his own impulses and motives.

In the classroom different incentives, hardly less strong, are brought into play. Obviously, a teacher is more than an instructor in the methods of dealing with problems. What he says to his pupils and how he says it, have much to do with the intensity of their involvement in these problems.

Since the advance of a child's ability to reason is so largely dependent on the guidance and intervention of adults, another important factor is the relative adequacy of language as a means of communication between them and him. The words of the adult in setting the problem before the child, the words of the child in attempting to solve the problem—these may have different ranges of meaning for each of them. We say, 'Put these in order—Put the *smaller* ones at this end, the *larger* ones at the other end'—'Which of these two glasses has *more* beads in it?'—'Give me the name of something which is *like* a lady's dress.' Now words of this kind denoting serial order, quantity, similarity are precisely those terms whose meanings for the child we are, at this stage of his development, striving to make more discriminatively abstract for him. To say that a child has the word 'in his vocabulary' is not, of course, to say that the concept it symbolises for him is the same as our own; but the word can certainly help him to achieve the concept.

In one task after another, in the course of the solution of problems, the child at this stage is called upon to recognise similarities and differences other than those which have emerged from his experiences and experiments. For him, as we have seen, the main similarities and differences between things have been those which are functional and orectic for him personally; now we adults call on him to recognise relationships which are much more cognitive and impersonal. For instance, for a child a Plasticine 'ball' and 'sausage' are likely to be functionally and orectically different; we ask him to recognise that they are alike in 'quality' or in 'weight'.

But we know very well that these terms, which for us symbolise abstract characteristics, for a child may still symbolise his own personal and orectically-influenced responses to particular objects.

Everyday observations of this kind are corroborated by the evidence of systematic investigations such as that of Lovell and Ogilvie. In a study of the concrete thinking of some three hundred children in junior schools, they find that many of them, at any rate up to the age of nine, use terms such as *longer, fatter, bigger, thicker, smaller* in ways that appear to an adult confused and confusing. A child struggling to describe the metamorphosis of ball into sausage said, 'It gets thinner and bigger, it doesn't get fat, though' (13).

If a child's ability to deal with problems depends in a measure on the guidance he gets from adults, then his misconceptions of what we tell and ask him, and our misinterpretations of what he is trying to tell us, must often impede rather than promote the development of his reasoning. But the remedy is not the exclusion of language from a child's attempts at problem-solving. It is rather that by the due introduction of language into the processes of his concrete thinking he will move forward in this and beyond this. There can be no doubt that one of the main factors in his progress in abstract thinking must be the acquisition of a vocabulary of abstract terms.

How this vocabulary may foster the development of thinking may be seen if we look in some detail at the place of language in the various specific tasks that may go to the solving of problems at this stage: the naming of things; classifying them simply or multiplicatively; seriation; the recall of a past situation; the formulation of principles of procedure.

(i) *The naming of objects*

No doubt children at this age often continue to perceive and attend to objects without naming them. But observations show that this is the time when in general there is a marked advance in the function of naming so strongly emphasised by Mead—that it establishes an object as that object for us (14). We have seen the beginnings of this in infancy, in a rudimentary form as early as the second year, in such observations as those of Shipinova and Surina; and its further development in early childhood, as shown by such workers as Pyles and Weir and Stevenson. The common observation that this function of naming makes a notable advance in later childhood is also borne out by the last-named observers. In choosing pictures of animals from collections that included incorrect pictures, half the children were required to name the animal before pointing to a picture, the other half merely to point. At every age from three onwards the 'naming group' were the more successful; and after the age of five the gap between these and the 'non-namers' steadily widened (15).

(ii) *Classification*

Very similar to this is the place of language in the classification of objects. For adults the names of things may have become indispensable in classifying them. But even for some adults, and certainly for many children, it is possible to recognise that an object belongs to a particular class of things without verbalising the concept of the class. Thus Vincent found that deaf children, given tests in classifying things by more than one criterion, used gestures to symbolise such class concepts as *blue* and *yellow*, *large* and *small*: and even imbecile children are capable of grouping together three objects without being able to name the class to which they belong. But the deaf children, in comparison with children with normal hearing, are retarded in ability to classify things; and those who have investigated the abilities of imbecile children also conclude that what they chiefly lack in the performance of tasks is the accompaniment of language (16).

For normal children, the help that naming gives in perceiving and recognising particular objects, also extends to the classification of objects. This has been shown by a number of investigators. Shepard and Schaeffer, for instance, presented children of twelve with one hundred geometrical figures—five copies of five different triangles, five different quadrilaterals, five different pentagons and five different 'nonsense-figures.' These were arranged in twenty-five sets of four—one of each kind of figure in each set. With the first set of four, the experimenter indicated that the triangle—without naming it—was the figure the children would be required to look for; they were then asked to indicate this kind of figure in the remaining twenty-four sets. After this they were given a 'concept-name' test consisting of eighteen figures, including five triangles, and asked to write the name of each figure under it. Those who used the word 'triangle' consistently and correctly were found to have been at a clear advantage—statistically significant—in the earlier task of recognising that the different triangles all belonged to the same class (17).

(iii) *Multiplication*

One of the tasks that Piaget found generally difficult for many children under twelve is what he calls multiplication; the ability to classify things in accordance with two or more criteria—for instance colour and shape. He suggests that a child's advance towards this achievement, with respect to different kinds of criteria—for instance, shape, colour, volume, weight—is to some extent a process of maturation; that the child gradually grows to the point where he can keep in mind and simultaneously deal with two or more relevant characteristics.

It seems clear from what he says that he would not exclude the effects of children's experiences in handling materials, nor of the effects of their use of language, whether spontaneous or suggested by others. But he does not emphasise either of these; and of language we can surely say that it must be valuable as a means of symbolising the criteria, especially where these are not immediately observable. A child, for instance, who can readily deal with the colours and the shapes of objects—because he can directly perceive these—can take account of their weights only by remembering them, once he has handled each object and laid it down again.

The importance of language in this may be inferred from the work by Vincent, mentioned on page 190, in which she investigated multiplicative classification by children between the ages of five and eight with impaired hearing, in comparison with children of the same age-range with normal hearing. The children were required to deal with three different kinds of geometrical figures—circle, triangle, square—in three sizes and three colours of each, classifying them by criteria taken two at a time, for instance, colour and shape. Vincent found that at each year of age the deaf children were retarded by more than one year; she ascribes this to the general poverty of their inner language (18).

(iv) *Seriation*

The ability to arrange things in a serial order in accordance with a criterion such as height, weight, volume or gradation of colour must involve some awareness of a relationship which subsists between successive members of the series. Here again we may assume that a child can sometimes arrange things in a series without verbalising the common factor. Certainly it is a matter of ordinary observation that a child of three who can build a tower of discs of regularly decreasing diameter may be quite unable to say why he arranges them in this way.

Language becomes more important in seriation as the task demands more than immediate perception—demands that the child shall carry particular characteristics of objects and their relationships 'in his mind.' As Burt and Susan Isaacs have pointed out, even a child of ten who can arrange five boxes of different size in serial order may fail when they are of the same size but different weights, for this demands 'the comparison of successive experiences of different modality, which therefore cannot be taken up in a single act of prehension, but involves a series of imaginative reconstructions' (19).

In serial ordering, as we have said of classification, language may help by providing names for what has to be kept in mind. This is evident of those children who achieve seriation which is relatively concrete and fail where the task is of a more abstract nature. Some of Piaget's subjects, for instance, who were able to arrange human figures in order of height, failed to serialise a corresponding group of sticks—a more abstract task. That this failure is partly due to their inadequate command of language is indicated by a study by Borelli, who tested deaf children between the ages of five and eight, in comparison with children of the same age-range with normal hearing. In arranging the human figures the two groups were equally successful by the age of six-and-a-half; but in arranging the sticks, while the normal children were successful some six months later, the deaf children needed another six months or more to reach the same level of success (20).

(v) *Recall of a past situation*

We come now to probably the most important characteristic of concrete thinking—what indeed chiefly marks it off as an advance in a child's development: the ability to deal with a new situation which is a transformation of a past situation. The child can now cope with a problem such as the 'ball and sausage' test, where he recognises that the ball and the sausage are equal in quantity—or weight—of Plasticine; the process, as Piaget calls it, of 'conservation' of substance or of weight, from the past ball to the present sausage.

Piaget's insistence that this conservation implies reversibility may may not be strictly valid for all children. Lovell and Ogilvie, testing children of junior school age, found that sometimes a child can see that the ball and the sausage are identical in quantity and yet be unable to envisage a reversion from the present sausage to the past ball. Other children can revert to the past situation without being able to bring this into relation with the present changed situation. In general, however, these investigations conclude that 'reversibility is the most frequently given reason for conservation at all ages' (21);

LANGUAGE AND CONCRETE THINKING

and it is clear that the most effective way of helping the child towards conservation is to cause him to revert to the past situation and relate this to the changed conditions in the present.

No doubt this double process of recall of the past and transition to the present may take place by non-verbal means—with the aid of visual or other symbols. But in adult life, as Bartlett and others have shown, we are normally influenced in the modification and reconstruction of a past experience by the intervention of language; how far is this true of the period of later childhood?

Here again there is direct evidence from the study of normal children and indirect evidence from the study of those with impaired hearing. For direct evidence we may cite the report by Smirnov of various investigations in the U.S.S.R. These show an interesting development during the present period in the relation between visual picturing and the use of language. The evidence is that in the earlier part of the period—up to about the age of nine—children tend to resort to pictures in the effort to understand language; for instance, they will often imagine or even draw pictures when called upon to interpret something read. As time goes on, these functions tend to be reversed. When it becomes necessary for the children to deal not merely with isolated visual impressions, but with relations between them, they bring in the aid of language.

In a study of English children, Hall found that by the age of eleven they were well on the way to the normal adult state of affairs—where what is visually perceived is constantly influenced by words. There was a general tendency for the recall of seen pictures and diagrams to be modified by what the children said at the time of the original presentation as well as subsequently. In the reproduction of the pictures and diagrams immediately, and then at successive moments up to one month later, the recall was rarely, if ever, unchanged. The increasing errors, in some cases; the increase in accuracy, in others, were found to be greatly influenced by the children's words. In the U.S.A., again, Kurtz and Hovland, with children from the age of eleven, compared the effects of pictorial and verbal presentation. One group saw only the printed names of certain objects while a parallel control group saw unnamed photographs of them. In tests given a week later, the 'verbalisation group' proved to be the more successful both in recognition and in recall (22).

All this, again, is borne out by evidence from the study of deaf children. They suffer from the inadequacy of their language where they are confronted with a problem that requires them to keep in mind a picture of a situation and bring it into relation with the actual situation before them. Among other investigations we may again cite the word of Chulliat and Oléron, already mentioned in Chapter 7 (page 124). Deaf children between the ages of five and twelve, when presented with practical problems which demanded the translation from the actual to an envisaged situation were, throughout the age-range, retarded in comparison with normal children. The deaf children were often eminently capable of reproductive recall by means of non-verbal symbolisation; what they found difficult was to re-organise this recall, to give it a new structure. Chulliat and Oléron, after reviewing the various factors that might cause this relative inflexibility, concluded that the most important by far is the impairment of language. For it is language, they say, which enables a person to disengage himself from a particular situation, so as to re-organise it or see it in relation to other situations (23).

The study of deaf children also reminds us that children greatly depend upon language for their ability to think of the future. Deaf children, because their ability to symbolise the future is relatively deficient, are not so well able to plan a course of action in dealing with a problem (24).

(vi) *The formulation of principles*

Finally, it would seem likely that children can be helped in the solution of problems by verbal statements of principles of procedure —'If you do this, then that happens.' There is obviously a wide range of possibilities here—from leaving the child to discover and formulate a principle entirely for himself, up to providing him with the stated principle ready-made. How best to help a child with a particular problem is likely to vary with the form and content of the problem and with the child's verbal and general development; but, in general, experimental evidence bears out a common observation of teachers that neither extreme is as effective as a due mixture of initiative by the child with some verbal help from others. Kittell, working with children of twelve, found that the effectiveness of this mixed

LANGUAGE AND CONCRETE THINKING

treatment showed itself in greater ability to 'transfer' readily to related problems, as well as in greater power of recalling the principles of solution after a lapse of time. He recognises that this is contrary to the normal experience of adults, who as a rule benefit most from discovering and formulating principles for themselves, but he points out that this is not really inconsistent with what is more beneficial for children. Adults have become accustomed to using language in their thinking; children are still engaged in learning to use language in this way and need our help in doing so (25).

LANGUAGE AND THE MEASUREMENT OF INTELLIGENCE

The end of the period of later childhood is the time when, in this country, the majority of children are subjected to tests of intelligence, by which we seek to estimate their aptitudes for the more scholastic forms of education. This, then, would seem to be an appropriate moment in our survey for a brief consideration of the relation between language and the intelligence we attempt to measure.

In the intelligence tests that we normally use, many of the problems are of the same kinds as the various tasks that have just been described. The recognition of the place of language in these tasks throws light upon some of the controversial issues that have long bedevilled the discussion of the nature of intelligence: the possibility of measuring innate intelligence, the relation between measured intelligence and family size and between measured intelligence and socio-economic background.

In the fifty years that have elapsed since the beginning of intelligence testing, it has gradually become clear that some, at any rate, of the controversy arises only from a failure to agree upon the definitions of terms. In particular we must recognise distinctions in the use of the term 'intelligence' itself, of the kind suggested by Hebb: Intelligence A, its innate basis; Intelligence B, the abilities shown in everyday life; Intelligence C, the abilities measured by our tests (26).

(i) *The possibility of measuring innate intelligence*

Nobody is in any doubt that with the tests that we actually use, we are measuring a combination of what is inborn and the influence of environment. But the hope is sometimes expressed that we might be able to devise a means of measuring purely innate intelligence—'culture-free' tests. Burt goes so far as to maintain that this can be done: 'Any psychologist who is adept in the construction of such tests will scrupulously avoid words or forms of scholastic skill that are likely to be harder for some children than for others; and so will arrange the tasks required, that the child's success in each turns solely upon his ability to solve diagnostic problems calling for no special training and no prior experience' (27).

Everything here obviously depends on what is meant by 'no special training and no prior experience'. Certainly it would seem to be true that the smaller the demand that a test makes upon special training and prior experience, the nearer does it come to measuring inborn intelligence. If, for instance, we use 'performance tests' which allow the actual physical manipulation of things, it seems likely that some of the effects of the environmental influences that are embodied in language may be excluded from measurement. Burt, in another piece of work, emphasises this. In attempting to estimate the contribution of heredity to measured intelligence, he cites a correlation of ·843 between identical twins reared apart, as compared with ·526 for non-identical twins reared together. But this wide difference, which must be due to heredity, is, he tells us, greatly reduced in the results obtained by Newman: ·670 and ·640 respectively. Explaining the discrepancy, Burt points out that whereas Newman had used the Stanford-Binet scale which is 'greatly influenced by differences in schooling and cultural background', his own figures 'were based on non-verbal tests of the performance type' (28).

Burt does not say that 'performance type' tests measure nothing but innate intelligence. But following a common usage he does call them non-verbal, and this is obviously a crucial issue. Are they really non-verbal? Can we say with certainty that when we set children performance tests we test abilities that are inevitably and absolutely free of the influence of language?

This at least can be said, that the evidence from testing deaf children shows that retardation in language may not be a handicap in dealing with performance tests. As we saw in Chapter 6, they do as well as, often better than, children of the same age with normal hearing. This would certainly suggest that performance tests, properly devised and carried out, can measure abilities in problem-solving which are comparatively free of the environmental influences that come through language.

It would, however, be going far beyond the evidence to assert that even performance tests are always completely independent of language. It is safe to say that today no child—even the child who is 'totally deaf'—grows up in a completely non-linguistic environment. Because every child lives in a world of speakers, some language, however minimal, must have entered his experience. If in no other way than this, his ability to solve problems in performance tests is likely to be influenced by his upbringing; and to some extent— however small—we may therefore be measuring the effects of his linguistic environment.

Still more is this so when we come to the tests which are normally used to ascertain the I.Q.s of children. As soon as a deaf child moves from a concrete situation, of which he can be immediately aware, to such symbolisations as pictures and diagrams, deficiencies of language begin to affect his success. So, too, when the situation becomes at all abstract—as with the children studied by Borelli, who were at a loss when required to put sticks in serial order.

It is true, therefore, that only a very limited range of tests can validly be called non-verbal—and these the tests which are least predictive of scholastic success, of the abilities that are most highly rewarded in a modern society. A child's competence to meet these demands must depend in part upon his upbringing.

This has long been understood—indeed it was clear to Binet, in the earliest days of intelligence-testing. What, however, has become equally well understood only of recent years is that the tests we give, because they are so largely tests of reasoning, demand the use of symbolisation in solving them; and that this symbolisation is likely to be linguistic—both from the nature of the tests themselves and from a child's normal life among others. As he himself uses language, as those about him speak to him, as their behaviour is permeated with language—to that extent will he be influenced to use language in solving problems. As a result, language may come into some of his responses to performance tests as well as to pictorial, diagrammatic and verbally-presented tests. Thus the I.Q.s that are derived from intelligence tests must in some measure reflect linguistic development—and it is these I.Q.s that are usually correlated with family size and socio-economic background.

FAMILY SIZE AND INTELLIGENCE

It has often been shown that there is a relationship between the measured intelligence of children and the size of their families—that, statistically speaking, children from larger families have lower I.Q.s than children from smaller families (29). Now there is no doubt that in part this is related to the socio-economic level of the home. In the recent past, at any rate, the larger families tended to be at the lower socio-economic levels, at which children were often at a disadvantage intellectually—as we have seen in Chapter 6.

But even apart from the general social and economic factors, the size of the family is still related to measured intelligence. Among others, O'Hanlon, Burt and Thomson have all found a negative correlation between family size and I.Q., with children from the *same* socio-economic level (30).

It is not impossible that this may in part be due to heredity—that there may be a genetic connection between fertility and mental ability. But it is also reasonable to ask whether there is not likely to be an environmental factor; so that membership of a large family may become detrimental to the development of ability to perform the tasks that constitute an intelligence test.

Everything that we have said here points to the hypothesis that an important factor must be the relative linguistic retardation which is likely to occur in a large family. The publication in 1949 of the data gathered for the Scottish Mental Survey prompted Nisbet to test this hypothesis. As a result of his investigation of more than five thousand children between eleven and twelve, he concluded that while other influences may also be at work, 'the environment of the large family constitutes a handicap to verbal development and that this verbal retardation also affects general mental development' (31).

From what we have seen of the environmental factors that influence linguistic development, we can readily say why this is so. In a large family the children may be in constant communication with each other rather than with their parents. For children to be living together, playing and speaking with each other, is certainly of value for their general personal and social growth, even their cognitive development; but for the fullest realisation of their cognitive potentialities, constant communication with adults is, as we have seen, essential. Thus when we seek to understand why membership of a large family tends to retard the development of measured intelligence, it is once more the influence of language which emerges as a powerful factor.

SOCIO-ECONOMIC LEVEL AND MEASURED INTELLIGENCE

Finally, we are confronted with another important way in which language may be related to measured intelligence: the influence of the socio-economic level of a child's home upon his linguistic development and so on his ability to deal with intelligence tests. In Chapter 6 we saw that these relationships are already strongly established in early childhood. To what extent are they likely to persist throughout school life? Among the problems of education in this country today, anything that throws light upon the assessment of mental abilities has become of paramount importance.

In the study of children's development, the connection between socio-economic level and measured intelligence has long been demonstrated and long been a subject of serious concern. In this country, a pioneer in investigating the facts and emphasising their significance for the welfare of the nation is Burt. He showed, for instance in a study of London schoolchildren, that those from the 'higher professional classes' had a mean I.Q. of 120 as against 90 for the children of unskilled workers. A multitude of investigators, particularly in this country and U.S.A., have come to similar conclusions (32).

The cause of major concern was the undoubted relationship between family size and socio-economic level. A quarter of a century ago the dysgenic implications of this caused much alarm, the echoes of which have not yet completely died down. It seemed evident that since the majority of the future population must come from the larger families, the average of the national intelligence must decline. Cattell warned us that within twenty years there must be a fall of three points of I.Q.; the estimates of Burt and of Thomson were little more reassuring—nearly two points in twenty years (33). To these, as to other investigators, the genetic factor appeared to be so powerful as to make the decline inevitable.

But these were statistical predictions, not checked by direct observations until the publication of the Scottish Mental Survey, 1949, and a smaller investigation by Cattell in the following year.

The Scottish Mental Survey compared groups of children after an interval of fifteen years. In 1932 an intelligence test had been given to all the eleven-year-olds in Scotland; in 1947 the same test was repeated with all the children then of that age. The result was startling. Within half a generation, the mean score had risen by two points. Corroboration came from Cattell's smaller investigation in 1950, comparing ten-year-olds in Leicestershire in 1936 and 1949. In thirteen years the mean I.Q. had risen by nearly one-and-a-half points.

Naturally there was much discussion of this reversal of the predicted decline. On the whole, both Thomson and Cattell were inclined to the view that a real decline was 'masked' by special conditions, as, for instance, the children having become 'sophisticated' in dealing with tests. Neither of them appeared to attach much importance to one fact which emerged at that very moment in the Report of the Royal Commission on Population, 1949: that the size of families in Great Britain had steadily been decreasing.

Penrose had indeed pointed out in discussion with Thomson that 'with universal family limitation, the mean I.Q. of the children would automatically rise.' In a comprehensive study of his own he agreed that if 'intelligence' were entirely determined by hereditary factors, there might be a decline of as much as two points of I.Q. in a generation; but cautiously pointed out that 'so far, no satisfactory direct evidence of declining intelligence in any modern community has been presented'; and added that a prediction of decline would 'be seriously invalidated if environment plays any considerable part in determining intelligence level'—this, before the Scottish Mental Survey had published its report (34).

No doubt there are hereditary factors in the pattern of family size, socio-economic level and measured intelligence. In addition to a possible hereditary factor in fertility there may well be a hereditary factor in the relation between socio-economic level and cognitive abilities. Those who are by nature less gifted to perform the more abstract tasks, for which there is so high a premium in a modern society, gravitate towards the lower social levels—and the children born into these homes may tend to inherit the cognitive potentialities of their parents.

But what is equally certain is that there are, as Penrose postulates, complementary influences of environment; and everything that we have seen of children's development points to language as among the chief of these influences. It is language that is a major environmental link between family size and measured intelligence; so that if care is taken, retardation can be lessened. And it is language which is a major link between socio-economic level and measured intelligence. Of course the relationship is complex. It is not only, as is so often said, that the parents are comparatively 'uneducated', that the homes lack books, that the children's experiences are restricted and that these deprivations constitute a handicap in ability to deal with tests of scholastic aptitude and, indeed, in ability to benefit from the more scholastic kinds of schooling. There is a much profounder and more permeative influence upon the children—the everyday language of family life.

We have brought evidence to show that vocalisation and the beginnings of speech in infancy; the perception of objects and the awareness of relationships, in early childhood; the passage from concrete to abstract thinking in later childhood—that all these owe much to the interchange of language between children and their elders. The ease of this intercourse, the scope and volume of vocabulary, the extent to which—as Bernstein has shown—the language reflects and promotes abstract ideas: all these characteristics of communication deeply affect the growing child's ability to cope with the demands of scholastic education. In measuring his intelligence by means of the usual tests, we are to some extent measuring the effects of his linguistic upbringing upon his cognitive development.

This would suggest that a child's measured intelligence may change; that his I.Q. is susceptible to modification in his environment. It is a conclusion unacceptable only by those who maintain that the level of intelligence is fixed at birth and thereafter unalterable, and who are satisfied to reject such evidence as the histories of children who have spent part of their lives in institutions.

The principle of the fixity of the I.Q. is sometimes thought to be implied in the very intention of measuring a child's intelligence at a particular moment in his life. Not so. At the very dawn of intelligence testing, Binet himself found it necessary to utter a manifesto against this view. He said, 'Some recent thinkers seem to have given their moral support to the deplorable conclusion which affirms that the intelligence of an individual is a fixed quantity, a quantity that cannot be increased. We must protest and react against this brutal pessimism; we shall try to demonstrate that it has no foundation. The mind of a child is like a field for which a skilful farmer has changed the mode of cultivation, with the result that instead of a fallow field we now have a harvest. It is in this practical sense—the only one open to us—that we say that the intelligence of children has been increased. We shall have increased that which constitutes the intelligence of a pupil, the capacity to grasp and assimilate instruction' (35).

The evidence we have reviewed in the present chapter leads to the conclusion that in any attempt 'to change the mode of cultivation' one of the chief means must be language. If this is true of a child's cognitive development, how far is it true of his orectic and ethical development? This is our next consideration.

11

Social and Ethical Development

AT the beginning of Chapter 9 we saw in broad outline the general pattern of orectic characteristics during this period of later childhood. We now look at these more closely, and particularly at their relations with language.

This is the period when strong forces combine to foster a child's allegiance to his contemporaries while at the same time promoting the emergence of his individual personality. We have to see how language serves the purpose of maintaining the cohesion of the contemporary group, how it helps to transmit the values of the group to its individual members and so influence individual attitudes, and how therefore it influences the growth of the child's awareness of what he is and what he might become.

The special characteristics of group-language, which mark it off from adult language, express and promote a child's allegiance to his contemporary group. At the same time, the freedom to explore the reaches of slang and scatology manifests children's belief that these are among the privileges and attractions of adult life which—from the perspective of an eleven-year-old—seem to promise self-sufficiency and freedom from authority. A third influence upon his language at this time is a child's identification of himself as a member of a sex-group. This is expressed in some sexual differentiation of language, which in turn, helps the child to form for himself a clearer and fuller picture of what he is and what he might become.

His growing individuality, as it takes shape from the strenuous enmities and amities of his social life, is manifested in a multivalence of attitudes towards his contemporaries and his elders. By turns he is aggressive or submissive, deeply involved or coolly reserved a follower or a leader. Language progressively takes over more and more the functions of expressing these attitudes, with greater power and discrimination the older he gets.

A further factor in this changing pattern of personal life is a child's growing awareness of rules of conduct—those which have the sanction of adult authority and those which emerge from and govern his relations with his peers. His individual reactions to these rules express his temperament and shape his personality. In conformity or rebellion he asserts himself and so comes to fashion for himself a body of principles which ultimately may be transformed into abstract fundamental ideals of conduct not necessarily in accord with those of his immediate society or the wider societies beyond this.

Because all this clearly involves the awareness of relationships, and the exercise of reasoning and judgment, his cognitive and his orectic development here as everywhere are closely interwoven. They are separable only in analysis, since they are aspects of his single and indivisible prehension of his world. In the growth of language during this period the complementary cognitive and orectic functions are very evident. The child must bring his cognitive abilities to bear upon the mastery of language if this is to be an instrument of his orectic development.

THE CHILD IS A MEMBER OF GROUPS,
ACTUAL AND POTENTIAL

In looking at the place of language in a child's social life at this time, we see that his relationships with his elders and his contemporaries are now more complex than at any earlier time in his life. Two social forces are now acting upon him: the continuing authority of his elders at home and in school, and his allegiance to his contemporary group. Each of these societies contributes to his linguistic development; but, more important than this, his linguistic development is the chief means of his membership of these societies. As Bernstein puts it strongly: 'The child learns his social structure through its language' (1). This, of course, is not simply a process of acceptance; each of the two societies may either secure a child's conformity or evoke his resistance—or both.

IN RELATION TO HIS ELDERS

A child's acceptance and rejection of adult authority is seen both in his language and in the ethical codes and patterns of conduct which this language symbolises. For their language, most children at this stage continue to accept the authority of parents and teachers, with some modification from the encroachments of the group-language. By the end of the period—as for instance, Templin found —the majority of children are able to show their grasp of the whole range of the usages of the mother tongue.

Two powerful forces combine to maintain a child's acceptance of adult authority in language. First—conservatism: the persistence of habitual forms of behaviour whose roots lie far back in the child's history. Secondly, the child as he approaches adolescence is constantly drawn towards adult ways of living as a recognition, to himself and others, that he is growing up towards adult stature.

But some children often, and most children sometimes, respond to adult linguistic authority with merely negative rejection or even positive resistance. There is a close relation between the consequent sub-literacy and the refusal to conform to adult rules of conduct that expresses itself in delinquency. Some observers would see the delinquency as the result of the backwardness. Schonell, for instance, cites a survey of two thousand delinquent children, 55 per cent of whom were 'markedly backward in reading and spelling'; he believes that 'the delinquencies of many such children are a direct result of their backwardness in school' (2). This may certainly be true of some of them, since a minimum achievement of literacy is so basic a demand on every child that a consciousness of inadequacy may bring with it an emotional upset that is expressed in delinquency.

But in some other cases, at any rate, delinquency is not simply the result of backwardness; both are manifestations of the same state of affairs in the child—two forms of his resistance to adult authority. His delinquency may be resistance to parental ethics, his sub-literacy a resistance to parental language. This is the conclusion of so experienced an investigator as Burt; some interesting instances are given by Stott (3).

ALLEGIANCE TO THE CONTEMPORARY GROUP

As a child acquires a sub-language of the kind that we described in Chapter 9, it may both express and foster his ethical behaviour as a member of the group. For while the use of the sub-language is an expression of each child's allegiance to the group, it is at the same time a means of promoting its cohesiveness. This is not only through the declarative function of the language in fostering feelings of communion; the language is also used manipulatively as a means of promoting group action—as in group games—or the belligerence of the group towards another group or a person.

An important result of a child's participation in a group sub-language is that for the first time he may become aware that a language is essentially social—that communication depends on the existence of a community. From the beginnings of the growth of his speech, language must have seemed to him as ubiquitous as the air he breathes. Unless he has learnt a second language—and perhaps even then—he may not have realised that different communities have different languages. This may now begin to dawn on him with his initiation into the group-language, as he becomes very conscious of the fact that this is a language that some others—particularly parents and teachers—do not speak and, it is supposed, do not understand. It is, of course, an important feature of a group-language that it shall be 'secret' or, at any rate, have some secret features; and it is disconcerting for children to discover that an adult does in fact understand. When this happens, the children often show a certain resentment that the adult is not quite playing the game, a feeling that he has no business to be prying into esoteric secrets.

We may now ask how the secrecy of a sub-language, with its various special characteristics, may serve to maintain the cohesion of a group and help it to present a united front against other groups and the encroachments of adult authority. We shall look at three of these characteristic features: an oral system of rituals often embodied in a special vocabulary; slang and 'secret codes' for communication; scatology.

(i) *A system of oral rituals.* Few characteristics of children's lives during this period so clearly evince their movement away from the family, and their integration into groups, as the language by which one group communicates with another. In particular there are rituals for securing a truce at a moment when necesssity demands the cessation of warfare. These rituals combine symbolic gestures with words of a special potency, many of them once current in the adult language but now obsolete.

Take one example from the many recorded by the Opies. Truce is offered and requested by showing crossed fingers and uttering the word of power:

'*Skinch*—you cross your fingers and walk to the other gang to tell them something.' (10-year-old boy) (4).

"*Fins*"

The study of these terms—as the Opies have shown—is a fascinating bypath of linguistic history. They have been preserved in rituals of ancient tradition, transmitted by word of mouth from generation to generation of children; and—from their very nature as orally-preserved words—have local dialectal forms, so that it is possible to draw a map showing the currency of each form. *Skinch*, for instance, is usual in Durham and Northumberland. Variants in other parts of the country include *barley*, *kings*, *keys*, *cree*, *fainites*.

These truce-terms are, of course, also used between individual children. We shall come back to this later. In the meantime we notice that a special vocabulary of this kind has the double effect of providing a sub-language for the contemporary group as a whole—helping to mark if off more distinctively from adult life—and at the same time promoting the cohesion of each gang within the wider contemporary group. Thus there is a powerful incentive to preserve the special traditional forms with the utmost rigour; and if—by the migration of children into a locality or from some other cause—a new form gains admission, this innovation is again preserved in its purity.

(ii) *Slang*. This is another linguistic means by which the special character of a group is maintained, not so much against other groups as in the face of adult authority. There is, first of all, the slang which while it is freely and openly used by adults is forbidden to the children. Even such comparatively innocuous slang as names for money —*lolly*, *dough*, *quid*, *bob*, *tanner*—may come under the ban. The usual adult justification for this prohibition is that slang is a corrupting influence on the young, degrading their language and frustrating their acquisition of 'good', 'correct' speech. One may suspect, however, that sometimes this is a rationalisation by adults of their discomfort in seeing their children growing up too fast, becoming too soon and too obviously like themselves in their less guarded moments. There can be little doubt that children, for their part, often sense this and are therefore all the more driven to assert their resistance to adult restrictions.

A second kind of slang may be called 'schoolboy slang.' This, perhaps because it is felt to be peculiar to childhood and not likely to persist into adult language as a corrupting influence, is more readily tolerated. None the less it serves to maintain and strengthen a sense of belonging to a contemporary group. *Honour bright*, for instance; if this comes into adult speech it is in a half-humorous way and with schoolboy overtones. It seems likely that this kind of slang is the one instance in which the written language has done something to preserve spoken words in a children's sub-language; the mummification of school-boy slang in school stories.

A third kind of slang are the 'secret' oral codes—contortions of the mother tongue—sometimes imitated from those current among adult sub-groups. Rhyming slang, for instance, as used by children:

almond rocks (socks); *apples and pears* (stairs); *tea-leaf* (thief).

Other oral codes—for instance, 'back-slang' and 'double-talk'—illustrate the lengths to which children will go in order to keep, as they think, their secrecy. An instance of back-slang given by the Opies consists in transferring the first consonant, or double consonant, to the end of a word and adding *ay*:

Unejay ithsmay isay igpay (June Smith is a pig).

Another kind of 'secret' slang inserts *arag* into each word:

Taragoo baraged, saragays slarageepy haraged (To bed, says Sleepyhead) (5).

The written codes so common among children during this period are also essentially 'secret' forms of slang. The assiduity and enthusiasm with which children devise and use all these attempts at secrecy attest the strength of their need to feel themselves members of a group, standing together in the face of outsiders, whether adults or other contemporary groups.

(iii) *Scatology*. It is doubtful whether the place of scatology in the life of a growing child is yet fully understood. During this period of later childhood, when its development is most striking, it already has the two essential characteristics of scatology as we find it in adult life—that it shall be indirect and yet still in a measure 'forbidden'. Younger children are often permitted and indeed encouraged by their parents to speak freely about their genitals and excretion, but now that in later childhood this direct reference is frowned on, it is replaced by veiled allusion to other parts of the body, underwear and the more or less concealed naming of excretion. It now becomes scatology, something mildly comic, to be spoken *sub rosa* and with a giggle rather than a laugh. This sense of transgression is no doubt in part due to children's growing self-consciousness and awareness of sex; but it is also reinforced by the veto of their elders which occurs quite normally in the ordinary course of everyday life. Even Susan Isaacs, with her strong belief in the importance of encouraging children to express themselves freely, felt that toleration was hardly desirable beyond the earliest years of childhood—'Children under five do need greater verbal freedom in these matters than it is useful for older children to have' (6).

A neat example which illustrates children's pleasure in rhymes, in puns and in veiled but clearly visible scatology is quoted by the Opies as a 'favourite poem' of a boy of seven:

> Up in the mountains, lying on the grass
> I saw a Chinaman sliding on his
> Ask no questions, tell no lies
> I saw a Chinaman doing up his
> Flies are a nuisance, flies are a pest
> I saw a Chinaman doing up his vest (7).

What, in general, is the function of scatology in children's lives? It would appear to serve two purposes. It can be, as we shall see later, a ready means of scoring off another child by causing him to utter what is forbidden and so expose himself, linguistically, to the public gaze. Here, where for the moment we are speaking of group-life, we see that because scatology is forbidden by adult authority, it takes on the chief characteristics of a 'secret' sub-language; it is at once a bond between children and a manifestation of growing up, a challenge to authority. A child—the more so if he is an only child—finds a certain pleasure in sharing this peculiarly intimate interest with other children. Parts of the body, the underwear associated with them, excretion—these have names which have acquired a powerful orectic colouring. The utterance that he is being trained to inhibit in adult company becomes one of the special pleasures to be shared within the community of children—a pleasure enhanced by an awareness that they are transgressing against the rules imposed by their elders.

The fact that while it remains secret it is a manifestation of growing up, is shown by the urgent need some children feel to take steps to let their elders know about their scatological behaviour in defiance of adult prohibition. So there is scribbling in school lavatories, and notebooks and 'secret' letters are found 'by accident' by parents and teachers.

MEMBERSHIP OF A SEX-COMMUNITY

A child's growing awareness of sex during this period shows itself not only in seeking the companionship of members of the same sex but also in some specific sexual characteristics of language. The quantitive differences apparent in infancy have by this age dwindled, the boys drawing level with the girls in the general mastery of forms and size of vocabulary. The differences are now mainly semantic—though today, with the growing approximation in the interests, behaviour and education of the sexes, the differences are less marked than in the past. They appear, first, in the verbal differentiation of things perceived and experienced; and secondly, in the different specific words used to denote characteristic personal attributes—these include some scatological words used only within each sex group.

(i) The distinctive vocabularies of boys and girls reflect and reinforce the selective perception and categorisation of the world around them—differences which probably have some innate sources and which certainly owe something to differences in upbringing. Although this differentiation of vocabulary has often been noted, there is still probably no complete survey for any one mother tongue. The observations of Burroughs and Walker do not go beyond the age of six-and-a-half; McCarthy summarises a number of systematic though limited studies (8). But everyday observation gives sufficient evidence of the reality of the differences. Boys generally have a wider range of words denoting mechanical things, and of measurable quantities such as weights, volumes, areas. Girls are more discriminative in naming colours, plants and—of course—dress. There are also distinctive differences in verbs, adjectives and adverbs.

(ii) There is also something of a distinctive vocabulary to denote personal characteristics: some words used by each sex only of itself, some words used only of the other sex:

'Among boys, to use the word *crying* is almost as sissy as the act itself. A lad must say *blubbing* or *bawling* or *squalling*, according to the custom of his school or the district in which he lives' (9).

Instances of words used on the whole by boys of boys are *tough guy* and *sissy*; of girls by girls, *sour-puss*, *copy-cat*. Words used by one sex only of the other are not easily brought into the open and there are probably not many; the Opies record, for instance, that *tart* is used by boys to denote, without any derogation, a nice well-dressed girl (10).

The distinctive scatological terms used only within the confines of each sex-group can, for the most part, only be guessed at, since in childhood they are kept secret from adults and are rarely recorded by them in recollection of their own childhood. But that they do exist there can be no doubt. Most of us can remember some from our own childhood; and it is probable that they amount to a few words denoting the physical characteristics of sex and sexual behaviour.

The sexual sub-languages of boys and girls—less distinctive though they may be today—have an important influence on their general development: they reinforce the children's awareness of sex, more powerfully than the more 'refined' language of the mother tongue sanctioned by adults. For where the adult language, reflecting a 'civilised' relationship between the sexes, has ceased to use differentiating terms, children's sexual sub-languages often continue to do so. And where the adult language—as D. H. Lawrence complained—uses colourless words for the physical characteristics of sex and for sexual behaviour, children's sexual vocabularies often retain a fuller orectic warmth. Thus during the period when it is important for a child's development that he should become increasingly aware of himself, a sexual sub-language may contribute to this by promoting his awareness of his personal sexual characteristics. But like so much else that is important for growth in later childhood, if this crudity of sexual language persists for too long during adolescence it may bring with it the problem of integrating sexual awareness in a mature personality.

LANGUAGE AND THE GROWTH OF SELF-AWARENESS

Three functions of language contribute, in ever-increasing measure during this period, to a child's awareness of himself. These functions
(i) relate the child as an individual to others, in friendship and hostility,
(ii) symbolise for him the pattern of his personality as it is and as it might become—his ego and his ego-ideal,
(iii) set out a pattern of conduct for his personal life.
We look at these in turn.

LANGUAGE IN A CHILD'S RELATIONS WITH OTHERS

We saw in Chapter 8 that in early childhood language has already gone a very long way towards becoming an instrument of relations between persons, superseding many of the earlier non-linguistic, physical manifestations of their relationships. In the present period —with the immersion of a child in the life of a group—there are rapid further developments in this direction, extending throughout the whole network of his relationships with others. Social behaviour is now highly verbal. Children now do verbal deeds to each other, deeds which matter more and more in their lives. Between individual children—as between groups—co-operation and competition are now expressed by symbolic patterns of behaviour, in which the verbal ritual is again the more important element.

We have already glanced at the faithfully observed rituals which regulate conduct between groups. More numerous and more frequently used are the co-operative rituals current between individual members within a group. Some of these are 'joining-in' rituals that promote the integration of a child in a group game; others are contractual rituals which serve to regulate relationships between children in a game or some other common activity.

(i) *'Joining-in' rituals.* A group game is essentially a system of routines organised by rules, and it is the routines rather than the rules that are verbalised. A child initiated into a game often learns how to take part by 'joining-in' and may continue to participate correctly without ever stating the rules or hearing them stated. Thus when Piaget induced the verbal formulation of the rules of games by questioning children, he found that during this period of later childhood they were unaccustomed to state rules, and were hazy and even inaccurate when urged to do so by an enquiring adult (11).

But to confine oneself to children's ability to state rules is to obtain a very limited and partial picture of the place of language in their games. For although language may not normally serve the purpose of formulating rules, it comes into games in a multiplicity of other ways, as any everyday observation of children will show. It may not come in as rules; it certainly plays its part in routines. For 'joining-in' there is a wealth of colourful verbal rituals: the shanties in speech and song, the 'counting-out' formulas and rhymes, the skipping rhymes and the ball-bouncing-rhymes which can be heard every day in any school playground. The physical routine itself may well have been learnt as a skill, with the minimum—or even the absence—of verbal formulation; the verbal ritual interwoven with it not only gives it a rhythmical pattern and a mnemonic structure for the child himself but also engages him in a pattern of play in a group.

(ii) *Contractual rituals.* Playing and living together engender a diversity of personal relationships, regulated by a host of rituals and traditional contractual undertakings each signified by physical act and verbal deed. In group games, the most important of these are the truce-rituals, as indispensable between individuals as we have seen them to be between groups. Here again the verbal formula is the dominant feature. The physical act—crossing one's fingers and the like—must of course be correctly performed. But the same act may be common to many contracts; it signifies truce only when the potent word is uttered.

> *Kings.* 'If one gets a stitch while playing chase, one crosses one's fingers and says "Kings", and the person who is "he" does not chase until one is ready'—twelve-year-old girl (12).

Within and beyond games, many other contractual rituals become supremely important during this period. The expansion of a child's social life with his fellows entails an intricate network of obligations and mutual undertakings: taking oaths; testing truthfulness; making bets and bargains; swopping, giving and gaining possession of things; claiming precedence. The fundamental ethical principle of these is, clearly, a 'law of mutuality', as Piaget and others have recognised; although here again, as in the rules of games, it is unlikely that the general principle is brought to a child's awareness by formulation in words, unless elicited by questions of the kind that Piaget put. As we shall see, conduct within a group is usually governed, not by formulated precepts, but by traditional rhymes of a gnomic and proverbial character.

The contractual rituals, by resolving actual or potential conflicts, substitute for anarchy a pattern of regulated relationships; they engage the children in symbolic behaviour in place of direct action. As in the narrower sphere of games, the ritual consists of a symbolic physical act coupled with a verbal formula, which is the dominant element. This is seen in the fact that some latitude is allowed in the performance of the physical ritual act:

Cross my heart. 'When one crosses one's heart one should do it with arms across the whole of one's chest, touching one's shoulders. Not everyone does it properly'—ten-year-old girl (13).

But the verbal formula must not be varied; it is the significant instrument of communication. To be able to live with his fellows, secure in the confidence that they, with him, are engaged in a common pattern of obligations, a child must know and understand the words of power. They serve to maintain his fellowship with others over the whole range of relationships, from the most peaceful co-operation to the alleviation of a sudden outburst of pugnacity. Where there is a friendly co-operative undertaking, the ritual sets its seal upon the agreement; at the other extreme, the actual and imminent hostility may be so intense that only the performance of the ritual prevents physical violence.

The ritual for a co-operative undertaking may be a solemn oath of affirmation:

> Cross my heart
> If I ever tell a lie
> Put a rope round my neck
> Then let me die.

Or an oath of secrecy:

> Prick of the finger, prick of the thumb,
> I won't tell what you've done.

Or an agreement to swop things:

'In Croydon they hook little fingers and shake, chanting:
> Touch teeth, touch leather
> No backsies for ever and ever' (14).

Rituals of this kind are an insurance against possible future conflict. Even more powerful than these are the rituals which take the place of conflict here and now. For instance, one of the commonest causes of strife in infancy and early childhood is the claim to personal property. A child will often try to regain a gift made in a burst of generosity or a moment of absent-mindedness. But in later childhood it has usually become a working rule that what is once given cannot be reclaimed. The child who attempts to re-assert his claim will have to submit to some such ritual as:

> Give a thing, take it back
> God will ask you, Where is that?
> You say you don't know,
> Then God will send you down below.

To secure precedence in a game of conkers, a child will say:

> Iddy, iddy onker
> My first conker;
> Iddy, iddy ack,
> My first smack (15).

(iii) *The expression of hostility*

While rituals allay, anticipate and even prevent conflict, they cannot of course entirely banish it. At any moment, in the constant friction of social living, a spark of hostility may burst into flame. When the fight is on—now much more a battle of words than in earlier childhood—the injuries though verbal are none the less hurtful. Now that the children are living in a social universe of verbalised relationships, because words are the instruments of law they are also the means of outlawry, of torture and punishment often harder to endure than physical violence.

The children themselves are only too sensitive to this, as the traditional response to verbal injuries betrays:

> Sticks and stones may break my bones
> But names will never hurt me;
> When I am dead and in my grave
> You'll be sorry for what you've called me (16).

What makes words so much more injurious to self-respect than they were in a child's earlier life is the fact that they now come to him with a social backing, in a context of social relationships within the group. Where the epithets are in the vocabulary and convention of the sub-language, they are so much the more expressive and hurtful because they are felt to be in the children's own language, not in the more refined and emasculated speech of one's elders. The epithet symbolises the feeling and attitude of one's peers, especially when it has a ritual pattern which brings with it something of the impersonal force of the whole group acting together. Even when spoken by a single child it suggests a chanting, mocking chorus:

> Inky pinky, pen and inky
> I smell a dirty stinky. (Eleven-year-old).

At the same time, the very ritualisation of the attack upon the child is a possible source of relief. Names will hurt him so much the less if he can participate in the ritual pattern and make the correct conventional reply:

> 'The trouble with you is that your nose was
> put too near your mouth' (17).

By mildly scoring off his opponent, by showing that he is capable of accepting disapproval without undue resentment, by expressing his feelings in an accepted verbal formula instead of resorting to blows—in all these ways he feels and lets the others feel that he remains within the orbit of the group.

SOCIAL AND ETHICAL DEVELOPMENT

In fact, so long as a child can maintain his membership of the community of speech, humiliation can be borne and injury endured. The moment of despair comes when words fail; as the Opies have said, 'To threaten physical action is to confess mental defeat' (18). Worst of all, this reversion to physical action may court the breaking-off of verbal communication—when the social bond is severed and one child says of another, 'I don't speak to him.' A few years earlier the two children could have played happily side by side in silence; now speech is the essential condition of any joint enterprise.

Nothing indeed matters so much to a child at this stage as his place in the verbal community. If he is singled out by a nickname and is made to feel different from the others, yet because the epithet is conventional, he still remains within the group. Although he may suffer painfully, there is still an element of social acceptance in the epithet, however unpleasant it may be.

It is evident that in so much of 'name-calling' the asperity is softened by a touch of friendliness: for the tall child, *Spindle-Dick*; the short, *Tich* or *Kipper*; the redhead, *Ginger for pluck*; the freckled, *Spotty-Dick*; the bespectacled, *Four-eyes*; the bright, *Clever-Dick*; the dull, *Dopey*; and even, for the timid, *Cowardy cowardy custard*. It becomes important that in response to the traditional epithet the object of it shall show that he takes it in the right spirit. If he does not he may be pilloried for asserting himself too strongly against the conventions of the group:

'In Glasgow, when having fun with somebody who does not take it as fun, they chant:

>'Roses are red
>Violets are blue,
>Lemons are sour
>And so are you' (19).

To the adult onlooker, children now—and often later—may seem to spend immense time and energy in finding new ways of scoring off and humiliating each other, with refinements of ruthlessness and cruelty. But the devices are only rarely invented; most of them are the heritage of tradition, handed over by the older to the younger children and from this very fact both gaining prestige and giving a special pleasure.

A common form of one-up-man-ship is the verbal trick by which a child is drawn into saying something which exposes him to ridicule: for instance, the pseudo-riddle:

'If frozen water is iced water, what is frozen ink?'

Or, by a pseudo-game, he is inveigled into inviting physical humiliation:

> 'Adam and Eve and Nipmewell
> Went in a boat to sea
> Adam and Eve fell out
> Who was left?'

Or:

> 'In Newcastle, a girl is told to say *soap*, and when she does so the others chorus, *Pull the rope*, suiting their actions to their words by pulling her hair' (20).

It is worth noticing that unless the prospective victim is willing to participate, the trick fails. The child's very eagerness to be socially acceptable, to join in with the others, lays him open to their designs upon him. It is of course true that often enough the victim takes it all in good part and may often quite sincerely join in the laugh against himself and even admire the cleverness of the trick that has been played upon him. It need hardly be added that he will immediately look around for another victim and that this is how a trick is handed on from generation to generation of children. So what is new in the experience of a particular child serves, through transmission, to promote the continuity of group life, maintaining in this way an uneasy equilibrium between established patterns of behaviour and the emergence of individuality.

It is to this emergence of individuality that we now turn. We have to consider the place of language in the two main aspects of personal development: a child's awareness of himself as he is and the growth of an 'ideal' picture of the person he may become.

LANGUAGE AND SELF-AWARENESS

Much that has already been said in this chapter implies that language plays an important part in the progressive emergence of clearer self-awareness out of the stresses of social life. It would be helpful if we could now survey specific and detailed systematic

SOCIAL AND ETHICAL DEVELOPMENT

observations of this development of individuality; but here, even more than for earlier childhood, we have to fall back upon incidental allusion and comment.

We have seen that from the beginning a child's awareness of himself has developed through his relations with others; that from birth he has been learning about himself from his daily physical—non-linguistic—experiences with people. When in infancy and early childhood language enters and becomes the medium of this social interchange, his awareness of himself is increasingly sharpened by the spoken word, heard and uttered. Now, in the present period, while his personality is influenced by his physical participation in the life of his group, it is linguistic interchange, particularly through the group language, which becomes the chief factor in this development. He continues to learn about himself from what others do to him and he does to them; but now he learns more, and more clearly, from what they say to him; from what he says to and about others and even from what he hears them say about each other. As a member of a group, in co-operation and competition; in verbal agreement or battle; suffering humiliation or scoring-off others, a child becomes aware of his own idiosyncratic traits and symbolises himself for himself. Language has now more than ever for him the special function that Mead ascribes to it: that it enables a person to become an object to himself (21).

It has long been a commonplace that self-awareness emerges from reciprocal relationships with others; what perhaps is not equally recognised is the part played in this by the special sub-language of a group. Our brief survey here would suggest that this is likely to foster a child's awareness of himself in a number of ways. Above all, it must constantly bring home to him the nature and strength of his own orectic attitudes. In the epithets applied by others to him he is made aware of the intensity of hostility or friendship in their attitudes towards him and so of their feelings about his attitudes towards them. *Tich*, for instance, is a more friendly nickname than *Little Squirt*. The child who is given the less friendly epithet is likely to feel that something about him has incurred the disapproval of others, and if he is perceptive enough may be led to recognise what this unacceptable trait is. Sometimes it will be brought sharply to his notice by being actually named by other children. If, for instance, in the stress of being teased he shows irritation, to be called *Spitfire* or *Pepperpot* or told *Keep your hair on!* will make him realise that others see him as unduly hasty and short-tempered. Again, when he himself uses an epithet to or about another child he will—more or less consciously—be comparing this child with others and so, to some extent, with himself. At the same time he may perhaps be made aware of his own attitude to this other child, as he sees how much support his epithet evokes in other members of the group; he will notice how far his approval or disapproval is group-sanctioned and therefore how far he is peculiar in this respect.

In the course of this constant comparison of himself with others he will become more clearly aware not only of his attitudes but of the forces that impel them and give coherence to them: his intentions (22). And as he becomes conscious of these intentions, it becomes more possible for him to direct his attitudes and his behaviour. His individuality takes on a character of its own.

Not only does all this help him to form a picture of his orectic and ethical characteristics, in very much the same way he is made aware of his skills and cognitive abilities. His intelligence is constantly being measured by judges who have no compunction in saying what they think and whose judgments are important to him: *You must be potty to do such a thing!* To have a remark of this kind made frequently to him must lead even a not very perceptive child to a judgment about himself.

While the growth of individuality owes so much to a child's membership if his contemporary group, it also owes something to his growing awareness of sex. The language which is linked with sex performs this important function: it adds to the concrete perceptible attibutes of sex a number of more abstract and conceptual characteristics which embody cultural attitudes. Thus from a very early age a child will, of course, have been aware not only of primary observable bodily differences but also of such culturally-determined differences as dress and length of hair. Now in this period of later childhood, the characteristic picture of each sex becomes richer by the accretion of more abstract features, many of them ethical; some sanctioned by elders, others by the contemporary group. Where there is conflict between these, it is the latter which are more likely to influence actual conduct.

From all this it is evident that the growth of a child's self-awareness during this period is largely the result of the changes that are taking place in his social life. There is the movement away from adults and towards contemporaries; with these, the enlargement of the social context—from interchange between individuals towards an intimate participation in group life; and a tendency for the growing consciousness of sex to be expressed in the segregation of groups of boys and girls.

The changes are gradual; but if we compare children of eleven or twelve with what they were five or six years since, we see marked differences in the impact of language upon their personal and social life. At the earlier stage, when a child is expressing approval or disapproval, he is experimenting with words of the mother tongue, whose meanings have the sanctions of adult usage; the interchange is largely between himself and another person—child or adult—as two individuals; and the epithets he uses become more discriminative as he becomes aware of the reactions evoked in this other person. Now, more and more, approval and disapproval are expressed within the context of the contemporary group. First, the epithets themselves are set patterns of the sub-language of the group; and secondly, their meanings become more discriminative for the child not simply from his awareness of the reactions of the individual to whom the epithet is applied, but in greater measure from the speaker's consciousness of the sanctions of the group of which he and the other child are both members. These sanctions are to some extent qualified by sex-differences in general behaviour and in language.

It is possible that in the growing importance of group-life for children we are today witnessing something of a change in human affairs. A number of recent developments combine to reinforce the tendency for children and adolescents to identify themselves with a group having a sub-culture and a sub-language of its own. The greater freedom which many societies now accord to their young, the acceleration of physical maturity, a readier command of money and other social resources—it is a commonplace that all these enhance the importance of his contemporary group in the life of a growing child. It is now more than thirty years since Piaget described the pattern of social life in later childhood as conforming to the 'principle of mutuality'. History has caught up with him; the principle has now an even greater descriptive validity than when he wrote. To what he said we are now able to add evidence of one of the chief means by which mutuality is promoted in a group of children: a sub-language. It is to be hoped that further studies of children's group-languages will show us even more strikingly how these, by deriving their sanctions from the children themselves, promote reciprocity in their behaviour with each other.

LANGUAGE AND THE GROWTH OF AN EGO-IDEAL

Looking finally at the formation of a child's picture of himself not only as he is, but as he may become, we see that language enters this in two ways: in the interchange of epithets and in the expression of principles of conduct.

(i) *Epithets*

Everything that contributes to a child's awareness of himself also leads him to form a picture of himself as he might be, an image of his 'ideal' self. Expressions of approval and disapproval that he hears and utters not only furnish criteria by which he may judge himself as he is; they also indicate goals towards which he may move. In particular, those epithets which come with the sanctions of his contemporary group must obviously be a powerful influence in this direction. This is true even of names for his characteristics as an individual—such as height, weight, strength, agility, intelligence; but the epithets that contribute most to the formation of an ideal image are those that name social conduct, ethical traits such as generosity, courage, loyalty—those traits in which a child is involved with other members of the group.

These epithets express group standards of conduct. By drawing attention to deviations from more or less clearly envisaged normality, they bring pressure to bear upon individual members to behave in ways conducive to living with others. Most of the time, no doubt, this pressure to conform is itself conventional rather than intentional; but occasionally it would seem to be quite deliberate. Certainly its influence upon the development of an ego-ideal is almost inescapable. Few children can resist the vigour of the epithets by which deviant behaviour is kept within bounds:

For greed and meanness: *greedy-guts*; *guzzler*; *mingy*; *stingy*
for failure to adapt oneself: *mardy*; *sulky-puss*; *sour-puss*; *peevy*; *shirty*
for disloyalty to one's peers:
   sucking up to elders: *creep-ass*; *grease-boy*
   sneaking: *snitch*; *blabber-mouth*
for appearing to steal a march in school work: *swotpot*
for considering oneself a cut above others: *swankpot*; *snobby* (23).

These are only a few from the copious collection made by the Opies and it is probable that there are many more that have not come their way. Expressing reproach more often than praise, they combine to present a picture of what, in the eyes of the group, an ideal fellow-member should be.

Throughout all this, it need hardly be said, a child's movement towards an ideal ego also remains powerfully influenced by criteria implied or expressed in the approval or disapproval of his elders. But almost everything in his life at this time goes to make these criteria less acceptable—at any rate, less openly acceptable—than the standards of the contemporary group. The need to live with his fellows, the fact that the sub-language is more concrete, more closely related to everyday life, more in harmony with the relative crudity and immaturity of the child's own attitudes—these combine to make the standards of the group more immediately powerful than the more abstract, more general, more remote ethical attitudes of his elders.

The complexity of children's responses, in acceptance or resistance, to all these ethical influences, from contemporaries on the one hand and from elders on the other, is reflected in the inconstancy and uncertainty of their development towards relatively stable patterns of ideal conduct.

For one very important result of the interchange of epithets is this: that as the child sees himself and others, now in this role now in that, he is gradually helped to recognise the network of relationships that constitute ethical behaviour (24). Regularities of conduct, approved by the group emerge; followed though not always formulated. But when they are symbolised in words, what forms do they take?

(ii) *The symbolisation of rules of conduct*

An ancient and commonplace principle of ethics is that the chief agent in the development of a child's ego-ideal must be his adoption of or resistance to parental precepts: the formulation by his elders of rules of conduct. No doubt Freud is right in saying that throughout a child's ethical growth he hears 'the voice of his father'. No doubt the precepts uttered by the parental voice have an ultimate influence upon his ego-ideal when he himself reaches adult life. But in the meantime, in later childhood and early adolescence, the effects of these parental precepts are largely latent rather than immediately operative. It is not simply that there is a gap between precept and practice, as there is for all of us throughout life. It is rather that parental precepts, though known to the child, are barely experienced; that though they make a cognitive impact upon him they are not taken up into his orectic and ethical concerns.

When Piaget turned from children's games to the conduct of their everyday lives, he was struck by the apparent paradox that a child may accurately repeat adult precepts—though these may have little or no relevance to his actual behaviour towards others—and yet at the same time be hardly aware of the principles of conduct by which he really lives (25). This is partly because much of his behaviour is governed by unformulated custom rather than law; partly because precepts are abstract generalisations, the force of which can barely be recognised by a child who is still at the stage of concrete thinking.

Piaget saw that it was very unlikely that the regularities of children's conduct could be entirely uninfluenced by language, but he could find no evidence of this other than the epithets they use to describe each other's behaviour (26). Since then, the observation of children's sub-languages has reminded us that there is a remarkable and highly specific means by which principles of their conduct are in fact symbolised; something which is transitional between the mere regularity of habit and the formulation of precepts; gnomic sayings, often in rhyme.

> Ask no questions
> And you'll be told no lies
> Shut your mouth
> And you will catch no flies.

> Mind your own business
> Fry your own fish
> Don't poke your nose
> Into my clean dish.

'One who blabs to a teacher or a senior is a "blabber-mouth"... Young children, in particular, will hound him (as we have witnessed) until he is almost pulp, a quivering sobbing heap having to bear the double agony of blows and reiterated refrain:

> Tell-tale tit
> Your tongue shall be slit
> And all the dogs in the town
> Shall have a little bit' (27).

These gnomic utterances have a warmth and an immediacy lacking in adult precepts, and a greater authority for the conduct that matters so much at this time—behaviour within the group. They are felt to arise and exist in the life of the group itself, not coming from above. A child who repeats an adult precept to other children runs the risk of being thought a prig, disloyal to the ethos of the group. In contrast with this, the gnomic saying commands approval because it expresses and demands allegiance to group ethics. In this way it becomes a main instrument in the development of 'mutuality' in children's conduct, for while acting as a means of co-ordinating their behaviour, it gives each child the experience of the force of common assent.

It is significant that the codes of conduct expressed in gnomic rhymes are not always in line with adult morality. Where, as in the case of sneaking, there is a conflict of loyalties, the group often demands and receives the primacy of loyalty to itself. And even when group morality is in direct opposition to adult ethics, then the code of the group may prevail:

'When we find anything,' declares an eleven-year-old, 'we say

> Finding's keepings
> Giving back's stealing.

'Every time we find anything we never give it back.' (28)

THE PLACE OF CHILDREN'S GROUPS IN THEIR ETHICAL DEVELOPMENT

But if group codes are at variance with adult codes, this does not mean that growth in later childhood is an aberration from the line of development that ultimately leads to a pattern of ideal adult conduct—an adult ego-ideal. On the contrary, unless a child is caught up and engaged in group-life with other children, his ethical development towards adulthood may suffer.

The road of this development leads from the regularities of home life, under adult authority and guidance, to the problems and formulated principles in membership of adult society. In later childhood and adolescence there would appear to be a deviation from this road to a mode of social life that strives to free itself from adult influences. But this apparent deviation is in fact a means by which a child may learn to live with those who are to be his fellows in adult life. It becomes the main task of ethical education to ensure that the social behaviour and experience of this prolonged period prepare the adolescent to meet the demands of adult life. In an industrialised society such as ours the one instrument deliberately devised to effect this transition is the school; the nature—and the shortcomings—of which are clarified for us by the contrast now so often made with the practice of simpler, more 'primitive' communities. In these, children are from an early age brought into active participation in adult life; we interpose a period of schooling, whose chief function is to wean the child from his home life and prepare him for adult living. The school attempts this by bringing him into a society made up of children and adults, organised and conducted by the adults for the benefit of the children. It continues to shelter and govern him while hoping to prepare him for the unsheltered responsibilities of adulthood. It attempts to equip him for the future by giving him practice in manipulating the instruments of adult life. With intentions preparatory rather than immediate, it tends to offer the child experiences that are vicarious—that is, symbolised—rather than direct.

Much of this would seem to be in opposition to the life of a child in his own contemporary group. Here his experiences instead of vicarious are direct; instead of preparatory, concerned immediately with his life here and now. But these experiences should be recognised as complementary rather than opposed to those of the school. For his group life with other children does some things for a child that the school can hardly do so well: presents him with codes of conduct which are brought to the test again and again in the daily intercourse of living, and brings him into the stresses of an unsheltered social life, in which he must often need to exercise personal responsibility.

Today we are only too clearly aware of the distractions in the growth of healthy personality that may result from these strains. We recognise that as a child moves into adolescence and asserts his independence through crudities of conduct and behaviour—amoral or even immoral by the ethical criteria of the adult society—it becomes increasingly the task of this society to harness the energy and independence of the incipient young man or woman to meet the problems that lie ahead.

Already in later childhood something may be achieved by recognising that the children's own group and the school, as disparate societies, have each a language with specific forms and functions appropriate to its way of life.

The language of the group is relatively simple in structure, with meanings concrete rather than abstract. Its structure has the syntactic characteristics of an oral language—simple sentences unvaried in form. This structure and its vocabulary are adapted for the purposes of communication within a limited group; the grounds on which adults commonly condemn the use of slang, that it limits the size of the community within which it has currency, constitute its special value for children in their groups. For the ethical problems of a child's daily life with other children, the group language provides ready-made solutions. A frequently recurring situation can be dealt with by making the appropriate ritual utterance and performing the ritual act. In a more equivocal situation the authority of a general principle can be invoked, not by enunciating a precept but by chanting a gnomic rhyme.

In contrast with all this, the language of the school is relatively complex in structure and abstract in meanings. Learning to read and write not only initiates the child into a language which has a structure and vocabulary of its own; it also influences those of his spoken language. Together, the spoken and the written language constitute a system for the symbolisation of abstract thinking; a system which serves not only the child's cognitive development but equally his social and ethical development. The linguistic education of the school sets out to provide him with an instrument of self-awareness and with a means of communication within a community as wide as the whole adult society, embracing the past as well as the present. Here lies the valid justification for the adult objection to slang: it may limit and inhibit the child's linguistic growth. If the linguistic education of the school succeeds in its task it will furnish the growing child with a medium for highly-generalised formulations of conduct, for deliberation and for the discussion of personal and social problems in the light of the formulated principles.

The task of the teacher, though fraught with difficulty and demanding great skill, is plain. He must remember that a child's language is an intricate pattern of habits, deeply rooted in his personal history and permeating every movement of his daily life. The linguistic education of the school is to be thought of least of all as 'an eradication of bad habits to make way for good ones'. Not much more valid is the notion of a child's own language as a building which can be partly demolished, then rebuilt and enlarged on the lines of a blue-print devised by experts in the architectonics of education.

If our survey of children's development here has shown anything, it is surely this: that at every successive moment the linguistic education of a child is a transformation of existing patterns of action. The schemata of his past are alive and active in the present. The child comes into the classroom an individual created by his home and by his life beyond his home, in the course of communication with his elders and his contemporaries. Interwoven in his individuality is the language of the home, the street and the playground. It is only by taking full cognizance of this basic language that the teacher can help the child to transform and extend its scope and power so that it will meet the needs of his coming adolescence and beyond this to his life as a fully adult person.

Notes

CHAPTER ONE

1. McCarthy in Carmichael 1954, 505 cites some evidence of vocalisation by a fœtus of five months.
2. There is some fœtal response to sounds, but the doubt is whether this is auditory or to tactual stimuli. Carmichael 1954, 154, and Pratt in Carmichael 1954, 235–40.
3. On the soothing effect of the human voice in the first week Ribble 1944, 632 gives evidence from the study of 600 infants. On the response of young birds: 'Following is usually elicited by auditory stimuli from the parents, such as the clucking of a broody hen. Although the auditory factors may be more effective than the visual ones, the auditory responsiveness is little more specific than the visual. Thus Collias and Joos found that repeated tapping on a table top would attract young ducks, and Ramsay's experiments suggest that the response of some ducklings to the calls of their parents is even less specific than this.' Thorpe and Zangwill 1961, 177.
4. Evidence summarised by McCarthy in Carmichael 1954, 584–6. The observations of Ribble 1944 are particularly notable, as also the detailed survey by Brodbeck and Irwin 1946, and by Gesell and Amatruda 1947. O'Connor 1956 emphasises the exceptions to this generalisation.
5. In attempting to record the sounds as they appear, at best one can make approximations to the sounds of adult speech. These are, however, sufficient for the important purpose of recognising the physiological formation of each sound-pattern as this is related to its function for the child. A closer analysis is attempted in Lewis 1951, Chapter III. The symbols used there, and here, may be interpreted broadly according to the following approximations:

a	French la	l	S. Eng. feel
ɑ	S. Eng. father	ŋ	S. Eng. thing
e	S. Eng. pen	h	S. Eng. horse
ɛ	French père	g	the voiced form of x
æ	S. Eng. man	x	Ger. doch
o	French pause	g	S. Eng. good
u	S. Eng. look	k	S. Eng. could
w	S. Eng. will	r	N. Eng. borrow

For front consonants, conventional letters. The 'dentals' t, d, n, are, more accurately, alveolar or gum-ridge sounds.

Detailed surveys of the order of occurrence of early sounds are summarised by McCarthy in Carmichael 1954, 509, particularly from the work of Irwin and Fisichelli, who find that back consonants predominate at first. She warns, however, against accepting this as completely valid. There is good evidence that w and l occur very early as discomfort-sounds; Lewis 1951, 24 onwards.

6. Darwin 1873, 151. A fuller discussion is in Lewis 1951, 27. The subsequent close study of numerous children has confirmed the accuracy of Darwin's observations. 'Vocal sounds are at first a component of mass activity. It is an interesting fact that the newborn infant utters very few non-crying sounds.... When the infant awakens before the feeding period and the time for it comes closer, the infant rolls the head, the mouth is opened in a wide rectangular manner, the body twists and jerks, bends, is thrown about, and the legs and arms kick and slash. Accompanying this mass activity there is much violent crying.' Irwin in Barker 1943.

7. Hebb 1949, 198 attempts an account of this learning process in the course of his consideration of the nature of learning. He suggests: (1) Hunger contractions result in restlessness in the infant; (2) 'the moving mouth is likely to make contact with the nipple'; (3) 'reflex sucking follows.' From this one can see how, in time, the infant may pass directly from (1) to (3); i.e., sucking-movements occur during hunger-contractions. If, then, these contractions are also expressed in a shrill cry, we get a cry interspersed with sucking-movements. Ribble 1944, 637–8

shows that normally the tendency to suck is reinforced; 'Fifty per cent of the children had to have considerable assistance from the nurse or mother in order to get vigorous sucking activity established.... If their primary sucking was not made easy or satisfying, their sucking activities gradually diminished, and they became either stuporous or resistive.... I am thoroughly convinced that a favourable sucking experience contributes considerably to the development of several aspects of structure and behaviour. The evidence indicates that sucking experience is important ... for the age at which speech appears and for the facility of the speech function.'

8. It would be reasonable to regard this perseveration as self-rewarding; i.e., the sucking-movements which gave satisfaction during feeding would when repeated give some pleasure in themselves.

9. *m* is the nasalised form of *b*; *n* of *d*. The nasal and pharyngeal structure and functioning of some infants may tend to give a nasal quality to many of their sound-patterns.

10. It is generally accepted that play with fingers and toes may occur within the first three months (Gesell and Amatruda 1947, 39). The recognition that vocal play may also occur as early as this has been slower: comfort-sounds at this time have been regarded either as 'aimless' and 'fortuitous' or as expressive of comfort. Even Stern, a pioneer in the study of children's language, uses *Lallen* to signify indiscriminately 'babbling' and 'expression' in states of comfort. Stern 1928, 153.

11. McDougall 1931. It has, of course, long been recognised that many other animals play; there now seems to be evidence of vocal play in birds. Thorpe in a study of chaffinches speaks of their 'sub-song, a somewhat irregular and indefinite vocal performance with no communicatory function, particularly characteristic of the early spring performance of first-year birds.' Thorpe and Zangwill, 1961.

12. Alexander 1933, 38.

13. Jesperson 1922, 106 Latif 1934.

14. There is evidence that chaffinches learn to imitate the song they hear in early life. The similarity with human growth is striking. Thorpe and Zangwill 1961, 212:

'Experiments on the song learning of the chaffinch serve to demonstrate the existence of an inborn ability to produce songs of the right duration (approximately two-and-a-half seconds). There must probably also be an inborn recognition of the tonal quality of the chaffinch's voice as providing an appropriate model for the imitative learning of the song and also almost certainly an inborn tendency to sing the song at intervals of from ten to twenty seconds. Beyond this it seems as if in the chaffinch almost all is learnt; although the readiness with which the bird learns, as the result of experience, to divide its song into three more or less well-defined sections, and still further the readiness with which it learns a simple flourish as appropriate to the termination of a song, suggests that there may be a very imperfectly inherited tendency to respond to and perform these features of the normal song—a tendency so slightly developed that it can never issue in action without the stimulus provided by the singing of another member of the species. The limitations of this blueprint of the song are shown by experiments in which previously isolated inexperienced birds are kept together during the song-learning period, but still out of earshot of experienced birds. When this is done these "Kaspar Hauser" birds will stimulate one another to sing songs of increasing elaboration, but the fine details of the song thus acquired may show little or no resemblance to the fine details of the normal performance of the species. But the songs of such isolated groups of naive birds do show a slight tendency to be broken up into two or three phases, although there is no evidence of any ability to produce a terminal flourish.'

15. Lewis 1951 Chapter VI for a detailed discussion.
16. Lewis 1951, 74, 279 for a discussion of Valentine's observations.
17. From this point onwards, children's speech is in conventional spelling. For a closer rendering see Lewis 1951. Recent work by Malrieu 1962, 140 gives more instances of children (in third and fourth months) 'imitating' by producing their own sounds.
18. McCarthy in Carmichael 1954, 584–6 for a general survey; for some effects of remedial treatment, O'Connor 1956; Lyle 1959, 1960.

CHAPTER TWO

1. For a detailed study of this development, Lewis 1951, Chapters IV and VII.
2. Lewis 1951, 40, 52. The view that the child's discriminative responses are not primary, but entirely due to learning, is expressed by Young 1947, 207 quoting Major 1906: 'If a child were accustomed to hearing soft words and being beaten at the same time, such words would come to arouse fear and trembling. If, on the other hand, gentle and caressing treatment were associated in the experience of the child with harsh sounds, the latter would soon come to be soothing and quieting.'
3. A detailed discussion of the child's response to the intonational characters of others' speech is in Lewis 1951, 112–16.
4. Pavlov 1927, 407. As is pointed out in Lewis 1951, Chapter VII, one of the main sources of the subsequent development of meaning is that, at first, heard speech evokes a physical act from the child. Malrieu 1962, 158 emphasises that it is 'un rôle que l'enfant est appelé a jouer.'
5. Lewis 1951, 340–2. Sherif 1958, 55 gives this instance: 'A year-old child, Cindy, used *mama* to designate anyone who waited on or cared for her; even her three-year-old brother and her five-year-old sister were called *mama*.'
6. This is discussed in detail in Lewis 1951, Chapter VIII.
7. Lewis 1951, 285 lists the first six words of twenty-six children— German, French or Danish—as given by Stern 1928, 172. Of these twenty-six children, six said *wow-wow*, or the like, with some reference to a dog, as one of the earliest half-dozen words.
8. Lewis 1951, 285–7.
9. 'Orexis: the conative and affective aspects of experience— impulse, attitude, desire, emotion.' Drever J., Dict. of Psychology 1952.
10. Simon 1957, 198; also Luria 1961, 10.
11. Meumann 1902, 156: 'Die ersten Wortbedeutungen des Kindes sind ausschliesslich emotioneller oder volitionaler Natur.'
12. From Lewis 1951, 340–3, and the discussion as listed there in the Index under *mama*.

13. A great deal of recent work has been devoted to the part played by 'symbolic mediation' in perception and therefore in thinking. Thus Morris 1946, 355 in a fundamental discussion of the relations between signs, language and behaviour defines a symbol as 'A sign that is produced by its interpreter and that acts as a substitute for some other sign with which it is synonymous: all signs not symbols are signals. Symbols may be *pre-language*, *language* and *post-language* symbols.' And Hallowell in Rohrer and Sherif 1951, 169 speaks of 'the ubiquitous role which symbolic mediation plays in building up a meaningful world in our species. . . . Human social life at its very root is functionally dependent upon the role which the symbolic representation of objects, events and relationships plays in establishing a novel kind of behavioural environment which transcends the more simply perceived world of the lower animals.' This is the 'mediating response' of Osgood 1953; all this work owes much to the influence of Mead 1934.
14. As, for instance, in Piaget 1953, Chapter I.
15. Bartlett 1932, 206; and in the critical discussion by Oldfield and Zangwill 1942. For Osgood 1953, 627 a schema is a 'mediating reaction' by which a person is 'set' by his past experiences to behave in a particular way in a given situation.
16. Price 1953, 277. 'A concept is a recognitional capacity which manifests itself also in absence.' He adds: 'In thinking, concepts are brought to mind . . . by such particulars as words, images, gestures, dumb-show, diagrams'; but 'a concept can be "had in mind" . . . when the corresponding symbol is not present' (254, 316).
17. Blanshard 1957, 63; Stout 1896, II, 174; Stout 1949, 540.
18. The full record and a detailed discussion is in Lewis 1951, Chapters VII, XI, XII.

CHAPTER THREE

1. For a fuller discussion of this see Lewis 1951, Chapter X.
2. Bartlett 1932, 201. For Brain 1961, 58 the hypothesis of schemata is fundamental in explaining the facts of speech. He postulates, among others, 'phonemic schemata'.

3. A summary of transformations in the speech of some English, French and German children is in Lewis 1952, Appendix III. Some striking instances of a child's assimilations of adult speech to his own forms are given by Cohen 1952, 223. At 1;8, *etati mama* for *elle est partie, maman* and *i po pa pape* for *je ne peux pas tomber*—two quite characteristic patterns of baby-language.
4. For a list of some of these observers see Lewis 1951, 189.
5. Romanes 1888, 283 says that he was told this by Darwin.
6. Chamberlain 1904, 265-6.
7. Lewis 1951, 192, 339.
8. Lewis 1951, 194-209. Osgood 1953, 361 discusses the nature of similarity as the basis of generalisation. The trend of his argument leads to the conclusion that the 'concept of similarity is meaningful only in terms of the behaviour of organisms.'
9. Lewis 1951, 352-3.
10. Keller 1904, 312
11. Even Stern appears to have committed himself to this view in his often-quoted remark that at a given moment (for his own three children in the middle of the second year) a child suddenly realises that everything has a name. We discuss this later in relation to children's 'naming-questions', Chapter 5, page 90.

CHAPTER FOUR

1. Lewis 1951, 192, 197, 206, 349-51.
2. Ames 1952, 207.
3. *ibid.* 207, 205, 206.
4. *ibid.* 206.
5. *ibid.* 201.
6. Ewing 1957, 326.
7. Kendall in Ewing 1957, 62; and many other observers.
8. Skeels and Dye 1939; Skeels and Harms 1948.
9. Bender 1953.
10. Moore 1947.
11. Harms and Spiker 1959. Four groups of children, mean ages 1;5, 1;9, 2;1, 2;8; twenty in each group. Speech 'recorded by trained observers'; tests—Kuhlmann and Cattell Scales. At the

youngest age-level, 'the correlation between intelligence and speech-sound production appears to be negligible (or slightly negative). For the three older age-levels, the relationship is positive and fairly high.'
12. Among others, Bowlby 1951, Clarke 1958, Goldfarb 1945, Lyle 1959, O'Connor 1956, Skeels and Dye 1939.

CHAPTER FIVE

1. Brain 1961, 3 takes reference to the absent to be the essential attribute of a symbol as distinct from a sign. Speaking of the cries of non-human animals, he says, 'They are never symbols; that is, they have no power to represent things in their absence.'
2. Lewis 1951, 234.
3. Halbwachs 1925, 377. 'Nous parlons nos souvenirs avant de les évoquer; c'est le langage, et c'est tout le système des conventions sociales qui en sont solidaires, qui nous permet à chaque instant de reconstruire notre passé.'
4. Isaacs in Appendix to Isaacs 1930, 294.
5. The details are: 94 per cent of the questions concerned the immediate situation; 46 per cent referred to human actions or relationships; 20 per cent were naming-questions. (Smith 1933, 201). Davis 1932, analysing 3650 questions of seventy-three children between 3;0 and 12;0 found that 88 per cent concerned the immediate situation.
6. Stern 1924, 162 and (a fuller account) 1922, 176. Among others, Vigotsky 1962 and Wallon 1924 have criticised Stern's view that a child in his second year arrives at a generalisation as to the naming-function of words. Wallon's paper is an excellent account of the basic affective, functional, imitative and social factors in the development of questioning.
7. For the full record see Lewis 1951, 365. Here no attempt has been made to render the child's pronunciation.
8. This function of self-addressed questions became clear to me from my own observations, first published in 1937 (Lewis 1951, 254), where I suggest that this is an important aspect of Piaget's 'egocentric' language. Vigotsky 1939, 39 emphasises the same

point in his criticism of Piaget; Luria, following him, calls language of this kind 'synpractic'; Luria and Yudovich 1959, 19; Luria 1961.
9. Piaget 1955, 360.

CHAPTER SIX

1. Vigotsky 1939, 39 and 1962, 6. He shows that egocentric speech is social in origin, growing out of communication, and that it helps the child to direct his behaviour; this is endorsed by the observations we have discussed in Chapter 5. In answer to Vigotsky's criticisms, Piaget has gone some way to meet him by agreeing that egocentric speech may be a point of departure for inner speech which may serve logical thinking. Piaget 1962, 7.
2. Luria and Yudovich 1959.
3. Ewing 1957, 47, 321.
4. Templin 1957, 134.
5. McCarthy in Carmichael 1954 brings this out very clearly in her review of studies of vocabulary.
6. Templin op. cit., 141.
7. Pestalozzi 1801, 98.
8. Summarised by Herrick in Eells 1951, Chapter II.
9. Jones in Carmichael 1954, 648.
10. *ibid*. 647.
11. Skeels and Harms 1948; Skeels and Dye 1939; Kirk 1958; Goldfarb 1945.
12. Herrick in Eells 1951, 14. Some verbal items may be more favourable to the lower socio-economic levels.
13. Kendall 1953, also Drever and Collins 1928; Hood 1949; Gaskill, L. G. Murphy, K. P. Murphy, summarised in Ewing 1957; Oléron 1957.
14. Emmett 1949.
15. Ananiev in Simon 1957, 137.
16. For positive correlations between linguistic and motor skills, Goodenough 1930; Eisonson in Cruickshank 1955, 197; for the effects of verbal instruction, Goodenough and Brian 1929; Simon 1957, 113—work of I. S. Dimanstein.

17. Many investigations point to this conclusion. One by Welch and Long 1940, with about one hundred children from four to seven, compared their ability to identify things with their ability to classify them: 'In some instances children can manipulate material which they cannot adequately identify; and vice-versa.'

CHAPTER SEVEN

1. Pyles 1932. As time goes on, children are less concerned with names for objects and more with the naming of relationships. A number of investigators have measured the decline of mere naming in children's spontaneous conversation. Broadly, it decreases from about 50 per cent of vocabulary at one-and-a-half years to about 10 per cent at four-and-a-half and about 7 per cent at nine-and-a-half years. McCarthy in Carmichael 1954, 571.
2. Weir and Stevenson 1959. Smith and Goss 1955 demonstrated the advantages for children four-and-a-half to five-and-a-half of using names in discriminating squares of different sizes.
3. Kuenne 1946. The repetition of Kuenne's experiments by Alberts and Ehrenfreund 1951 confirms her conclusions, but is not altogether reliable because of the somewhat crude design of their experiments. Wohlwill 1960 investigating the development of number concepts in children from four to seven concludes that 'the mastery of verbal labels designating the numbers plays a prominent role.'
4. Oléron 1957.
5. Piaget 1953. The difficulties of interpreting Piaget's work are well known. His ideas and terminology are novel and he is not always well served by his translators. We discuss 'concrete', 'conservation' and 'reversibility' more fully when we come to consider later childhood; see Chapter 9 and notes 2 and 3; and Chapter 10 and notes 1 and 2.
6. Isaacs 1960, 35: 'The chronological linkages [in Piaget's account] are no more than an approximate method of marking out the *sequence* of the distinguishable phases of growth, the order in which they follow one another.'

NOTES: CHAPTER 7, PAGES 122–132   239

7. Simon 1957, 220.
8. Luria in Simon 1957, 117–20; Zaporozhets, op. cit., 113; see also page 116 and Chapter 6, note 16.
9. Bartlett 1958, 85.
10. Bartlett 1932, 205; Oldfield and Zangwill 1942, 148; see also Chapter 5.
11. Hildreth 1944.
12. Bussmann 1946.
13. A typical problem consisted in having a sweet attached to the wall at a height of six feet, with tables, chairs and wooden rods lying about in the room, and indicating to the child that the sweet was his if he could reach it. The words of Chulliat and Oléron are: 'Le langage permet d'organiser l'expérience et de fixer les schèmes qui ont été mis en oeuvre. . . .Une autre fonction du langage est de permettre les "éxperiences mentales".' Chulliat and Oléron 1955, 303. Pintner and Paterson 1917 found that in the immediate recall of visually presented digits, deaf children over seven were considerably retarded in comparison with hearing children.
14. Ewing 1957, 321.
15. Bryan 1934, 52.
16. A systematic study by Guanella 1934 confirms the common observation that this is a normal feature of solitary play by the beginning of the third year.
17. Nunn 1945, Chapter VII, in his illuminating expansion of the theses of Pestalozzi, Froebel and Groos; Griffiths 1935; Isaacs 1930, 104.
18. Goodenough and Brian 1929.
19. Carey and Goss 1957. The evidence is conflicting, partly because of the difficulty of determining how far a pattern of sounds is a 'nonsense-word' for the child: Smith and Goss 1955 and Spiker and Terrell 1955.
20. Nielsen 1951.
21. Luria and Yudovich 1959.
22. McCarthy in Carmichael 1954, 572
23. In Isaacs 1930, 332.
24. McCarthy in Carmichael 1954, 581.
25. In Isaacs 1930, 328.

CHAPTER EIGHT

1. Allport 1949, 48.
2. Freud, as he himself tells us, changed his views from time to time. To obtain a coherent account of his picture of human development, one has to piece together statements from the wide diversity of his writings. A convenient way is to follow the epitome by Rickman 1937; the references here are to pages 255, 136, 266, 231. Freud varied his terminology; 'ego-ideal' and 'super-ego' are synonymous—Rickman 259.

   Freud's profound insight into the nature and functions of language is first shown in his study of aphasia, 1891—a work almost forgotten until re-issued in an English translation by E. Stengel in 1953. In this Freud recognised, almost alone in his time, the importance of the work of Hughlings Jackson which, says Stengel, 'had a decisive influence on Freud's thinking.' Since Jackson, through Head and Bartlett, has also had a decisive influence on psychology in Great Britain, he stands at the source of two major contributions to our understanding of the place of language in human behaviour.
3. E.g., Peel 1959. A study of the replies of thirty children, from about eight to fifteen, to questions on moral issues, endorses Piaget's account of the last three stages. In a survey of relevant work, Johnson 1962 reports general agreement with Piaget's stages, though not with his explanations.
4. 'There is in the very functioning of sensori-motor operations a search for coherence and organisation.... How then will the mind extract norms in the true sense from this functional equilibrium? It will form structures by means of an adequate conscious realisation.... Social life is necessary if the individual is to become conscious of the functioning of his mind and thus to transform into norms properly so called the simple functional equilibria immanent to all mental and even all vital activity.' Piaget 1932, 406–7.
5. Bossard 1948, Chapter VIII and page 177; Bernstein 1958, 1960, and in Halsey, Floud and Anderson 1961.
6. Isaacs 1933, 260, 276, 387–8.
7. *ibid*, 395.

8. *ibid*, 390, 392, 425. Mead 1934, 138.
9. Isaacs, 1933, 33.
10. *ibid*, 93, 103, 105, 107, 108.
11. Many observations of this, e.g., Bridges 1931, 85.
12. Isaacs 1933, 105, 97, 98, 94, 109.
13. *ibid*, 42, 48, 44, 42, 43, 66, 70.
14. *ibid*, 36, 43, 38, 44, 66, 44, 46, 57, 52.
15. *ibid*, 73, 74, 77, 79, 80, 83, 88; 247 onwards.
16. Ames 1952, 212; Isaacs 1933, 36, 35, 35, 38, 36.
17. Isaacs 1933, 31, 67; Ames 1952, 218, 222; Isaacs 139.
18. Ames 223; Isaacs 172, 183, 176, 182.
19. Isaacs 1933, 172, 182, 184, 180, 180.
20. 'Il y a souvent, comme dit Stern, "convergence" entre le langage des parents et le style enfantin, c'est à dire que les parents emploient d'instinct des expressions faciles, concrètes, et mêmes animistes ou anthropomorphiques pour se mettre au niveau de l'enfant.' Piaget 1923, 130.
21. Ames and Learned 1946.
22. Isaacs 1933, 313.
23. Minski 1957, 16; Ewing 1957, 326; Bradway 1937; Pintner, Eisonson, Stanton 1941, 164–5; 199–200; Burchard and Myklebust 1942. Kendall 1953, 395 finds that deaf children, in their social as well as in their intellectual development, are comparatively retarded in ability to deal with a novel situation and tend to rely upon others to help them in this. Chulliat and Oléron 1955, 305, in their investigation with deaf children over the age of five, conclude that poverty of language retards their development in disengaging themselves from a situation and se seeing themselves objectively.
24. Heider and Heider 1941, 23.
25. Kendall 1953, 388.
26. Levine 1956, 141.
27. Getz 1953, 67.
28. The problem is summarised in Masland, Sarason, Gladwin 1958, 374–6.
29. Pringle and Tanner 1958.
30. Goldfarb 1945.
31. Haggerty 1959.

CHAPTER NINE

1. Jones, reviewing the work of Bayley, draws attention to the successive changes in the influence of parents' educational level upon the measured 'intelligence' of their children. In the first year the correlation is negative; then parental influence is manifested in a rapidly increasing positive correlation up to the age of about four. Thereafter, with the growing assertion of the child's individual characteristics combined with the effects of school and other influences beyond the home, the increase in the correlation slows down, and after the age of about seven remains stationary. Jones in Carmichael 1954, 646.
2. Piaget 1932, Chapters I, III.
3. Piaget's term 'concrete' is liable to misinterpretation. Thus Peel says, 'Concrete operations have a particular restriction in that they are carried out by children only with reference to objects and materials which are visibly and tangibly present' (Peel 1960, 82). But on page 72 of his book he cites children's answers to questions about Alfred the Great as 'answers at a concrete level'.
4. Davis 1937a, 134 finds that up to the middle of the tenth year, the superiority of girls in almost all aspects remains; the boys, however, being more spontaneous and asking more questions. That these differences are influenced by environment is shown by their decrease as the children grow older; by Templin's evidence that the differences are smaller than twenty-five years ago because of the decreasing differentiation in the upbringing of the sexes (page 109 above); and by Davis's evidence (supported by McCarthy, in Carmichael 1954, 579) that linguistic sex-differences are more marked in the lower socio-economic levels —for it is here that the approximation in upbringing is least likely to occur.
5. Templin 1957, 134; see Chapter 6 above.
6. Bernstein's fundamental principle is this: 'Receptivity to a particular form of language structure determines the way relationships to objects are made and an orientation to a particular manipulation of words.' From this he goes on to show that a

'working-class' child acquires 'a language where the stress is on emotive terms employing concrete, descriptive, tangible and visual symbolism. The nature of the language tends to limit the verbal expression of feeling.' A 'middle-class' child acquires, by contrast, a language which symbolises 'an ordered rational structure.... A value is placed upon the verbalisation of feeling.' At school the middle-class child is better fitted to enter into the modes of thought and language current among educated people. Bernstein 1958; see Chapter 8 above.

7. For a survey of resistance of this kind, Lewis 1953, Chapter VII.
8. Opie and Opie 1959.
9. *ibid*, 107–9.
10. Bartlett 1932, particularly Chapter X.
11. Opie op. cit., 22; 80, 81. Many teachers recognise that children's enjoyment of parody and nonsense-rhymes may be a step towards creative writing.

CHAPTER TEN

1. Piaget 1953, 8. Lovell and Ogilvie 1961 find themselves 'at variance with Piaget on this point.' In studies of the conservation of substance and of weight by junior-school children they found that many children 'capable of reversibility' were not yet at the stage of conservation: these children were able 'to return in thought to the initial situation after various spatial transformations'. But isn't there ambiguity in the use of the word 'reversibility'? A child might be able to *revert* in thought to the previous appearance of the two containers, and yet when confronted with the new situation he might still be incapable of performing a *reversible* operation, as this term is used in physics and mathematics and intended by Piaget. The actual process consists of establishing 'equilibrium': 'It is this equilibrium between assimilation and accommodation that seems to explain to us the functioning of the reversible operations.... Reversibility is a logical idea, while equilibrium is a causal idea.' Piaget 1961, 279.
2. Piaget 1947, 175. 'Les "groupements" demeurent relatifs aux types de notions concrètes (c'est-à-dire d'actions mentalisées) qu'ils ont effectivement structurées.'

3. Lunzer 1960.
4. Thus Peel 1960, on Piaget's work, confines his references to language entirely to the stages before and after the period of later childhood.
5. Piaget 1947, 195. 'Il est, en effet, bien difficule de comprendre comment l'individu parviendrait à grouper de manière précise ses opérations, et par consêquent transformer ses représentations intuitives en opérations transitives, réversibles, identiques et associatives, sans l'échange de pensée.'
6. Piaget 1947, 190: 'Mais il va de soi que, à cette collection, l'enfant commence par emprunter ce que lui convient, en ignorant superbement tout ce qui dépasse son niveau mental.' The English translation (Piaget 1950, 159) gives 'disdainfully ignorant' for 'superbement ignorant'. The quotation from Lunzer is in L, 1960, 4);
7. Peel 1960.
8. See Chapter 6 above. Vigotsky 1939, 39 and 1962, 6. Luria in Simon 1957, 120; and again in Luria 1961. Cofer 1957.
9. Galperin in Simon 1957, 217.
10. Ascoli 1950. 'D'une façon plus générale nous avons constaté que lorsqu'il s'agit d'objets qui ne sont pas caractéristiques par leur forme ou leur couleur mais par une propriété que l'enfant n'est pas en mesure d'apprécier (par l'usage par exemple comme dans la question, "Dis-moi quelque chose de semblable à une robe") l'enfant indique bien un autre objet semblable par l'usage, mais il justifie son choix par des réponses qui font appel à d'autres qualités qu'il connaît mieux, telles la forme ou la couleur. Il y a un décalage net entre la possibilité d'évoquer un objet semblable par l'usage et la capacité d'éxprimer cette similitude.'
'Voici des pourcentages qui expriment ce décalage:
A: pourcentage choix guidés par l'usage,
B: choix guidé et justifié par l'usage.

Age	5.0	6.0	7.0	8.0	9.0	10.0
A	34	50	90	85	100	100
B	0	5	22	30	20	60

11. Churchill 1958, II 33, 42; Hood 1962, 53, 280–1.
12. Page 103 above. Neilsen 1951, in a study of the development of sociability in children, points out that a child cannot benefit from the attempts of others to solve a problem until 'le problème en question lui est devenu actuel.' Page 127 above.
13. Lovell and Ogilvie 1960. In the ball and sausage test the child sees a piece of Plasticene divided in halves and each rolled into a ball, one of which is then drawn out as a 'sausage'.
14. Mead 1934; see page 141 above.
15. For Shipinova and Surina and Pyles see pages 36 and 118 above. Weir and Stevenson 1959; see page 119 above.
16. For adults, Mowrer 1960, 241: In classifying blocks 'the subject applies certain verbal terms to the blocks and then makes the classification on the basis of *their* similarity.' For deaf children, Vincent 1957. For imbecile children, Hermelin and O'Connor 1958. For the absence of 'accompanying' language in imbecile children, Clarke and Clarke 1958.
17. Shepard and Schaeffer 1956.
18. Vincent op. cit., 455, 462. At all ages the median scores of the deaf groups were below the lower quartile scores of the hearing groups.
19. Isaacs 1930, 68.
20. Piaget and Szeminska 1941, Chapter V. Borelli 1951—the criterion of success was that 59 per cent of the group achieved the seriation. 'L'opération resterait chez le sourd-muet plus longtemps fragile et relative au material utilisé, parce qu'informulée faute de moyens d'expression' (page 237).
21. Lovell and Ogilvie 1960, 1961.
22. Smirnov in Simon 1957, 34; Hall 1936; Kurtz and Hovland 1953.
23. Chulliat and Oléron 1955, 299, 305.
24. Heider and Heider 1941, 24, 32.
25. Kittell, 1957; Haslerud and Meyers 1958 explain the discrepancy between Kittell's results and the normal experience of adults as due to their verbal and general maturity.
26. Hebb 1949, 294; the C is added by P. E. Vernon in Univ. of London Inst. of Educ. Studies, 7, 1955, 193.
27. Burt and Howard 1957, 58.

28. Burt 1958, 287.
29. Nisbet 1953, summarising forty-four investigations. In thirty-eight of these, there was a negative correlation between family size and I.Q.
30. O'Hanlon 1940; Burt 1946; Thomson 1946.
31. Nisbet 1953.
32. Burt 1943; a general account and a classified list of investigations is Halsey 1956.
33. Cattell 1936; Burt 1946; Thomson 1946.
34. Penrose's discussion with Thomson is in Thomson op. cit., Appendix; the quotations from Penrose, 1949, 122. Maxwell 1961, in a cautious review of the Scottish Survey, maintains that in fact there is no significant change in mean I.Q. between 1932 and 1947. But, he adds, there has been no decline. He mentions also that the evidence is insufficient to show whether this absence of decline is connected with the decrease in the number of larger families.
35. Binet 1909, 141, 146. My translation. Skeels and Dye 1939, quoting this passage with approval, translate 'au lieu de *friches*, nous avons maintenant une récolte,' as 'instead of a *desert*...' This rendering of 'friches' has no support from the standard dictionaries. Binet's point here, of course, is that the child's mind, though not yet cultivated, has potentialities.

CHAPTER ELEVEN

1. Bernstein in Halsey *et. al.* 1961, 307.
2. Schonell 1942, 508; for a discussion of resistance and sub-literacy see Lewis 1953, Chapter VII.
3. Burt 1945, 23; Stott 1950, 154.
4. Opie 1959, 142.
5. Opie 321.
6. Isaacs 1933, 449.
7. Opie 94.
8. McCarthy in Carmichael 1954, 577–81; Burroughs and Walker 1959.
9. Opie 186.

10. Opie 327.
11. Piaget 1932.
12. Opie 142.
13. Opie 129.
14. Opie 124, 141, 132.
15. Opie 133, 138.
16. Opie 160.
17. Opie 48.
18. Opie 46.
19. Opie 169–85.
20. Opie 58, 60, 204.
21. See page 141. At first sight, Sherif would appear to express a contrary view, that awareness of self must *precede* reciprocity in relations with others: 'The child cannot carry on, for any appreciable time, give-and-take relationships with other individuals, including children, because this requires seeing himself and the other person from the point of view of both.' (Sherif 1948, 210). Similarly Piaget 1932, 87: 'In order to co-operate, one must be conscious of one's ego.' But the tenor of their discussion, in both cases, is that self-awareness arises out of relationships with others and that these in turn cannot develop very far without self-awareness.
22. Piaget, 1932, 187. 'It is co-operation which leads to the primacy of intentionality, by forcing the individual to be constantly occupied with the point of view of other people so as to compare it with his own.'
23. Opie, 155–92.
24. Strauss 1954, in an investigation with children playing imaginary parts, concludes that in this period of later childhood they learn rules of behaviour as they come to recognise different mutual roles of persons in groups. This, in his view, endorses the generalisation of Mead on the ethical effects of taking different roles. We have seen, in Chapter 8, the importance of this in early childhood, and the handicaps that deaf children may suffer because of the poverty of their role-taking in imaginative play. (Heider and Heider 1941.)
25. Piaget 1932, 131.
26. Piaget 1932, 292–3. 'The interrogatory shows . . . the contrast of

two moralities—that of authority and that of equalitarian solidarity. The style of speech used by children in this connection is highly significant, and one may say that the terms used by children to describe behaviour in school are sufficient to differentiate the two types of reaction.'

27. Opie 183, 189.
28. Opie 136.

References

The place of publication, if in Great Britain, is not mentioned.

ALBERTS E. AND EHRENFREUND D. 1951. *J. Educ. Psychol.* 41.
ALEXANDER S. 1933. *Beauty and other forms of value.*
ALLPORT G. W. 1949. *Personality: a psychological interpretation.*
AMES L. B. AND LEARNED J. 1946. *J. Genet. Psychol.* 69.
AMES L. B. 1952. *J. Genet. Psychol.* 81.
ASCOLI G. 1950. *Enfance* 3.
BARKER R. G. 1943. *Child behaviour and development.*
BARTLETT F. C. 1932. *Remembering.*
BARTLETT F. C. 1958. *Thinking.*
BENDER I. 1953. *Aggression, hostility and anxiety in children.* Springfield, Ill.
BERNSTEIN B. 1958. *Brit. J. Sociol.* 9.
BERNSTEIN B. 1960. *Brit. J. Sociol.* 11.
BINET A. 1909. *Les idées modernes sur les enfants.* Paris.
BLANSHARD B. 1957. *The nature of thought.*
BORELLI M. 1951. *Enfance* 4.
BOSSARD J. H. S. 1948. *The sociology of child development.*
BOWLBY J. 1951. *Maternal care and mental health.* Geneva.
BRADWAY K. P. 1937. *Amer. Ann. Deaf* 82.
BRAIN R. 1961. *Speech disorders.*
BRIDGES K. M. B. 1931. *The social and emotional development of the pre-school child.*
BRODBECK A. J. AND IRWIN O. C. 1946. *Child Develpm.* 17.
BRYAN A. I. 1934. *Arch. Psychol.* 24.
BURCHARD E. M. L. AND MYKLEBUST H. R. 1942. *Amer. Ann. Deaf* 87.
BURROUGHS G. E. R. AND WALKER H. 1959. *Educ. Rev.* (Univ. of Birmingham) 11.

REFERENCES

BURT C. 1945. *Brit. J. Educ. Psychol.* 15.
BURT C. 1946. *Intelligence and fertility.*
BURT C. 1958. *Brit. J. Educ. Psychol.* 28.
BURT C. AND HOWARD M. 1957. *Brit. J. Statist. Psychol.* 10.
BUSSMANN E. 1946. *Le transfert dans l'intelligence pratique chez l'enfant.* Paris.
CAREY J. E. AND GOSS A. E. 1955. *J. Genet. Psychol.* 87.
CARMICHAEL L. (Ed.) 1954. *Manual of child psychology*, 3rd Ed.
CATTELL R. B. 1936. *Eugen. Rev.* 28.
CATTELL R. B. 1950. *Eugen. Rev.* 42.
CHAMBERLAIN A. F. AND I. C. 1904. *Ped. Sem.* 11.
CHULLIAT R. AND OLÉRON P. 1955. *Enfance* 8.
CHURCHILL E. M. 1958. *Univ. of Leeds Res. and Stud.* Pts. I and II.
CLARKE A. N. AND CLARKE A. D. B. (Ed.) 1958. *Mental deficiency: the changing outlook.*
COFER C. N. 1957. *J. Gen. Psychol.* 57.
COHEN M. 1952. *Enfance.* 5.
CRUICKSHANK W. M. 1955. *Psychology of exceptional children and youth.* New York.
DARWIN C. 1873. *The expression of the emotions in man and animals.*
DAVIS E. A. 1932. *Child Developm.* 3.
DAVIS E. A. 1937. *The development of linguistic skill in twins, singletons with siblings and only children.* Minnesota.
DREVER J. AND COLLINS M. 1928. *Performance tests of intelligence.*
EELLS K. 1951. *Intelligence* and *cultural differences.* Chicago.
EMMETT W. C. 1949. *Brit. J. Statist. Psychol.* 2.
EWING A. W. G. (Ed.) 1957. *Educational guidance and the deaf child.*
FAHEY G. L. 1942. *J. Genet. Psychol.* 60.
GESELL A. AND AMATRUDA C. S. 1947. *Developmental diagnosis.* 2nd Ed. New York.
GETZ S. 1953. *Environment and the deaf child.* Springfield, Ill.
GOLDFARB W. 1945. *Amer. J. Psychiat.* 102.
GOODENOUGH F. L. 1930. *Child Developm.* 1.
GOODENOUGH F. L. AND BRIAN C. R. 1929. *J. Exp. Psychol.* 12.
GRIFFITHS R. 1935. *A study of imagination in early childhood and its function in mental development.*
GUANELLA F. M. 1934. *Arch. Psychol.* 24.
HAGGERTY A. D. 1959. *J. Genet. Psychol.* 94.
HALBWACHS M. 1925. *Les cadres sociaux de la mémoire.* Paris.
HALL V. 1936. *Brit. J. Psychol.* 18.
HALSEY A. H. 1956. *Brit. J. of Sociol.* 7.

REFERENCES

HALSEY A. H., FLOUD J. AND ANDERSON C. A. 1961. *Education, economy and society*. New York.
HARMS I. E. AND SPIKER C. E. 1959. *J. Genet. Psychol.* 94.
HASLERUD G. M. AND MEYERS S. 1958. *J. Educ. Psychol.* 49.
HEBB D. O. 1949. *The organisation of behaviour*. New York.
HEIDER F. K. AND HEIDER G. M. 1941. *Psychol. Monogr.* 53.
HERMELIN B. AND O'CONNOR N. 1958. *J. Ment. Defic. Res.* 2.
HILDRETH G. 1944. *J. Genet. Psychol.* 64.
HOOD H. BLAIR 1949. *Brit. J. Educ. Psychol.* 19.
HOOD H. BLAIR 1962. *Brit. J. Psychol.* 53.
ISAACS S. 1930. *Intellectual growth in young children*.
ISAACS S. 1932. *Social development in young children*.
JESPERSEN O. 1922. *Language: its nature, origin and development*.
JOHNSON R. C. 1962. *Child Developm.* 33.
KELLER H. 1904. *The story of my life*.
KENDALL D. C. 1953. *The mental development of young deaf children*. Unpub. Thesis. Manch. Univ.
KIRK S. A. 1958. *Early education of the mentally retarded*. Urbana, Ill.
KITTELL J. E. 1957. *J. Educ. Psychol.* 48.
KUENNE M. R. 1946. *J. Exp. Psychol.* 36.
KURTZ K. H. AND HOVLAND C. I. 1953. *J. Exp. Psychol.* 45.
LATIF I. 1934. *Psychol. Rev.* 41.
LEVINE E. S. 1956. *Youth in a soundless world*. New York.
LEWIS M. M. 1951. *Infant speech*. 2nd Ed.
LEWIS M. M. 1953. *The importance of illiteracy*.
LOVELL K. AND OGILVIE E. 1960. *Brit. J. Educ. Psychol.* 30.
LOVELL K. AND OGILVIE E. 1961. *Brit. J. Educ. Psychol.* 31.
LUNZER E. A. 1960. *Recent studies ... on the work of J. Piaget*. N.F.E.R. London.
LURIA A. R. 1961. *The role of speech in the regulation of normal and abnormal behaviour*.
LURIA A. R. AND YUDOVICH F. IA. 1959. *Speech and the development of mental processes in the child*.
LYLE J. G. 1959. *J. Ment. Defic. Res.* 3.
LYLE J. G. 1960. *J. Ment. Defic. Res.* 4.
McDOUGALL W. 1931. *An introduction to social psychology*. 31st Ed.
MALRIEU P. 1962. *J. de Psychol.* 59.
MASLAND R. L., SARASON S. B., GLADWIN T. 1958. *Mental subnormality*. New York.
MAXWELL J. 1961. *The level and trend of national intelligence*.
MEAD G. H. 1934. *Mind, self and society*. Chicago.

MEUMANN E. 1902. *Die Entstehung der ersten Wortbedeutungen beim Kinde.* Leipzig.
MINSKI L. 1957. *Deafness, mutism and mental deficiency in children.*
MOORE J. K. 1947. *J. Exp. Educ.* 16.
MORRIS C. 1946. *Signs, language and behaviour.* New York.
MOWRER O. H. 1960. *Learning theory and the symbolic processes.* New York.
NEILSEN R. F. 1951. *Le développement de la socialité chez l'enfant.* Geneva.
NISBET J. D. 1953. *Family environment.*
NUNN T. P. 1945. *Education: its data and first principles.* 3rd Ed.
O'CONNOR N. 1956. *Acta Psychol. Amst.* 15.
O'HANLON G. S. A. 1940. *Brit. J. Educ. Psychol.* 10.
OLDFIELD R. C. AND ZANGWILL O. L. 1942. *Brit. J. Psychol.* 32, 33.
OLÉRON P. 1952. *Enfance* 5.
OLÉRON P. 1957. *Recherches sur le développement mental des sourds-muets.* Paris.
OPIE I. AND OPIE P. 1959. *The lore and language of schoolchildren.*
OSGOOD C. E. 1953. *Method and theory in experimental psychology.* New York.
PAVLOV I. P. 1927. *Conditioned reflexes.* Trans. G. V. Anrep.
PEEL E. A. 1956. *The psychological basis of education.*
PEEL E. A. 1959. *Brit. J. Educ. Psychol.*
PEEL E. A. 1960. *The pupil's thinking.*
PENROSE L. S. 1949. *The biology of mental defect.*
PESTALOZZI J. H. 1801. *How Gertrude teaches her children.* Trans. Holland L. E. and Turner F. C. (1894).
PIAGET J. 1923. *Le langage et la pensée chez l'enfant.* Neuchâtel.
PIAGET J. 1932. *The moral judgment of the child.*
PIAGET J. 1947. *La psychologie de l'intelligence.* Paris.
PIAGET J. 1950. *The psychology of intelligence.* Trans. M. Piercy and D. E. Berlyne.
PIAGET J. 1953. *Logic and psychology.*
PIAGET J. 1955. *The child's construction of reality.* Trans. M. Cook.
PIAGET J. 1961. *J. Educ. Psychol.* 52.
PIAGET J. 1962. *Comments on Vigotsky.* Mass. Institute of Technology.
PIAGET J. AND SZEMINSKA A. 1941. *La genèse du nombre chez l'enfant.* Paris. New York.
PINTNER R., EISONSON J. AND STANTON M. 1941. *The psychology of the physically handicapped.*
PINTNER R. AND PATERSON D. G. 1917. *J. Exp. Psychol.* 2.
PRICE H. H. 1953. *Thinking and experience.*

PRINGLE M. L. K. AND TANNER M. 1958. *Lang. Speech* 1.
PYLES M. K. 1932. *Child Developm.* 3.
RIBBLE M. A. 1944. *Infantile experience in relation to personality development*, in McV. Hunt J., *Personality and the behaviour disorders*. New York.
RICKMAN J. 1937. *A general selection from the works of Sigmund Freud*.
ROHRER J. H. AND SHERIF M. 1951. *Social psychology at the crossroads*. New York.
ROMANES G. J. 1888. *Mental evolution in man*.
SCHONELL F. J. 1942. *Backwardness in the basic subjects*.
SHEPARD W. O. AND SCHAEFFER M. 1956. *Child Developm.* 27.
SHERIF M. 1948. *An outline of social psychology*.
SIMON B. (Ed.) 1957. *Psychology in the Soviet Union*.
SKEELS H. M. AND DYE H. B. 1939. *J. of Psychol-asthenics* 44.
SKEELS H. M. AND HARMS I. 1948. *J. Genet. Psychol.* 72.
SMITH M. E. 1933. *Child Developm.* 4.
SMITH S. S. AND GOSS A. E. 1955. *J. Genet. Psychol.* 87.
SPIKER C. C. AND TERRELL G. 1955. *J. Genet. Psychol.* 86.
STERN C. AND W. 1928. *Die Kindersprache*. 4te Aufl. Leipzig.
STERN W. 1924. *The psychology of early childhood up to the sixth year of age*.
STOTT D. H. 1950. *Delinquency and human nature*.
STOUT G. F. 1896. *Analytic psychology*.
STOUT G. F. 1949. *A manual of psychology*. 4th Ed.
STRAUSS A. L. 1954. *Child Developm.* 25.
TEMPLIN M. C. 1957. *Certain language skills in children*. Minneapolis.
THOMSON G. H. 1946. *Eugen. Rev.* 38.
THORPE W. H. AND ZANGWILL O. L. 1961. *Current problems in animal behaviour*.
VIGOTSKY L. S. 1939. *Psychiatry* 2.
VIGOTSKY L. S. 1962. *Thought and language*. New York.
VINCENT M. 1957. *Enfance* 10.
WALLON H. 1924. *J. de Psychol.* 21.
WEIR M. W. AND STEVENSON H. W. 1959. *Child Developm.* 30.
WELCH L. AND LONG L. 1940. *J. Psychol.* 9.
WOHLWILL J. F. 1960. *J. Genet. Psychol.* 97.
YOUNG K. 1947. *Personality and problems of adjustment*.

Index

ABSENT, reference to, 80
Adults, intervention of, 21, 82, 84, 103, 105, 127, 177, 179, 182, 187–188, 201
Alberts, E. and Ehrenfreund, D., 238
Alexander, S., 21
Allport, G. W., 134
Ames, L. B., 152, 235; and Learned, J., 156
Ananiev, B. J., 116
Animals, names of, 50–54
Animism, 155
Approval, awareness of, 76; differentiation of, 61; about others, 69, 145; of playthings, 154; towards others, 68, 143
Ascoli, G., 184
Aversion, expression of, 69

BABBLING, beginning of, 20; and imitation, 24
Baby-language, basic, 33; secondary, 34
Bad, 70
Bartlett, F. C., 40, 121, 123, 125, 136, 173, 193, 234
Bender, I., 76
Bernstein, B., 140, 171, 201, 204, 246
Binet, A., 112, 197, 200
Birds, imitation in, 231; vocal play of, 231
Blanshard, B., 41
Blind children, questioning by, 131
Borelli, M., 197, 245
Bossard, J. H. S., 140, 158, 160
Bowlby, J., 236
Bradway, K. P., 241
Brain, R., 234, 236
Bridges, K. M. B., 241
Brodbeck, A. J. and Irwin, O. C., 229
Bryan, A. I., 125
Burchard, E. M. L., 241
Burroughs, G. E. R. and Walker, H., 210

Burt, C., 110, 191, 196, 198–199, 205, 245
Bussmann, E., 124

CAREY, J. E. AND GOSS, A. E., 239
Cattell, R. B., 199
Causal relationships, 128–129
Causality, awareness of, 96, 144
Chamberlain, A. F. and I. C., 235
Chulliat, R. and Oléron, P., 124, 128, 194, 241
Churchill, E. M., 185
Clarke, A. N. and A. D. B., 236, 245
Classification (Piaget), 177, 189
Clean, 68
Cofer, C. N., 182
Cognitive development in infancy, 37; in early childhood, 110; in later childhood, 168–169; play and, 126–127; and questions, 131; retardation, 75–76, 78, 159; schema, 52; skills in ethical behaviour, 134
Cohen, M., 235
Comfort sounds, early, 14; sequence of, 16; source of, 18
Companion, imaginary, 141, 156–158
Conceptual thinking, 41, 54, 75
Concrete operations, 120, 122, 168, 176–178, 185
'Conservation' (Piaget), 120, 123–124, 177, 192
Conservatism, 48, 205
Consonants, back, 18; front, 18, 19
Contraction of meanings, 49, 54
Contrast, effects of, 66
Cries, discomfort, 12, 14, 15, 16

DARWIN, C., 230
Davis, E. A., 236, 242
Deaf children, 'classification' by, 190; cognitive retardation of, 75, 78, 120, 190–191; linguistic retardation of, 14; orectic retardation of, 157; 'free drawing' by, 158; group language of,

INDEX

106; inflexibility of, 124, 128, 158–159, 194; perception by, 40; and 'performance' tests, 115, 196; planning by, 194; play of, 105, 128, 158; questioning by, 94, 131; 'transposition' by, 124
Declarative speech, 31, 54, 67, 69, 144, 206
Delinquency and retardation, 205
Dimanstein, I. S., 237
Dirty, 65, 146
Disapproval, awareness of, 76; differentiation of, 64–66; expression of, 69; of playthings, 154
Discomfort cries, 12, 14, 15, 16
Drever, J. and Collins, M., 237

Ego, 136, 218 f.
Egocentric language, 82, 182
Ego-ideal (super-ego), 136, 222 f.
Eisonson, J., 237
Emmett, W. C., 237
Epithets and ego-ideal, 222; and self-awareness, 219; social effects of, 217, 221
Ethical development, 42, 67, 166
Ewing, A. W. G., 75, 105, 125, 157, 237
Exhibitionism, 72, 152
Expansion of meanings, 49, 54
Expressive utterance, 19

fa (flower), 59
Fahey, G. L., 129
Family size and intelligence, 198, 200
First word, 30
Foetal responses, 14
Formal thinking, 177
Freud, S., 136–138, 224
Froebel, F. W. A., 239
Future, reference to, 86

Galperin, P. Ia., 183
Gaskill, P., 237
Gesell, A. and Amantruda, C. S., 229, 231
Getz, S., 241
'Gnomic sayings', 224
Goldfarb, W., 114, 161, 236
Goodbye! response to, 28
Goodenough, F. L., 112, 237; and Brian C. R., 116, 237, 239
Grammatical correctness in early childhood, 107
Griffiths, R., 239
Groos, K., 239
Group allegiance, 206; ethics and ego-ideal, 226; language, 171–172, 203; membership, 204; standards of conduct, 222
Guanella, F. M., 239
Guilt, expression of, 152, 155

Haggerty, A. D., 161
Halbwachs, M., 236
Hall, V., 193
Hallowell, A. I., 234
Halsey, A. H., 246
Harms, I. E. and Spiker, C. E., 235
Haslerud, G. M., 245
Hebb, D. O., 195, 230
Heider, F. K. and G. M., 158, 245, 247
Hermelin, B. and O'Connor, N., 245
Herrick, V. E., 115
Hildreth, G., 123
Honey, reference to, 81, 86
Hood, H. B., 186, 237
Hostility about others, 149; co-operation in, 149; expression of, 215; towards others, 146

I, use of, 72, 74
Iconographic words, 35
Id, 136
Identification, 137
Imagination and language, 125–129
Imitation, 22; and babbling, 24; in play, 141; in questioning, 90
Immaturity, orectic, 76, 159
Individuality, expression of, 172, 220
Infantile speech, 144
Inhibition of others' actions, 71
Institution, life in an, 14, 24, 76, 78, 94, 106, 113, 159
Intelligence and family size, 198–200; tests, 78, 110, 115, 195
Intention in child's speech, 32
Internalisation, 82, 93, 104
Intonation, response to, 27, 86
Intonational patterns, 76
Irwin, O. C., 230
Isaacs, N., 87, 121, 129, 131–132
Isaacs, S., 126, 140, 142–143, 145–146, 148–150, 152, 154, 156, 191, 209

Jespersen, O., 231
Jones, H. E., 113, 242

Keller, Helen, 56, 235
Kendall, D. C., 115, 158, 235, 237, 241
Kinæsthetic experience, 15, 29
Kings, 213
Kirk, S. A., 113

INDEX

Kittell, J. E., 194
Kuenne, M. R., 119
Kurtz, K. H., 193

LANGUAGE AND CONCRETE THINKING, 187; group, 171–172; and ethical behaviour, 135, 139–142, 145; and pictures, 193; and play, 126, 'secret,' 172, 206; self-addressed, 92, 126, 130
Latif, I., 231
Levine, E. S., 241
Linguistic intercourse, 83, 85
Lovell, K. and Ogilvie, E., 188, 192, 243
Lunzer, E. A., 178, 180
Luria, A. R., 104, 122, 127, 182, 233, 237
Lyle, J. G., 232, 236

MALRIEU, P., 232–233
Mama, Mummy, 19, 30, 32–33, 37–40, 42, 68, 74
Manipulative speech, 31, 89, 206
Masland, R. L., 241
Maxwell, J., 246
McCarthy, D., 210, 229, 230, 232, 237, 238, 239, 242
McDougall, W., 20, 141, 231
Mead, G. H., 141, 189, 219, 234, 247
Meaning, beginnings of, 25; in early speech, 29; response to, 27
Memory, social influence on, 86
Meumann, E., 37
Minski, L., 157
Moore, J. K., 235
Moral judgment, Piaget on, 138–139
Morris, C., 234
Motivation and communication, 187
Motor skills and language, 116
Mowrer, O. H., 245
'Multiplication' (Piaget), 177, 190
Murphy, L. G., 237
Murphy, K. P., 237
'Mutuality' (Piaget), 214, 221–222, 225

NAMING, 57, 90, 95, 118, 189
Nasalisation, 16
Naughty, 66, 70
Nielsen, R. F., 127, 245
Nice, 63
Nisbet, J. D., 198, 246
No!, 28, 43–45, 72, 147
Nonsense-words and memory, 127
Nunn, T. P., 239

O'CONNOR, N., 229, 232, 236

O'Hanlon, G. S. A., 198
Oldfield, R. C. and Zangwill, O. L., 234, 239
Oléron, P., 115, 120–121, 124
Onomatopœic words, 35
Operations, concrete, 120, 169; psychological, 128
Opie, I. and P., 167, 171–175, 206 f.
Oral rituals, 206
Orectic, attitudes, discrimination of, 58; behaviour, 43; definition of, 35; immaturity, 76, 157–159; response, 37; schema, 52; similarity, 63; speech, 38
Osgood, C. E., 182, 234, 235
Ownership, expression of, 73

PAST, reference to, 84
Pavlov, I. P., 29, 36, 122, 184
Peel, E. A., 180, 240, 242, 244
Penrose, L. S., 200
Perception, 39, 115
Personality, definition of, 134, 136, 141–142, 148, 151; development of, 72, 136, 142, 212, 218, 222
Pestalozzi, J. H., 111, 239
Phonetic symbols, 229
Piaget, J., on cognitive development, 40, 97, 120, 123, 126, 128, 132, 144, 168–169, 177, 184, 190–192, 236–237, 241, 243; on ethical development, 138–139, 155, 166–168, 213–214, 221, 224, 247 and Szeminska, A., 245
Pictures and language, 193
Pintner, R., 157; Eisonson, J. and Stanton, M., 241; and Paterson, D. G., 239
Play, babbling, 20; and deafness, 128; imitative, 141; linguistic, 170; make-believe, 126, 155; projection in, 153; in questioning, 90, 92; social patterns of, 102
Pre-natal responses, 13; vocalisation, 13
Pretty, 61
Price, H. H., 41
Principles, ethical, 135, 224
Pringle, M. L. K. and Tanner, M., 160
Problem-solving, adult intervention in, 182–183; and naming, 118, 189; and play, 127; principles in, 120, 194; 'transfer' in, 119
Pyles, M. K., 118

QUESTIONS, confirmatory, 97; differentiation of, 94; in early childhood,

129–133; as exploration, 91; functions of, 87; imitation in, 90; naming, 95; to oneself, 92; play in, 90; rudimentary, 88; on sources of actions, 95

REFLEX, conditioned, 36
Relationships, awareness of, 119; personal, 212
Remembering, and language, 123–125; and nonsense-words, 127
Response to, intonation, 28; meanings, 27; pre-natal, 13
Retardation, cognitive, 75–77, 159; and delinquency, 205; linguistic, 77; orectic, 76, 159; scholastic, 171, 205
'Reversibility' (Piaget), 120, 123, 177, 192
Ribble, M. A., 230
Rituals, contractual, 213; 'joining-in', 213; oral, 206
Role-taking, 223
Romanes, G. J., 235

SCATOLOGY, 209, 211
Schema, definition of, 41; cognitive, 52; in concrete thinking, 180; in ethical behaviour, 135–136, 138, 174; functional, 52; and imagining, 123, 125; orectic, 52; in questioning, 96; symbolisation of, 84, 123; in 'transfer', 121
Schonell, F. J., 205
School, entrance into, 140; functions of, 227
Scottish Mental Survey, 198–200
'Secret' language, 206, 208–209
Self-assertion, 71, 142; awareness, 71, 74, 135, 151, 212, 218; criticism, 152; justification, 148; objectification, 141
'Seriation' (Piaget), 177, 191
Sex, differences in language, 108, 170, 211; groups, 210; and individuality, 220
Shee (sea), 60
Shepard, W. O. and Schaeffer, M., 190
Sherif, M., 233, 247
Shipinova and Surina, 36
'Signal-systems' (Pavlov), 122, 184
Similarity, functional, 52, 188; orectic, 188
Skeels, H. M. and Dye, H. B., 113, 235–6, 246; and Harms, I., 113, 235

Skinch, 207
Slang, 207, 227
Smirnov, A. A., 193
Smith, M. E., 90
Smith, S. S., 238–239
Social influences on thinking, 178
Socio-economic influences, 108, 112, 129, 170–171, 199
Sounds, sequence of, 17
Spatial relationships, 128–129
Spiker, C. C. and Terrell, G., 239
Stern, W., 90, 112, 153, 231, 233, 235
Stott, D. H., 205
Stout, G. F., 41
Strauss, A. L., 247
Symbolic mediation, 40
'Synpractic' language (Vigotsky), 92, 103–104

TEMPLIN, M. C., 107, 170, 205
Temporal relationships, 128–129
Terman, L. M., 112
Tests, 'performance', 115, 196; 'non-verbal', 196
Thomson, G. H., 198–199, 200
Thorpe, W. H. and Zangwill, O. L., 229, 231–232
'Transfer' in problem-solving, 119, 195
Transformations in speech, 47–49
Truce-terms, 207
Twins, private language of, 106; retardation of, 104, 127

VALENTINE, C. W., 23
Verbal tricks, 218
Vernon, P. E., 245
Vigotsky, L. S., 103, 182, 236
Vincent, M., 190–191, 245
Vocabulary, measurement of, 107
Vocalisation, pre-natal, 13
Voice, response to, 14

WALLON, H., 236
Weir, M. W. and Stevenson, H. W., 119, 189
Where?, 91
Wohlwill, J. F., 238
Word, 'first,' 30

YERKES, R. M., 112
Yes!, 43–45, 72
Young, K., 233

ZAPOROZHETS, A. V., 239

manipulative + declarative speech - 31
deictic   35, 57
self-assertion + self-awareness - 70
reference to the absent + thought - 84
present - past - future
dvlpmt of interrogation - 94
causality v. juxtaposition - 97
recap of interrogative behavior - 98